Cowboy and Western Songs

Cowboy and Western Songs
A Comprehensive Anthology

Edited by

Austin E. and Alta S. Fife

Music Editor: Mary Jo Schwab

with illustrations by J. K. Ralston

BRAMHALL HOUSE · NEW YORK

To
Geordie,
for roots across the land

This 1982 edition is published by Bramhall House,
a division of Clarkson N. Potter, Inc.,
distributed by Crown Publishers, Inc.

Manufactured in the United States of America

ISBN: 0-517-387689
h g f e d c b a

Acknowledgments

Many folklorists, musicologists, folksong collectors and singers, and friends have contributed to the building of this collection. Beyond the specific citations that appear with each song, we are grateful to Ray B. Browne, Richard M. Dorson, Edith Fowke, Gail I. Gardner, Frank Goodwyn, Chuck Haas, Herbert Halpert, Wayland D. Hand, Frank Hoffmann, Arthur Holmgren, F. W. Keller, William E. Koch, Rae Korson, Ben G. Lumpkin, Mrs. Joe O. Naylor, Hermes Nye, John Donald Robb, Scott K. Schwab, Ellen J. Stekert, Allen W. Stokes, Clifford P. Westermeier, and D. K. Wilgus.

We appreciate also assistance and materials provided by the John Simon Guggenheim Foundation, the Archive of Folk Songs of the Library of Congress, the Arizona Folklore Archive, the Kansas State Historical Society, the Pacific Northwest Farm Quad, and the Texas Historical Society.

Especially we wish to express our gratitude to Utah State University and to Dr. D. Wynne Thorne, Vice-President for Research, whose sustained confidence and support have made it possible to bring this work to publication.

—AUSTIN AND ALTA FIFE

Logan, Utah

Contents

Introduction

If there is any one trait that marks this mid-century generation it is its frenzied quest for the ethnic: ethnic dress and demeanor, ethnic morals and manners, ethnic art, ethnic dance, and ethnic music. It is as though we are compelled to turn backward toward our origins proportionately to our mad propulsion forward toward this nebulous but sacred cow called "progress," whose latest achievements suggest that we may fracture things more precious than the atom. In any case, the term "progress" has lost much of its magic, and our society is ripe for some as yet unnamed Janus-faced totem that looks backward as well as forward—earthbound roots give the tree as much of its life and meaning as does its sky-searching foliage.

We have watched the growth of interest in ethnic music for thirty years and may, indeed, have become a part of the process itself. In this period the worth in the marketplace of a top-flight "folk" singer has gone from one to four digits per appearance. Collectors have combed the backcountry for ethnic music, and the generally known repertoire of "folk" songs has been expanded a thousandfold. The guitar has replaced the piano in living room and honky-tonk; pseudoethnic strumming and singing styles are preferred to bel canto with piano or orchestration, and a good song must have deep ethnic meanings—put there forcibly, if need be, by the city-billy singer who is cultures removed from Bugtussle or Upper Volta where his favorite song is presumed to have been hatched. Yet, despite the many ridiculous aspects that the movement offers, we find it basically wholesome, especially when we compare it with the "popular" (i.e., commercially synthetic) music of the decades between the two great wars ("Yes, We Have No Bananas!" "One Meat Ball," "Barney Google").

It is not easy to say precisely what constitutes the "ethnic" music of Anglo-America. Some even say that no such music exists, that all in our popular musical heritage deserving the name "ethnic" originated across the Atlantic. Without arguing the point, let us merely advise the reader that we believe Anglo-America does have its own ethnic songs and that by their New World settings, images, language, and expressed or implicit code, they speak as candidly of the roots of Anglo-America as did the Iliad of Ancient Greece or the Song of Roland of eleventh-century France. To support our case we invoke particularly spirituals and revivalist hymns, blues and work songs, lumberjack songs, the mid-nineteenth century vaudeville repertoire, hillbilly music, and songs of the overlanders, western miners, railroaders, sodbusters, cowboys.

It is with cowboy songs in particular, and with other "western" songs, that we are concerned in this book. Their importance as an expression of pioneering and frontier life has been noted by a few perceptive critics since the dawn of our century. N. Howard (Jack) Thorp went out of his way to collect and preserve them in the late 1880's, editing and printing the first slender volume in 1908.* Two years later John A. Lomax, encouraged by the notable George Lyman Kittredge of Harvard, published a considerably larger collection which has since been enlarged and reedited by him and by his son Alan several times. In the '20's and '30's many other cowboy and western songs were printed either as collections or as single items contributed to the *Journal of American Folklore, The*

---

* *Songs of the Cowboys.* A facsimile edition with variants, commentary, notes, and lexicon by Austin E. and Alta S. Fife was published by Clarkson N. Potter, Inc., New York, 1966.

Idaho Farmer, Adventure Magazine, Western Folklore Quarterly, to plains and intermountain newspapers, and other periodical or esoteric imprints.* During the same period a score of popular entertainers crooned cowboy and western songs over the radio and recorded them on 78 rpm records, millions of which were sold throughout the land. They appeared also in sheet music, and cowboy and western song folios were published giving words, melodies, piano arrangements, and tablatures for guitar or banjo.

Since World War II, awareness of the ethnic significance of this music has become general, and the field collecting of "folk" songs, including cowboy and western songs, has gone full steam ahead. A score or more of significant private collections have been made in the plains and intermountain states. Several universities have accumulated field recordings and established modest archives, and the Library of Congress has, in its music division, assembled field recordings made by several collectors who have given attention to the cowboy and western repertoire. Thus the archival resources now available for the study of cowboy and western songs are many times greater than was the case when previous books of cowboy and western songs were edited.

All the previous published collections of cowboy and western songs, even the pretentious Lomax books, were based on relatively small and fragmentary field resources. Nearly all were made when it was not yet evident that the cowboy culture had passed, and hence they suffer from subjectivity and limited historical perspective. Song selection in most of them was determined principally by the song available, not by which songs said the most about cowboys and the West.

Resources for the present volume are of a different order. With the passage of time the substance, images, and code of the cowboy begin to emerge. The stereotypes and clichés—candid vehicles for myth—become recognizable by their sheer persistence and generality. The songs offered here have been selected from among several thousand possible choices: all the previously published collections, plus some forty volumes of notes and transcriptions of field recordings made by the authors and their colleagues in a dozen western states. For each song, we have chosen from among many

variants one or more texts that ring truest to the cowboy mode. We have not made up "synthetic" texts by combining the "best" stanzas from sundry sources, although, in a few cases where the text selected is defective, we have offered stanzas from other sources with clear indication that the stanza (or stanzas) in question is not integral to the text it accompanies. We have avoided polishing up the grammar, vocabulary, meter, or morals, preferring to preserve the original punctuation and spelling from our sources. We have, however, given standard English spellings in lieu of pseudo-phonetic orthography which frequently makes a song unreadable without making it any more authentic: *there* for *thar,* them for *'em,* far for *fer,* etc.

Wherever possible we have used texts and tunes that come to us together, "in holy wedlock," so to speak. However, in several cases the most significant texts are without accompanying tunes. This has forced us to seek elsewhere for a traditional melody; we hope that the resulting "shotgun marriages" do not do violence to the songs. Users of this volume must appreciate, however, that musically illiterate singers—genuine folk singers, that is—synchronize words and tune by various spontaneous devices. Syllables that fall on the beat and the melodic contours are pretty well fixed: other rhythmic and prosodic features can be and are bent to the needs of the moment so that in the very same song, for example, a single solid stressed note or the same note with one or even two notes on the upbeat are considered musically equivalent:

On ă cóld Septémbĕr mórn
'Twăs on ă cóld Septémbĕr mórn
Ĭt wăs on ă cóld Septémbĕr mórn

In every case the musical notation offered here presumes the same flexibility on the part of users of this book that our informants availed themselves of; otherwise we should have to give a musical transcription for each separate stanza.

We wish we were able to inform singers concerning cowboy and western singing styles. And, while we can volunteer a few suggestions, it remains for ethnomusicologists more skilled than we are to arrive at sound conclusions based on more, and more carefully made, observations. In its most typical setting a cowboy or western song functioned as a self-inflicted exercise to ward off loneliness or to capitalize for oneself the aesthetic value of a meaningful theme. Histrionics, modulations, vibratos, crescendos, decrescendos, syncopations, and other interpretive hanky-panky were of

---

* The most notable early collectors of cowboy and western songs after N. Howard Thorp and John A. Lomax are Louise Pound, Margaret Larkin, Jules Verne Allen, J. Frank Dobie, Myra Hull, Sharlot Hall, Robert Frothingham, Robert W. Gordon, and Charles A. Siringo.

little value indeed where there were at best only cattle or coyotes to listen, and where, in any case, the melody was little more than a vehicle for ideas and moods. If there was an instrumental accompaniment—and this was by no means obligatory—it consisted of the simplest possible support to tune and rhythm. The ending of a song required no cadence, the ending often being of little consequence since facts extraneous to the song itself in all probability determined when a Westerner stopped singing or started up again.

On this simple bedrock of ethnic singing style, of course, the professional radio crooners of the '30's used the cowboy and western song repertoire as a vehicle to enchant a whole nation of listeners, injecting therein interpretive devices that minstrels have used since they first captivated an audience. And while we may be intrigued by the schmaltzy velvet-lined phrases of a Burl Ives or the acrobatic lyricism of Jimmy Rogers' blue yodels, when it comes right down to cowboy songs per se we prefer less sophisticated artists like Harry McClintock, the late Woodie Guthrie, or Slim Critchlow, who avoid gimmicks that distract the listener's attention from the content of the song itself.

To conclude this introduction, it seems important to situate "cowboy and western" songs in time and in space. In a sense the whole history of our nation is the history of a movement "west" so that this word had acquired mythical properties even before there was any such thing as a "cowboy." Still the impact of the term "west" is maximized and fixed in our culture only when it gets applied to the last American frontiers: the Missouri basin, the Texas plains, the Rocky Mountains. It is here that the Anglo-American will have his final confrontation with the Red Man, here that Europeans will finally gain ascendency over malign nature with its ruggedness of terrain and climate, its exotic flora and fauna. It is here that the horse, which had carried Western man to all his conquests since the dawn of recorded history, will render his last faithful service prior to his burial by steel, steam, the combustion engine, electricity, and ultimately, fission.

It all began in the 1830's with the migration of Anglo-Americans into Texas, then the war with Mexico, and finally the opening of the Southwest through the exploitation of its animal resources by the killing of the buffalo and the advent of cattle raising on the open ranges. Sodbusters (homesteaders) and prospectors will follow close behind, subjecting the open range to fencing, land to the plow, and the earth to pilferage of its subterranean treasures. In a bit more than half a century this whole vast domain will have been subdued, fenced, road-riddled, and railroaded: man had at last placed his brand upon the cattle and upon the earth itself. Laws, economic conventions, and social restraints had brought order and conformity to a land of erstwhile lawlessness and high adventure.

The best of the cowboy songs came into being after 1870 and before 1930. Their real substance consists of the candid and dramatic way in which they reveal the human condition in those decades of frontier life when men lived, labored, loved, and died where laws, conventions, and tradition were lacking or ineffectual. To the present generation, which feels the omnipresence of law, moral codes, economic and social conformity, and the tyrannies of technology, the *ethnic* significance of cowboy and western songs may well reside in the singer's (and listener's) vicarious experience with a moment of freedom and high adventure that is no longer possible in real life. We wonder, indeed, if, at their best, all artistic expressions—either ethnic or highbrow—may not find their ultimate meaning as therapeutic agents for human beings weighted down by the overburden of their own institutions. If this is so then the best of the cowboy and western songs may do service for a time yet as purges for congestion of the soul.

—AUSTIN AND ALTA FIFE

Sources and Abbreviations

Complete references accompany all texts and melodies from published sources used in this anthology. However, many materials are from esoteric local publications, newspapers and other periodical literature of the American West, sheet music and popular song folios, popular recorded music of the 78-rpm era, our own field recordings and those of a score of fellow researchers who have contributed their significant cowboy and western items, ballet books, and sundry other manuscript resources. These resources which are not accessible in good research libraries have been assembled and entered in the ten volumes of the Fife Mormon Collection (FMC) and the forty-two volumes of the Fife American Collection (FAC). Tapes (or acetate recordings on the earlier items) are preserved of all songs gathered from oral sources.

Large private collections, entered into the Fife Collection as integral volumes, are identified by appropriate independent abbreviations. They are as follows:

Gordon: two volumes extracted from the Robert W. Gordon Collection at the Library of Congress.

Hendren: seven volumes from the private collection of Stella M. Hendren of Kooskia, Idaho.

JL: three volumes extracted from the manuscript collections of John A. Lomax in the archives of the Texas Historical Society, Austin.

PC–F: one volume from the private collection of Edwin Ford Piper at the State University of Iowa.

PNFQ: three volumes from the manuscript collection of the Pacific Northwest Farm Quad, Spokane, Washington.

In addition to these abbreviations, the *Publications of the Texas Folklore Society* are designated as *PTFLS.*

Part One

The West Before the Cowboy

No. 1
Shenandoah

From the 1600's onward, America loomed in the eyes of venturesome Europeans as a wild land of exotic adventure where common seamen wooed, won, and abandoned (or were rebuffed by) the bronzed daughters of Indian chieftains. Though of oceangoing origins, this song eventually got "landlocked" on the Missouri River, artery of the hinterland: it was a favorite of rivermen and of soldiers at frontier outposts. (Melody and text: W. B. Whall, *Sea Songs and Shanties* [Glasgow: Brown, Son and Ferguson, 1910], pp. 1–2.)

SHENANDOAH

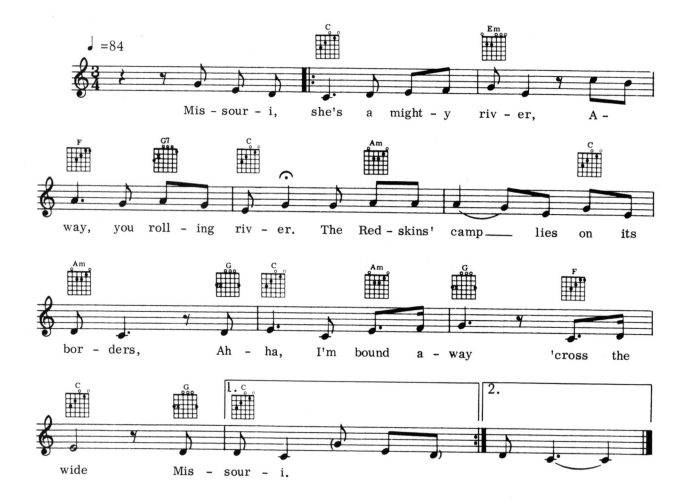

Mis - sour - i, she's a might - y riv - er, A-
way, you roll - ing riv - er. The Red - skins' camp___ lies on its
bor - ders, Ah - ha, I'm bound a - way 'cross the
wide Mis - sour - i.

Oh, Missouri, she's a mighty river,
    Away you rolling river.
The Red-skins' camp lies on its borders,
    Ah-ha, I'm bound away 'cross the wide Missouri.

The white man loved the Indian maiden,
    Away you rolling river.
With notions sweet his canoe was laden.
    Ah-ha, I'm bound away 'cross the wide Missouri.

"O Shenandoah, I love your daughter,
    Away you rolling river.
I'll take her 'cross yon rolling water."
    Ah-ha, I'm bound away 'cross the wide Missouri.

The chief disdained the trader's dollars:
    Away you rolling river.
"My daughter never you shall follow."
    Ah-ha, I'm bound away 'cross the wide Missouri.

At last there came a Yankee skipper,
    Away you rolling river.
He winked his eye, and he tipped his flipper.
    Ah-ha, I'm bound away 'cross the wide Missouri.

He sold the chief that fire-water,
    Away you rolling river.
And 'cross the river he stole his daughter,
    Ah-ha, I'm bound away 'cross the wide Missouri.

"O Shenandoah, I long to hear you,
    Away you rolling river.
Across that wide and rolling river."
    Ah-ha, I'm bound away 'cross the wide Missouri.

No. 2
The Buffalo Hunters

The western image of ideal masculinity demands toughness of mind and body and the spirit of adventure: witness this song, written in 1872 (according to one source) by "Whiskey" Parker, a college man who had wandered into the Black Hills with a gold watch, a Testament given him by his mother, and a "fallen angel." Together they reared a brood of native sons whose offspring are now peers of our Midwest kingdom. (Melody: J. Frank Dobie, "A Buffalo Hunter and His Song," PTFLS [Vol. XVIII, 1943], p. 5 [published by permission of the Texas Folklore Society]. Text: Gordon 3782.)

THE BUFFALO HUNTERS

Come— all you pret-ty fair maids, these lines to you I write; We're go-ing on the range____ in which we take de-light, We're go-ing on the range____ as we poor hunt-ers do, While those ten-der-foot-ed fel-lows do stay at home with you.

Come all you pretty fair maids, these lines to you I write;
We're going on the range in which we take delight,
We're going on the range as we poor hunters do,
While those tender-footed fellows do stay at home with you.

Our game it is the antelope, the buffalo, elk and deer;
They roam these broad prairies without the least of fear;
We rob them of their robes in which we think no harm,
To buy us chuck and clothing for to keep our bodies warm.

The buffalo is the largest and the noblest of the van,
He sometimes refuses to throw us up his hands,
With shaggy mane uplifted, and face toward the sky,
As if to say, "I'm coming, so hunter mind your eye!"

All the day long we go tramping around,
In search of the buffalo that we may shoot them down;
Armed with our trusty rifle and belt of forty rounds,
We send them up Salt River to their happy hunting grounds.

While armed with the Sharps rifle or the Needle gun so true
We cause the "buff" to bite the dust for they send their bullets through;
For when we come upon them, if our guns have no defects,
We cause them to throw up their hands and pass us in their checks.

Our houses are made of buffalo hides, we build them tall and round;
Our fires are made of buffalo chips, our beds are on the ground.
Our furniture is the camp kettle, the coffee pot and pan;
Our chuck is buffalo beef and bread intermingled well with sand.

Our neighbors are the Cheyenne, the Arapaho and Sioux;
Their mode of navigation is the buffalo hide canoe.
And if they all should emigrate I'm sure we wouldn't care,
For a peculiar way they have of raising hunters' hair.

The hunters are jolly fellows, they like their lager beer,
The hunters are jolly fellows, they drink their whiskey clear;
And now you've heard my song you must not think it queer,
If I take a drink of whiskey or a glass of lager beer.

No. 3
The Wild Rippling Water

This song forms a bridge between cowboy songs and Old World ballads concerning the seduction of a maiden by the enchantment of music. Having satiated the maiden's love for music by his expertise at "fiddling," the cowboy turns suddenly brutal in his talk about the wife back home in Arizona. In an equal number of songs the cowboy is left to pine while the maiden moves on to better game. (Melody and text: FAC I 232, as sung by Frank Goodwyn.)

THE WILD RIPPLING WATER

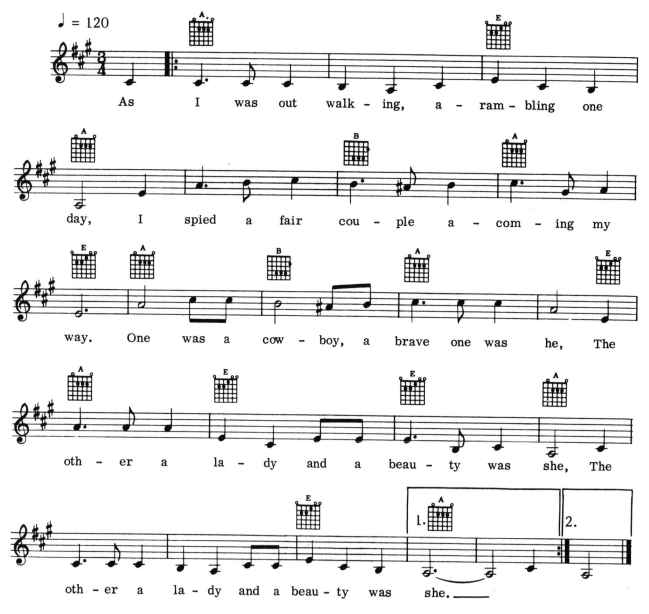

As I was out walking, a-rambling one day
I spied a fair couple a-coming my way.
One was a cowboy, a brave one was he,
The other a lady and a beauty was she,
The other a lady and a beauty was she.

Say, "Where are you going, my pretty fair maid?"
"Just down by the river, just down by the shade,
Just down by the river, just down by the spring,
To see the wild water and hear the nightingale sing,
See the wild rippling water and hear the nightingale sing."

They hadn't been gone but an hour or so
When he drew from his satchel a fiddle and bow.
He tuned up his fiddle all on a high string
And played a tune over and over again,
And played a tune over and over again.

"Now," says the cowboy, "I should have been gone."
"No, no," said the maid, "just play one more song.
I'd rather hear the fiddle played on one string
Than to see the wild water and hear the nightingale sing,
See the wild rippling water and hear the nightingale sing."

He tuned up his fiddle and rosined his bow
And played her a lecture, he played it all low.
He played her a lecture all on the high string.
"Hark, hark," said the maid, "hear the nightingale sing,
Hark, hark," said the maid, "hear the nightingale sing."

She says, "Dear cowboy, will you marry me?"
"No, no, pretty maid, that never can be.
I've a wife in Arizona, a lady is she,
One wife and one ranch are plenty for me.
One wife and one ranch are plenty for me.

"I'll go to Mexico and I'll stay there one year,
I'll drink a lot of wine, I'll drink a lot of beer.
If I ever come back it will be in the spring
To see the wild water and hear the nightingale sing,
See the wild rippling water and hear the nightingale sing."

Come all you young ladies, take warning from me,
Never place your affections in a cowboy so free;
He'll go away and leave you as mine left me,
Leave you rocking the cradle, singing "Bye, oh baby,"
Leave you rocking the cradle, singing, "Bye, oh baby."

No. 4
A Hunting Tale

Since primitive times, if we are to judge from the lore of the folk, men have talked big to hide awareness of their frailty in the face of malign nature. In "A Hunting Tale" the bragging transcends both the plausible and the coherent—becomes indeed cosmic. Scores of cowboy and western songs offer us such "tall talk" of amazing variety and exuberance. (Melody and text: FAC I 559, as sung by Ezra Barhight, collected by Ellen J. Stekert.)

A HUNTING TALE

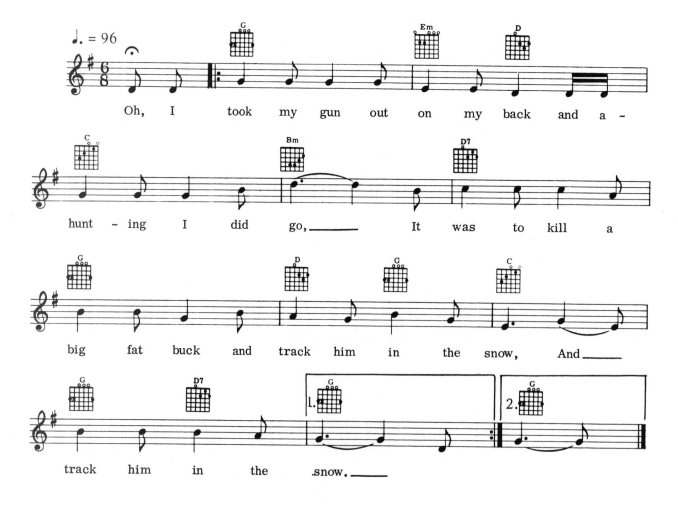

Oh, I took my gun out on my back and a-hunt-ing I did go, _____ It was to kill a big fat buck and track him in the snow, And _____ track him in the snow. _____

Oh, I took my gun out on my back and a-hunting I did go,
It was to kill a big fat buck and track him in the snow,
    And track him in the snow.

I followed him to that river that runs up on yonders hill;
At the bottom of that river this herd of deer did dwell,
    This herd of deer did dwell.

When I came in sight of them like divers they dove down,
They dove into the bottom and they squat upon the sand,
    They squat upon the sand.

I took my gun all in my hand, out into the water ran;
It was to kill all those that fled, that was my whole intent,
    That was my whole intent.

When I was under water five thousand feet or more
I fired off that rifle, like a cannon it did roar,
    A cannon it did roar.

I fired all in among them, I chanced for to kill one,
The rest stuck up their bossets and at me they did come,
    And at me they did come.

Their horns were in the velvet, [the fiery ship could mask?]
And like so many streams of lightning, why, they pitched my body past,
    They pitched my body past.

Till it became like a riddle and a bulldog could jump through,
I threw all in a passion, my naked sword I drew,
    My naked sword I drew.

Five hours I held them battle, six hours I gave them play.
Well, I killed about five thousand and the rest all ran away,
    Why, the rest all ran away.

Well, I gathered up my venison, all out the water went,
It was to kill all those that fled that was my whole intent,
    That was my whole intent.

Then I bent my gun a circle and I shot around the hill.
Then out of four and twenty a thousand I did kill,
    A thousand I did kill.

Then I gathered up my venison and I started out for home,
It was a hot and summer day, and a blustery squall of snow,
   And a blustery squall of snow.

Well, I traveled o'er hills and mountains, and over hills so high
That when I stood a-gazing I could almost reach the sky,
   I could almost reach the sky.

As I stood a-gazing the sun came running by,
And I gathered up my venison, I jumped on as it passed by,
   I jumped on as it passed by.

It carried me all 'round the world and o'er the swelling tide,
And I sold my venison to the stars so merrily I did ride,
   So merrily I did ride.

Just as the sun was going down it gave a sudden whirl,
Then I let loose my hold, I landed in the other world,
   Landed in the other world.

But as Saint Providence would have it I lodged upon the moon
And in course of a half of day or so I landed safe at home,
   I landed safe at home.

Then I gathered up my money for venison and for skin,
And I took it to the big frame barn, it wouldn't near half go in,
   It wouldn't near half go in.

The rest I dealt out to the poor, bright guineas out of hand,
And now I think it's time to stop and live again to man,
   And live again to man.

Now the man that made up this song, sir, his name was Bango Bang,
And if you can tell a bigger lie I swear you ought to hang,
   I swear you ought to hang.

No. 5
Old Rosin the Beau

The rugged individualism, which is a tag of Westerners, is already evident in this song, very popular on the frontier since 1838, possibly earlier. It also contains other aspects of what will become the code of the cowboy: a taste for strong drink, preoccupation with death, the ritual of burial. (Melody and text: FAC I 556, collected by Frank Hoffmann.)

OLD ROSIN THE BEAU

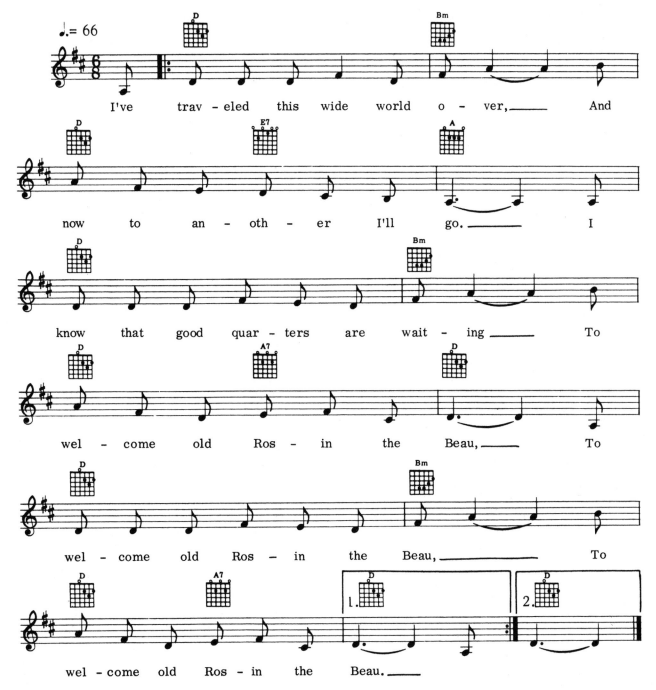

I've trav-eled this wide world o-ver,——— And now to an-oth-er I'll go.——— I know that good quar-ters are wait-ing——— To wel-come old Ros-in the Beau,——— To wel-come old Ros-in the Beau,——— To wel-come old Ros-in the Beau.———

I've traveled this wide world over
  And now to another I'll go,
I know that good quarters are waiting
  To welcome Old Rosin the Beau,
  To welcome Old Rosin the Beau,
  To welcome Old Rosin the Beau.

When I'm dead and laid out on the counter
  A voice you'll hear from below
Singing out, "Whiskey and water,
  To drink to Old Rosin the Beau,
  To drink to Old Rosin the Beau,
  To drink to Old Rosin the Beau."

And when I am dead I reckon
  The ladies will want to, I know,
Just lift off the lid of my coffin
  And look at Old Rosin the Beau,
  And look at Old Rosin the Beau,
  And look at Old Rosin the Beau.

You must get a dozen good fellows
  And stand them all 'round in a row,
And drink out of half gallon bottles
  To the name of Old Rosin the Beau,
  To the name of Old Rosin the Beau,
  To the name of Old Rosin the Beau.

Get four or five jovial good fellows
  And let them all staggering go,
And dig a deep hole in the meadow
  And toss in it Rosin the Beau,
  And toss in it Rosin the Beau,
  And toss in it Rosin the Beau.

And get you a couple of tombstones,
  Place one at my head and my toe,
And do not fail to scratch on it
  The name of Old Rosin the Beau,
  The name of Old Rosin the Beau,
  The name of Old Rosin the Beau.

I feel the grim tyrant approaching,
  That cruel, implacable foe,
Who spares neither age nor condition,
  Nor even Old Rosin the Beau,
  Nor even Old Rosin the Beau,
  Nor even Old Rosin the Beau.

No. 6
The Wagoner's Lad

Parental intrusions upon the course of true love must be as old as the family itself. The lover may seek a coward's consolation by isolation on a mountaintop, or, as in this cowboy text, he may induce the enamored maiden to elope with him. Out West there was plenty of room to get lost. (Melody: William A. Owens, *Texas Folk Songs* [Austin: Texas Folklore Society, 1950], p. 278 [reproduced by permission of the author]. Text: FAC II 133, from "Songs o' th' Cowboys" corraled by "Chuck" Haas.)

THE WAGONER'S LAD

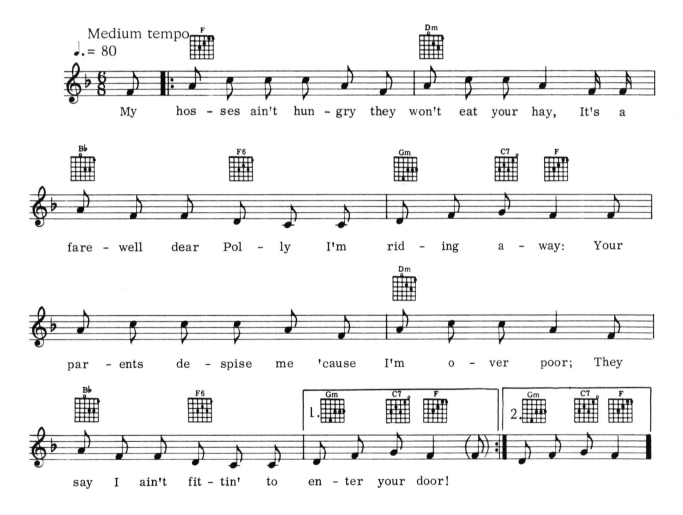

My hos-ses ain't hun-gry they won't eat your hay, It's a fare-well dear Pol-ly I'm rid-ing a-way: Your par-ents de-spise me 'cause I'm o-ver poor; They say I ain't fit-tin' to en-ter your door!

"My horses ain't hungry, they won't eat your hay,
It's farewell dear Polly, I'm riding away:
Your parents despise me 'cause I'm over poor;
They say I ain't fittin' to enter your door!

"I'm just a poor cowboy, I don't own no herd;
I ain't got much money, but give you my word,
I'm handy at roping up poor loneful strays,
An' we'll sure be rich 'fore the end of our days!

"Dear Polly, you promised to be my own wife,
You vowed for to wed me and share all through life,
So mind your words, Polly, I've not long to stay:
Please pack up your duds and we'll ride far away!"

"You know I'm your Polly, your sweet loving dear;
'Cause my kin despise you, don't you have a fear.
Just calm down your feelings and raise up your head;
I know you're the fittin' man for me to wed!

"Yes, Tom, I'll go with you, though you're poor, I'm told,
But it's love I'm wanting, not silver or gold—
Tie on my belongings, we'll ride till we come
To some far-off cabin, and there make our home!

"I mourn for to leave maw, she treats me so fine,
But I've given my promise to you, cowboy mine!
So I'll bid good-bye to my parents this day,
Then we'll mount our ponies and lope far away!

"Far over the mountains we'll come to a rest
In a pretty valley, and build us a nest:
We'll raise a big herd, and a fine family,
And live out our lives there, Tom, all happily!"

No. 7

Bonny Black Bess

Exaltation of the horse as the noblest of creatures was fixed in Anglo-Scottish tradition long before the West was won: "Bonny Black Bess" is a valiant example and became one of the most beloved ballads sung on the frontier. We give it here both in its extended literary form and in the terse intensity to which it is reduced most typically in oral tradition. (Melody and text A: FAC I 106, sung by Kathy Dagel. Text B: Hendren 508.)

BONNY BLACK BESS

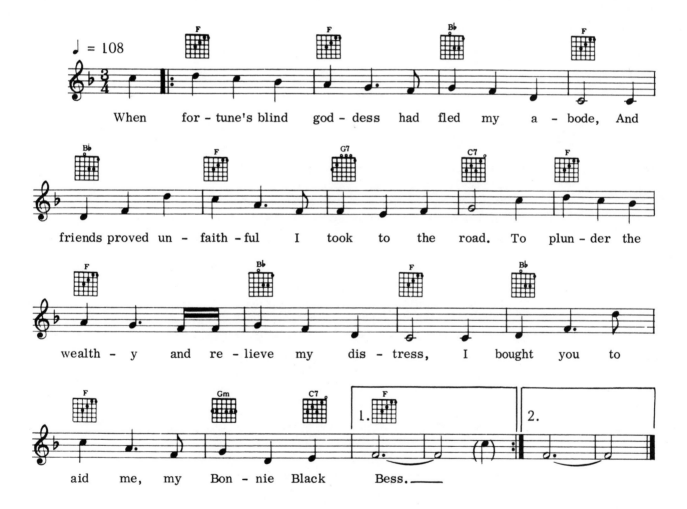

When for - tune's blind god - dess had fled my a - bode, And friends proved un - faith - ful I took to the road. To plun - der the wealth - y and re - lieve my dis - tress, I bought you to aid me, my Bon - nie Black Bess.

When fortune's blind goddess had fled my abode,
And friends proved unfaithful I took to the road.
To plunder the wealthy and relieve my distress,
I bought you to aid me, my Bonnie Black Bess.

How silent you stood when the carriage I stopped,
The gold and the silver its inmates would drop;
No poor man I plundered, nor e'er did oppress
No widows or orphans, my Bonnie Black Bess.

When Argus-eyed justice did me hot pursue
From Yorktown to London like lightnin' you flew;
No toll bars could stop you, the waters did breast,
And in twelve hours you made it, my Bonnie Black Bess.

But hate darkens o'er me, despair is my lot,
And the law does pursue me for the many I've shot;
To save me, poor brute, thou hast done thy best,
Thou art worn out and weary, my Bonnie Black Bess.

They never shall have thee, the law I defy,
So noble and gentle and free, thou must die.
My fate some will pity and some will confess
'Twas kinder to kill thee, my Bonnie Black Bess.

No one can e'er say that ingratitude dwelt
In the bosom of Turpin, 'twas a vice never felt.
I will die like a man and soon be at rest,
Now farewell forever, my Bonnie Black Bess.

Let the lover his mistress' beauty rehearse,
And laud her attractions in languishing verse;
Be it mine, in rude strain but with truth, to express
The love that I bear to my Bonny Black Bess.

From the west was her dam, from the east was her sire;
From the one came her swiftness, from the other her fire.
No peer of the realm better blood can possess
Than flows in the veins of my bonny Black Bess.

Look! Look! how that eyeball glows bright as a brand,
That neck proudly arching, those nostrils expand;
Mark that wide-flowing mane, of which each silky tress
Might adorn prouder beauties, though none like Black Bess.

Mark that skin, sleek as velvet and dusky as night,
With its jet undisfigured by one lock of white;
That throat branched with veins, prompt to charge or caress,
Now is she not beautiful, bonny Black Bess?

Over highway and byway, in rough or smooth weather,
Some thousands of miles have we journeyed together;
Our couch the same straw, our meals the same mess,
No couple more constant than I and Black Bess.

By moonlight, in darkness, by night or by day,
Her headlong career there is nothing can stay,
She cares not for distance, she knows not distress;
Can you show me a courser to match with Black Bess?

Once it happened in Cheshire, near Dunham, I popped
On a horseman alone, whom I suddenly stopped;
That I lightened his pockets you'll readily guess,
Quick work makes Dick Turpin when mounted on Bess.

Now it seems the man knew me. "Dick Turpin," said he,
"You shall swing for this job, as you live, do you see?"
I laughed at his threats and his vows of redress;
I was sure of an alibi then with Black Bess.

The road was a hollow—a sunken ravine,
Overshadowed completely with woods like a screen.
I clambered the bank, and I needs must confess
That one touch of the spur grazed the side of Black Bess.

Brake, brook, meadow and plowed field Bess fleetly bestrode;
As the crow wings his flight we selected our road.
We arrived in Hough Green in five minutes or less,
My neck it was saved by the speed of Black Bess.

Stepping carelessly forward, I lounged on the green,
Taking excellent care that by all I was seen;
Some remarks on time's flight to the squires I addressed,
But I say not a word of the flight of Black Bess.

I mention the hour—it is just about four,
Play a rubber at bowls, think the danger is o'er,
When athwart my next game like a checkmate in chess
Comes the horseman in search of the rider of Bess.

What matter details? Off with triumph I came.
He swears to the hour, and the squires swear the same.
I had robbed him at four, while at four they profess
I was quietly bowling—all thanks to Black Bess.

No. 8

Squeball

This is another song of British heritage preserved in western American tradition both in its extended broadside form and in a greatly reduced, intensified, and Americanized form which is typical of songs that live in oral tradition. From accounts of Squeball's valiant race to a score of ballads about the fleet and dangerous races of western horses, such as Pattonio or Chopo, is an easy, indeed inevitable, transition. Note, moreover, that Text A gives witness to precedence for the notion that there are horses who can talk! (Melody: Library of Congress #906A2, recorded by John A. Lomax. Text A: PNFQ 435. Text B: JL 21.)

SQUEBALL

Come la - dies, come la - dies, come gen - tle - men and all: I'll sing you the prais - es of the no - ble Sque - ball; I'll sing it to you so you'll un - der - stand, He was owned by Squire Mar - ble, the king of the land, And by his bold ac - tions, so I have been told, He was chal - lenged to run for a large sum of gold.

Come ladies, come ladies, come gentlemen, and all:
I'll sing you the praises of the noble Squeball;
I'll sing it to you so you'll understand
He was owned by Squire Marble, the king of the land,
And by his bold actions, so I have been told,
He was challenged to run for a large sum of gold.

The day was appointed, the horses brought forth,
The people all gathered from south and from north;
From north and from south they all did declare,
"We will gamble our money on the Valued Gray Mare."
From north and from south they all did declare:
"I will gamble my money on the Valued Gray Mare."

Then up stepped Squire Marble, who walked the plains round,
Said he, "Ladies and gentlemen, the money's laid down,
Nine thousand one hundred, I'll stand you all,
I'll venture to bet on my noble Squeball.
Nine thousand one hundred, I will stand you all,
I will venture to bet on my noble Squeball."

When Squeball stripped his blanket and was brought on the track,
The people all shouted, "You had better go back,
For to run with Miss Hopkins, the Valued Gray Mare,
She is the queen of the turf on the Plains of Kildare.
For to run with Miss Hopkins, the Valued Gray Mare,
She's the queen of the turf on the Plains of Kildare."

The riders were mounted, so I heard them say,
"Look out for the horses and please clear the way";
If you had been there to see them come 'round,
You'd a thought that those horses weren't touching the ground,
If you had been there to see them go by,
You'd thought to your soul that those horses did fly.

When Squeball was about in the midst of his course,
Then he and his rider began to discourse,
Said he, "Noble rider, can you tell to me,
How far is that Valued Gray Mare before me?"
"Oh yes," says the rider, "we'll run in high style,
She is sporting down close to an English half mile."

"Then stick to my saddle, hang on to my hair,
And we ne'er shall be challenged by the Valued Gray Mare;
It's stick to my saddle, hang on to my mane,"
And like the swiftness of a bullet along past they came.
"It's stick to my saddle, hang on to my mane,"
And like the swiftness of a bullet along past they came.

When Squeball was about to pull through the last pole,
Said he, "Noble rider, we'll drink from the bowl,
We'll drink it to those lost on the Gray Mare,
So that they'll remember the Plains of Kildare.
We'll drink it to those lost on the Gray Mare,
So that they'll remember the Plains of Kildare."

TEXT B

Come all you little riders that gamble all day,
I'll tell you of a race horse that was great in his day,
He was raised in New Boston, he was rode in St. Paul,
And the name they gave him was noble Squeball.

If you had a-been there when the horses came round
You'd swore by your Saviour that they'd never touch ground;
The women they shouted and the children all bawled,
The men, they all hollered, "Just catch old Squeball."

Come all you little riders that gambles on the square,
Don't bet your last dollar on the iron-gray mare,
She reels and she staggers, she's liable to fall,
Ten thousand gold dollars in on old Squeball!

He gave her the starting, she led a good piece,
Old Squeball overtakes her, overtakes her by speed.
Give me beef steak when I'm hungry, corn whiskey when I'm dry,
Give me green backs when I need them, sweet heaven when I die.

Go rap on your counter and the waiter will bring
A glass of corn whiskey for the cowboys to drink.
The train it is coming, it is ready to go,
Old Squeball will neigh at the union depot.

No. 9

Johnny Cake

In folk song, the battle of the sexes is sometimes more provocation than battle: this is the case with a song we choose to call "Johnny Cake," though it appears under a score or more of titles. It has British origins, was as popular on the frontier as whiskey or whiskers. For those who must hear folk songs as an exercise in depth psychology, "Johnny Cake" is probably a causative agent for babies, and when "baked brown," there are scatological overtones: there are texts which clarify these matters. Strangely, Text A uses a stanza from a song of the Mormon Battalion as a refrain. The song has been adapted to fit the young men of half the states in the Union. (Melody and Text A: commercial recording, Len Nash. Text B: Library of Congress #1732A3, recorded by John A. Lomax. Text C: FAC II 492, collected by Hermes Nye. Text D: Gordon 3431.)

JOHNNY CAKE

Come all girls pay at - ten - tion to my voice, Don't you

fall in love with the Kan - sas boys, ____ For

if you do your for - tune it will be, Hoe - cake, hominy, and

sas - sa - fras tea. ____ (After every *second* verse, go to the Chorus) Oh,

CHORUS

On the road to Cal - i - for - ney, It was a hard and

te - di - ous jour - ney, Far a - cross the Rock - y Moun - tains,

Crys - tal springs and flow - ing foun - tains. ____

TEXT A. ON THE ROAD TO CALIFORNIA

Come all girls, pay attention to my voice,
Don't you fall in love with the Kansas boys,
For if you do your fortune it will be
Hoe-cake, hominy, and sassafras tea.

They'll take you out on the jet black hill,
And they'll take you there much against your will,
Leave you there to perish on the plains,
For that is the way with the Kansas range.

CHORUS:
> Oh, on the road to Californey
> It was a hard and a tedious journey,
> Far across the Rocky Mountains,
> Crystal springs and flowing fountains.

When they go to meeting the clothes that they wear
Is an old brown coat all fixed and bare.
An old white hat small-rimmed and crowned,
And a pair of cotton socks that they wore the year around.

Some live in a cabin with a huge log wall
And a-nary a window in it at all,
A sandstone chimney and a punch board floor,
A clap board roof and a button-hole door.

When they go to milk they milk in a gourd
And they heave it in the corner and they cover it with a board.
Some get plenty and some get none
For that is the way with the Kansas run.

When they go a-fishin' they take along a worm
And they put it on a hook just to see it squirm.
The first thing they say when they get a bite
Is, "I got a fish as big as Johnny White."

When they go a-courtin' they take along a chair
And the first thing they say, "Has your daddy killed a bear?"
The second thing they say when they sit right down
Is, "Madam, your johnny cake is baking brown."

TEXT B. HAD A LITTLE FIGHT IN MEXICO

Had a little fight in Mexico,
Wasn't for the girls, the boys wouldn't go.

CHORUS:
> Sing tol de rol, sing tol de ray,
> Sing tol de rol, sing tol de rol de ray.

Come to the place where the blood was shed,
The girls turned back and the boys went ahead.

And the girls and the boys where they did meet
They laughed and talked and kissed so sweet.

You better get up, you're mighty in the way,
Choose you a partner and come along and play.

O that little fight in Mexico,
None was killed but John Taylor-o.

I had an old hat with a flop-down brim,
It looked like a toad frog setting on a limb.

I had an old cow and I milked her in a gourd,
Set it in a corner and covered it with a board.

I want to go to Texas, and to Texas I'll go,
And I'll vote for old John Taylor-o.

I went to the fight in Mexico,
Fighting for the gunboats all in a row.

Come to the place where the blood was shed,
The girls turned back and the boys went ahead.

And the girls and the boys where they did meet
They laughed and talked and kissed so sweet.

I started out a-courtin' and I knew where to go,
I went to a man's house here below.
The kids cried for bread and the old folks gone,
And the girls they were mad and their heads not combed,
And the girls they were mad and their heads not combed.

The old dirty clothes was hanging on the loom,
The house not swept for they had no broom.
There was a long-tailed coat greased all around
And an old leather bonnet with a hole in the crown,
And an old leather bonnet with a hole in the crown.

Well, I stayed and sparked till I got ashamed,
Every once in a while they would ask me my name.
I told them it was Johnny and they seemed satisfied,
For they giggled and they laughed till they both cried,
For they giggled and they laughed till they both cried.

Well, they called me to dinner and I thought it was to eat,
And the first thing I saw was a big hunk of meat,
Cooked half done and as tough as a moll,
And an old corn dodger baked bran and all,
And an old corn dodger baked bran and all.

I had an old dull knife and nary a fork,
Well, I sawed and sawed and I couldn't make a mark.
So I kept on sawin' till I got it on the floor,
Then I up with my foot and kicked it out the door,
Then I up with my foot and kicked it out the door.

In came the old man with a double-barreled gun
And the girls said, "Johnny, you'd better run."
But I stood and I fought him as brave as a bear,
And I tangled my fingers in the old man's hair,
And I tangled my fingers in the old man's hair.

TEXT D. MISSISSIPPI GALS

Come all you Mississippi girls and listen to my noise,
If you happen to go West don't you marry those Texian boys.
For if you do your fortune it will be
Cold johnny cake and beefsteak, that's all that you will see,
Cold johnny cake and beefsteak, that's all that you will see.

When they come a-courting here's what they wear,
An old leather coat and it's all soiled and tore;
And an old brown hat with the brim tore down,
And a pair of dirty socks they've worn the winter round,
And a pair of dirty socks they've worn the winter round.

When one comes in, the first thing you hear
Is, "Madam, your brother has killed a deer."
And the next thing they say when they sit down
Is, "Madam, the johnny cake is too damn brown."

They live in a hut with a hewed log wall,
But it ain't got any windows at all;
With a clapboard roof and a puncheon floor
And that's the way all Texas o'er,
And that's the way all Texas o'er.

They will take you out on a mesquite hill
And there they will leave you against your will;
They will leave you on the prairie, starve you on the plain,
For that is the way with the Tex-i-ans,
For that is the way with the Tex-i-ans.

When they go to preaching let me tell you how they dress,
Just an old black shirt without any vest.
Just an old straw hat with more brim than crown,
And an old sock leg that they wear the winter round,
And an old sock leg that they wear the winter round.

For your supper there'll be beef and corn bread,
There it is to eat when the ceremony's said.
And when you go to milk you'll milk into a gourd.
And set it in a corner and cover it with a board.
Some gets little and some gets none,
For that's the way with the Tex-i-ans,
For that's the way with the Tex-i-ans.

No. 10
Rigby Johnson Chandler

There are songs for every mood: here laughter is evoked by a sharp contrast between the absurdity of images and the gravity of musical expression. Each stanza plus the refrain is a complete expression: length of the song is limited only by the singer's ingenuity in coining new stanzas. (Melody and text: FAC I 26, recorded by Rosalie Sorrels.)

RIGBY JOHNSON CHANDLER

Old man went out to plow, Rig - by John - son Chand- ler, Old man went out to plow, And he hooked up a hog with a jer - sey cow,__ Rig - by John-son Chand - ler; that's e - nough for me. It's

Refrain:

frost - y on the prai - rie and the sun is shin - ing down, It's thun - der in the moun-tains and it's rain - in' all a - round.

Old man went out to plow,
  Rigby Johnson Chandler,
Old man went out to plow,
And he hooked up a hog with a jersey cow.
  Rigby Johnson Chandler, that's enough for me.

CHORUS:
  It's frosty on the prairie and the sun is shining down,
  It's thunder in the mountains and it's rainin' all around.

Old man died on the railroad track,
  Rigby Johnson Chandler,
Old man died on the railroad track,
And they carried him home in two gunny sacks.
  Rigby Johnson Chandler, that's enough for me.

Had an old hen and she learned to fly,
  Rigby Johnson Chandler,
Had an old hen and she learned to fly,
And she laid an egg two miles high.
  Rigby Johnson Chandler, that's enough for me.

Two old maids sittin' in the sand,
  Rigby Johnson Chandler,
Two old maids a-sittin' in the sand,
Each of 'em wishes that the other was a man.
  Sing Rigby Johnson Chandler, that's enough for me.

I took my woman down to town,
  Rigby Johnson Chandler,
I took my woman down to town,
And she went to the circus and run off with the clown.
  Rigby Johnson Chandler, that's enough for me.

I went in a joint to drink some beer,
  Rigby Johnson Chandler,
I went in a joint to drink some beer,
A man came in with a big long tommy gun
And he looked around and said, "There's too many people here."
  That's the tommy gun.
    [Last line spoken while striking repeatedly on guitar.]

Part Two

Westward Ho!

No. 11
Root Hog or Die

This remarkable specimen of frontier realism is among the earliest of our ruggedly American folk songs. It appears localized at the Boston Tea Party, in the War of 1812, as a Negro minstrel ditty, as an anti-Union song during the Civil War, as a Gold Rush satire, as a cowhand work song, and, most typically, as the classical ballad of the bullwhackers who made the first link between western frontier towns and supply points farther east. These hardy teamsters are the mythical forebears of the railroad engineers, truckers, and pilots of times less remote. (Melody: Library of Congress #2321B2, A4, recorded by Alan Lomax. Text A: FAC II 466, published by permission of the collector, Herbert Halpert, Memorial University, St. John's, Newfoundland. Text B: *Out West,* April 1911, p. 336.)

ROOT HOG OR DIE

TEXT A. ROOT HOG OR DIE

I am a jolly driver of the Salt Lake City line,
I can whip the rascal who would yoke an ox of mine.
You'd better bring him out; you bet your life I'd try,
I would sprawl him with an ox bow, root hog or die.

I tell you how it is when you first get on the road,
You have an awkward team and a very heavy load,
You cut and you slash, if you swear it's on the sly,
Punch along your team, boys, root hog or die.

There's many strange sights for to see along the road,
Antelopes and deers and big sand toads,
Buffaloes and elks where the rabbits jump so high,
Where all those bloody Injuns are. Root hog or die.

Times on Bitter Creek—they are hard to beat,
Root hog or die's on every wagon seat.
The sand's within my throat and the dust is in my eyes,
So bend your back and bear it, boys, root hog or die.

Every day there is something to do,
If nothing else there's an ox for to shoe.
You trip him with a rope and there you make him lie
While you tack on the shoes, boys, root hog or die.

I suppose you'd like to know what we have to eat:
A little piece of bread and a dirty piece of meat,
Little old molasses and sugar on the sly,
Potatoes when you get them, boys, root hog or die.

When we arrived in Salt Lake City, 'twas the twenty-fifth of June,
The people were surprised to see us come so soon.
We are the bold bull-whackers on who you can rely,
We're tough and we can stand it, boys, root hog or die.

Text B. A Philosophical Cowboy

On the Double Circle Range where the grass grows green,
The cattle get wild and the broncs get mean,
And the calves get bigger as the days go by,
So we got to keep a-rimming, boys, it's root hog or die.

If you ride them out of horses you've got to keep them shod,
If you can't shoe them standing then lay them on the sod.
You can tack the iron on them if you're a mind to try,
So get busy, boys, for it's root hog or die.

In the morning after breakfast about daylight,
Throw your saddle on a horse and pull your cinches tight;
Your bronc may jump crooked or he may jump high,
But we all got to ride them, boys, it's root hog or die.

Oh, the hills are rough and rocky but we got to make the drive,
When you start a bunch of cattle you better come alive.
If you ever get a maverick you must get him on the fly,
So you better take to them, boys, it's root hog or die.

When the long day is over you'll be glad to see the chief
With a pot of black coffee and another full of beef,
And some sour dough biscuits to take the place of pie.
When he hollers, "Come and git it," it's root hog or die.

In the middle of the night it is sometimes awful hard
To leave your warm blankets when you're called on guard,
And you pass the weary moments while the stars are in the sky
Humming to the cattle, boys, it's root hog or die.

Sometimes it's dreadful stormy and sometimes it's pretty clear,
You may work a month and you might work a year,
But you can make a winning if you'll come alive and try,
For the whole world over, boys, it's root hog or die.

No. 12

Joe Bowers

Joe Bowers, from Pike County, Missouri, is among the best known of the Forty-Niners. The ballad has pervaded American folk song for more than a hundred years. Joe's mock-tragic vein on receipt of news of Sally's marriage and motherhood, especially his concern about the color of the baby's hair, is one of the high points in the whole gambit of American folk humor. (Melody: FAC I 520, sung by Jay Bailey. First seven stanzas of text from W. E. Connelley, *Doniphan's Expedition* [Topeka, Kansas, 1907], pp. 10–11; last stanza from Gordon 785.)

JOE BOWERS

My name it is Joe Bowers and I've got a broth-er Ike; I came from Old Mis - sour - i, and— all the way from Pike. I'll tell you why I left there, and— why I came to roam, And leave my poor old mam-my,— so far a - way from home.

My name it is Joe Bowers, and I've got a brother Ike;
I came from Old Missouri, and all the way from Pike.
I'll tell you why I left there, and why I came to roam,
And leave my poor old mammy, so far away from home.

I used to court a gal there—her name was Sally Black;
I axed her if she'd marry me; she said it was a whack;
Says she to me, "Joe Bowers, before we hitch for life,
You ought to get a little home to keep your little wife."

"O Sally, dearest Sally, O Sally, for your sake,
I'll go to California and try to make a stake."
Says she to me, "Joe Bowers, you are the man to win;
Here's a kiss to bind the bargain"—and she hove a dozen in.

When I got to that country I hadn't nary red;
I had such wolfish feelings, I wished myself 'most dead;
But the thoughts of my dear Sally soon made those feelings git,
And whispered hopes to Bowers—I wish I had 'em yit!

At length I went to mining, put in my biggest licks;
Went down upon the boulders just like a thousand bricks.
I worked both late and early, in rain, in sun, in snow;
I was working for my Sally, it was all the same to Joe.

At length I got a letter from my dear brother Ike;
It came from Old Missouri, and all the way from Pike;
It brought to me the darndest news that ever you did hear—
My heart is almost bursting, so pray excuse this tear.

It said that Sal was false to me, her love for me had fled;
She'd got married to a butcher, and the butcher's hair was red;
And more than that, the letter said—it's enough to make me swear—
That Sally has a baby, and the baby has red hair!

And now you've heard the story of Bowers and his woes,
I'll give to you the sequel and let the story close.
Smallpox had knocked the butcher out
When Joe soon wandered back, married Sally and the Shop,
And now he has the red-haired boy to drive the butcher cart.

No. 13
Ox Driving Song

Many work songs—drilling songs, track lining songs, hoisting or rowing songs, etc.—manifest amazing joviality and exuberant rhythms: it is as if the song opened up a world of fantasy in which consciousness of harsh muscular exertion is submerged. (Melody and text: Library of Congress #2648A2, recorded by Ruby T. and John A. Lomax.)

OX DRIVING SONG

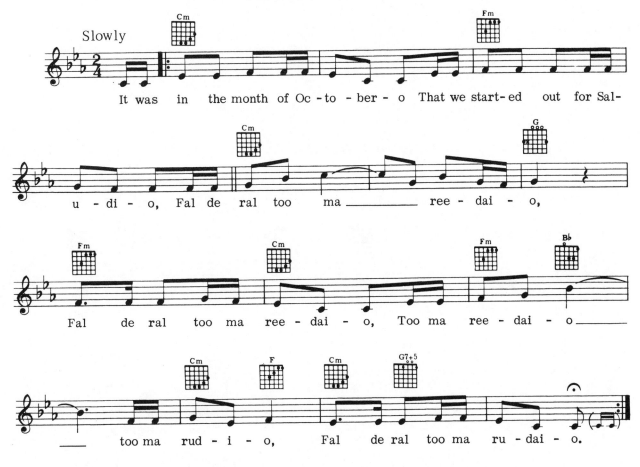

It was in the month of October-o
That we started out for Saludio.

CHORUS:
Fal de ral too ma reedaio,
Fal de ral too ma reedaio,
Too ma reedaio, too ma rudio,
Fall de ral too ma rudaio.

I'll bid adieu to the whip and line
And drive no more in the winter time.

I pop my whip, I bring the blood,
I make my leaders take the mud.

It would make any tender-hearted person weep
To see my oxen pull and slip.

When I get home I'll have revenge,
I'll land my family among my friends.

No. 14
A Ripping Trip

A much used route for migration to the Pacific Coast was by steamer to Panama, by rail across the Isthmus (earlier by mule train), and by ship again to San Diego, Monterey, San Francisco. Some took an even longer voyage around the Horn, often halting in Hawaii before bending back to the Pacific Coast. This song evokes the hazards of such a trip in language that is realistic and flamboyant. (Melody is traditional "Pop Goes the Weasel." Text: *Put's Golden Songster* [San Francisco: D. Appleton and Co., 1858], p. 46.)

A RIPPING TRIP

You go a-board of a leak-y boat and sail for San Fran-cis-co, You've got to pump to keep_ a-float, you have that, by jin - go. The en - gine soon be - gins_ to squeak, but nar - y thing to oil her, Im - pos - si - ble to stop the leak, rip goes the boil - er.

You go aboard of a leaky boat and sail for San Francisco,
You've got to pump to keep afloat, you have that, by jingo
The engine soon begins to squeak, but nary thing to oil her,
Impossible to stop the leak—rip goes the boiler.

The captain on the Promenade looking very savage,
The steward and the cabin maid fighting 'bout a cabbage,
All about the cabin floor passengers lie sea sick,
Steamer's bound to go ashore—rip goes the physic.

Pork and beans they can't afford to second cabin passengers,
The cook he has tumbled overboard with forty pounds of "sassengers,"
The engineer, a little tight, bragging on the Mail Line,
Finally gets into a fight—rip goes the engine.

The cholera begins to rage, a few have got the scurvy,
Chickens dying in their cage, steerage topsy turvy,
When we get to Panama, greasers want a back load,
Officers begin to jaw—rip goes the railroad.

When home you'll tell an awful tale and always will be thinking
How long you had to pump and bail to keep the tub from sinking.
Of course you'll take a glass of gin, 'twill make you feel so funny,
Some city chap will rope you in—rip goes your money.

No. 15

The California Brothers

"The California Brothers," known perhaps most often as "The Dying Californian," has appeared hundreds of times since its earliest printing in 1850. The mournful mood is reminiscent of traditional white spirituals. It is filled with the clichés of frontier religiosity and sentimentality: God, mother, father, wife, brother, sister, and the imperishable soul are all present, yet a tragic note prevails. Despite its obvious literary origins it is popular in oral tradition. (Melody A: FMC I 969, sung by Effie Carmack. Melody B: FAC I 554, recorded by Frank Hoffman. Text: *Beadle's Dime Song Books*, No. 1 [New York, 1859], p. 47.)

THE CALIFORNIA BROTHERS

Lay up near - er, broth - er, near - er For my limbs are grow-ing cold, And thy pres - ence seem - eth dear - er When thy arms a-round me fold. I am dy - ing, broth-er, dy - ing, Soon you'll miss me in your berth And my form will soon be ly - ing Be-neath the o - cean's brin - y surf.

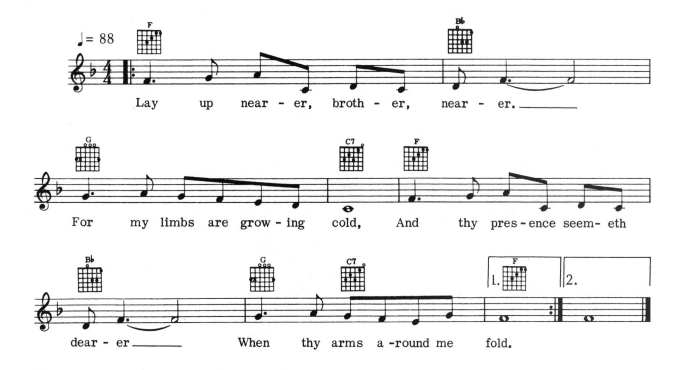

Lay up nearer, brother, nearer
  For my limbs are growing cold,
And thy presence seemeth dearer
  When thy arms around me fold.

I am dying, brother, dying,
  Soon you'll miss me in your berth
And my form will soon be lying
  Beneath the ocean's briny surf.

Hearken to me, brother, hearken,
  I have something I would say
Ere this veil my vision darken
  And I go from hence away.

I am going, surely going,
  But my hopes in God are strong,
I am willing, brother, knowing
  That He doeth nothing wrong.

Tell my father, when you greet him,
　That in death I prayed for him,
Prayed that I might one day meet him
　In a world that's free from sin.

Tell my mother, God assist her
　Now that she is growing old,
Tell her son would glad have kissed her
　When his lips grew pale and cold.

Hearken to me, catch each whisper,
　'Tis my wife I speak of now,
Tell, oh tell her how I missed her
　When the fever burned my brow.

Hearken to me, closely listen,
　Don't forget a single word,
That in death my eyes did glisten
　When the tears her memory stirred.

Tell her then to kiss my children
　Like the kiss I last impressed,
Hold them fast as last I held them
　Folded closely to my breast.

Give them early to their Maker,
　Putting all their trust in God,
And He will never forsake her,
　He has said so in His word.

Oh my children, heaven bless them,
　They were all my life to me,
Would I could once more caress them
　Ere I sink beneath the sea;

'Twas for them I crossed the ocean,
　What my hopes were I'll not tell,
But they have gained an orphan's portion,
　Yet He doeth all things well.

Tell my sisters I remember
  Every kindly, parting word,
And my heart has been kept tender
  By the thoughts their memories stirred.

Tell them I never reached the haven
  Where I sought the precious dust,
But I've gained a port called heaven
  Where the gold doth never rust.

Urge them to secure an entrance
  For they will find their brother there,
Faith in Jesus and repentance
  Will secure for them a share.

Hark, I hear my Savior calling,
  'Tis, I know His voice so well,
When I'm gone, oh don't be weeping,
  Brother, hear my last farewell.

No. 16

Steamboat Bill

The Mississippi was the gateway to the cowboy kingdom. "Steamboat Bill," cousin, if not indeed the sire, of the immortal railroader "Casey Jones," evokes the virility and flamboyance of the river towns and steam-driven boats that churned the whiskers of the silted old monarch from St. Paul to the Gulf. (Melody: FAC I 335, sung by Eda D. Smith. Text: *Hobo News Folio*, No. 10, n.d.)

STEAMBOAT BILL

Down the Mis-sis-sip-pi steamed the *Whip-poor-will*, Com-
mand-ed by the pi-lot, Mis-ter Steam-boat Bill. The
own-ers gave him or-ders on the strict Q. T., To
try to beat the rec-ord of the *Rob-ert E. Lee.*

CHORUS
Repeat after every *second* verse

Oh, Steam-boat Bill, steam-in' down the Mis-sis-sip-pi, Steam-boat Bill, a

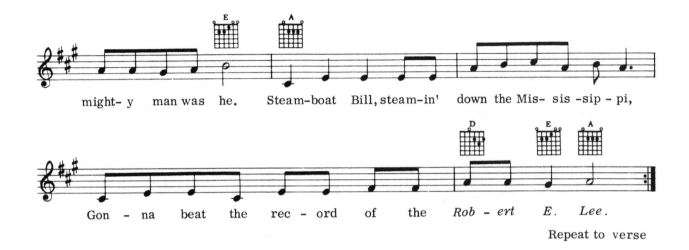

might-y man was he. Steam-boat Bill, steam-in' down the Mis- sis -sip - pi,

Gon - na beat the rec - ord of the *Rob - ert E. Lee.*

Repeat to verse

Down the Mississippi steamed the *Whippoorwill*
Commanded by the pilot, Mister Steamboat Bill.
The owners gave him orders on the strict Q.T.
To try to beat the record of the *Robert E. Lee.*

Just speed up your fire, let the old smoke roll,
Burn up all your cargo if you run out of coal.
"If we don't beat that record," Billy told the mate,
"Then the *Maiden Care*'ll beat us to the Golden Gate."

CHORUS NO. 1:
    Oh, Steamboat Bill, steamin' down the Mississippi,
      Steamboat Bill, a mighty man was he.
    Oh, Steamboat Bill, steamin' down the Mississippi,
      Gonna beat the record of the *Robert E. Lee.*

Up then stepped a gambling man from Louisville
Who tried to get a bet against the *Whippoorwill.*
Billy clasped the roll and surely was some bear,
The boiler it exploded, blew them up in the air.

The gambler said to Billy as they left the wreck,
"I don't know where we're going but we're neck and neck."
Said Billy to the gambler, "Tell you what I'll do:
I'll bet another thousand I'll go higher than you!"

CHORUS NO. 2:
    Oh, Steamboat Bill, he tore up the Mississippi,
      Oh, Steamboat Bill, the pilot made him swear.
    Oh, Steamboat Bill, he tore up the Mississippi,
      An explosion of the boiler put him up in the air!

The river's all in mourning now for Steamboat Bill.
No more you'll hear the popping of the *Whippoorwill,*
There's crepe on every steamboat that plows the stream,
From Memphis right to Natchez, down to New Orleans.

The wife of Mister William was at home in bed
When she got the telegram that Steamboat's dead.
Said she to the children, "Blessed Honey Lambs,
The next papa that you have'll be a railroad man!"

CHORUS NO. 3:
    Oh, Steamboat Bill, missing 'long the Mississippi,
      Oh, Steamboat Bill is with an angel band.
    Oh, Steamboat Bill, missing 'long the Mississippi,
      He's a fireman on a ferry in the Promised Land!

No. 17
That Is Even So

This is a song of stark realism about the disappointments of the gold seekers, and of the cold reception the Mormons gave them as they crossed the Great Basin en route to California. (Melody from D. H. Mansfield, *The American Vocalist* [Boston, 1849], quoted by Richard A. Dwyer and Richard E. Lingenfelter, *The Songs of the Gold Rush* [Berkeley and Los Angeles: The University of California Press, 1964], p. 47. Text: *Put's Golden Songster* [San Francisco: D. Appleton and Co., 1858], pp. 53–55.)

THAT IS EVEN SO

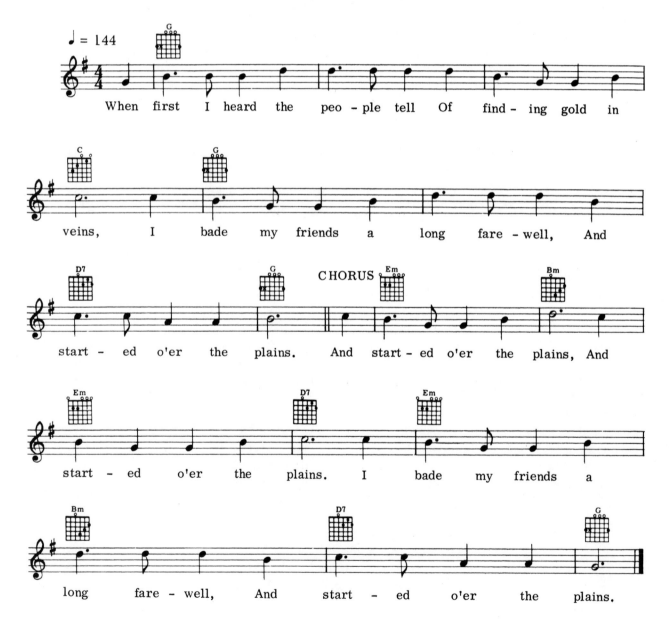

When first I heard the peo-ple tell Of find-ing gold in veins, I bade my friends a long fare-well, And start-ed o'er the plains. And start-ed o'er the plains, And start-ed o'er the plains. I bade my friends a long fare-well, And start-ed o'er the plains.

When first I heard the people tell
  Of finding gold in veins,
I bade my friends a long farewell
  And started o'er the plains.
  And started o'er the plains,
  And started o'er the plains,
I bade my friends a long farewell
  And started o'er the plains.

I joined a train and travelled on,
  And all seemed satisfied,
Until our grub was nearly gone,
  And I got alkalied.
  And I got alkalied,
  And I got alkalied,
Until our grub was nearly gone
  And I got alkalied.

My bowels soon began to yearn,
  My legs began to ache;
My only show was to return
  Or winter at Salt Lake.
  Or winter at Salt Lake,
  Or winter at Salt Lake,
My only show was to return
  Or winter at Salt Lake.

The Mormons knew that Uncle Sam
  Had troops upon the route,
And Brigham prayed the Holy Lamb
  Would help to clean them out.
  Would help to clean them out,
  Would help to clean them out,
And Brigham prayed the Holy Lamb
  Would help to clean them out.

The distance then, one thousand miles,
  Me in the face did stare,
For Brigham swore no damned Gentiles
  Again should winter there.
  Again should winter there,
  Again should winter there,
For Brigham swore no damned Gentiles
  Again should winter there.

I reached the mines with "nary red,"
  Was treated rather cold,
I found no lumps but found instead
  I'd been completely sold.
  I'd been completely sold,
  I'd been completely sold,
I found no lumps but found instead
  I'd been completely sold.

I hope and pray that every man,
  If mineral lands are sold,
Will drop his shovel, pick and pan
  And leave the land of gold.
  And leave the land of gold,
  And leave the land of gold,
Will drop his shovel, pick and pan
  And leave the land of gold.

No. 18
The Wells and Fargo Line

Stagecoach robberies have become a standard theme in the Western movies. This song evokes the most famous of the western stagecoach lines, and the depredations wrought thereon by Major Thompson, Jim Hughes, Black Bart, and others. As in many ballads, there are a stereo-typed beginning and conclusion that suggest a comfortable barroom setting more than the wide-open spaces. (Melody and text: JL 446.)

THE WELLS AND FARGO LINE

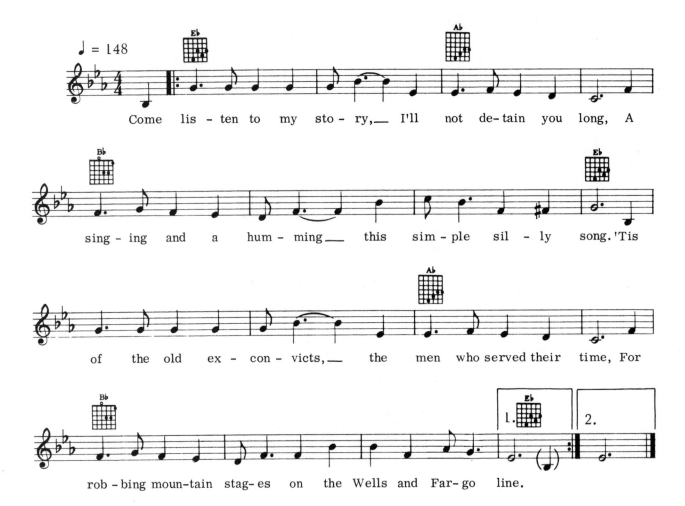

Come lis-ten to my sto-ry,— I'll not de-tain you long, A sing-ing and a hum-ming— this sim-ple sil-ly song. 'Tis of the old ex-con-victs,— the men who served their time, For rob-bing moun-tain stag-es on the Wells and Far-go line.

Come listen to my story, I'll not detain you long,
A-singing and a-humming this simple silly song.
'Tis of the old ex-convicts, the men who served their time
For robbing mountain stages on the Wells and Fargo line.

There was Major Thompson turned up the other day,
He said that he would hold them up or hell would be to pay,
For he could hold a rifle and draw a bead so fine
Upon those shotgun messengers of the Wells and Fargo line.

And there was Jimmy Miner who thought he was a thief
But he did surely prove himself to be a dirty sneak;
And now behind San Quentin's walls he's serving out his time
For giving tips to Old Jim Hughes on the Wells and Fargo line.

And there was still another who well did play his part,
He's known among the mountains as the highwayman, Black Bart.
He'd ride those mountain jerkies, to him it was but pleasure,
He'd ride the trail both night and day for the Wells and Fargo treasure.

And now my story's ended, I've not detained you long,
A-singing and a-humming this simple silly song.
And though the nights are long, boys, and weary grows the time,
But when we are out we'll ride again the Wells and Fargo line.

No. 19

Sweet Betsey from Pike

"Sweet Betsey" is the most sung of all frontier women. Her Odyssey with Long Ike offers a rollicking specimen of frontier humor and the stereotype of a rugged pioneer woman having no counterpart in this puritanized generation of ours. The song has been recorded, printed, sung, copied innumerable times: there are many stanzas not offered in this 1858 text, including some that "don't look good in print." (Melody: Library of Congress #1697A1, recorded by John A. Lomax. Text: *Put's Golden Songster* [San Francisco: D. Appleton and Co., 1858], pp. 50–52.)

SWEET BETSEY FROM PIKE

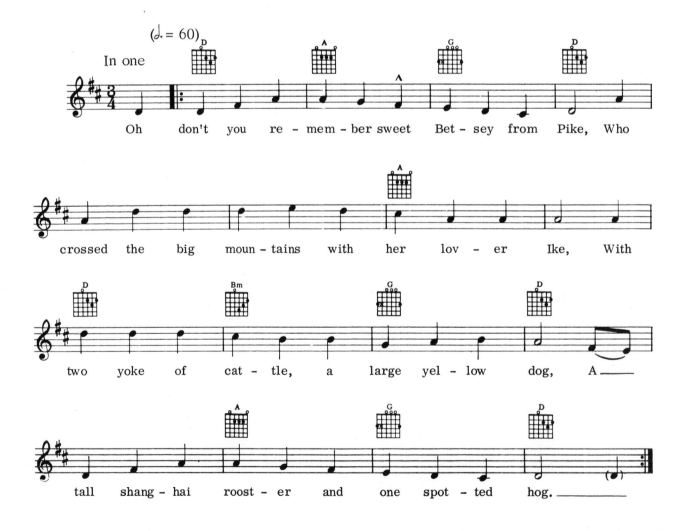

Oh don't you re-mem-ber sweet Bet-sey from Pike, Who crossed the big moun-tains with her lov-er Ike, With two yoke of cat-tle, a large yel-low dog, A ___ tall shang-hai roost-er and one spot-ted hog. ___

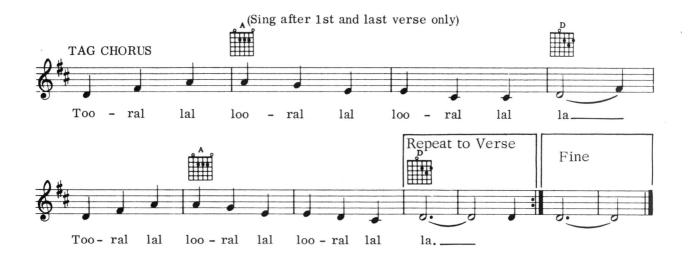

TAG CHORUS

(Sing after 1st and last verse only)

Too - ral lal loo - ral lal loo - ral lal la_____

Repeat to Verse   Fine

Too- ral lal loo - ral lal loo - ral lal la._____

Oh, don't you remember sweet Betsey from Pike,
Who crossed the big mountains with her lover Ike,
With two yoke of cattle, a large yellow dog,
A tall shanghai rooster and one spotted hog.

CHORUS:
  Too-ral lal loo-ral lal loo-ral lal la,
  Too-ral lal loo-ral lal loo-ral lal la.

One evening quite early they camped on the Platte,
'Twas near by the road on a green shady flat,
Where Betsey, sore-footed, lay down to repose,
With wonder Ike gazed on that Pike County rose!

Their wagon broke down with a terrible crash,
And out on the prairie rolled all kinds of trash,
A few little baby clothes done up with care,
'Twas rather suspicious, though all on the square.

The shanghai ran off and their cattle all died,
That morning the last piece of bacon was fried.
Poor Ike was discouraged and Betsey got mad,
The dog drooped his tail and looked wondrously sad.

They stopped at Salt Lake to inquire the way,
When Brigham declared that Sweet Betsey should stay;
But Betsey got frightened and ran like a deer
While Brigham stood pawing the ground like a steer.

They soon reached the desert, where Betsey gave out,
And down in the sand she lay rolling about;
While Ike, half distracted, looked on with surprise,
Saying, "Betsey, get up, you'll get sand in your eyes."

Sweet Betsey got up in a great deal of pain,
Declared she'd go back to Pike County again;
But Ike gave a sigh and they fondly embraced,
And they travelled along with his arm 'round her waist.

They suddenly stopped on a very high hill,
With wonder looked down upon old Placerville;
Ike sighed when he said, and he cast his eyes down,
"Sweet Betsey, my darling, we've got to Hangtown."

Long Ike and Sweet Betsey attended a dance;
Ike wore a pair of his Pike County pants;
Sweet Betsey was covered with ribbons and rings;
Says Ike, "You're an angel, but where are your wings?"

A miner said, "Betsey, will you dance with me?"
"I will that, old hoss, if you don't make too free;
But don't dance me hard, do you want to know why?
Dog on you, I'm chock full of strong alkali!"

This Pike County couple got married of course,
And Ike became jealous, obtained a divorce.
Sweet Betsey, well satisfied, said with a shout,
"Good bye, you big lummox, I'm glad you've backed out!"

No. 20
Freighting from Wilcox to Globe

Freighting by wagon and team (oxen, horses, mules) continued in isolated areas into the first two decades of our own century. There were well-organized corporations like Wells Fargo, but, typically, goods were moved by frontiersmen whose only capital was a wagon and a span of horses. Their margin was precarious, and most did well to hold body and soul together: witness the stark realism of this vigorous song. (Melody and text: University of Arizona Folklore Archive, sung by A. J. Busby.)

FREIGHTING FROM WILCOX TO GLOBE

Come all you jol - ly freight- ers__ who trav-el up-on the road, That

ev - er hauled a load of coke from Wil - cox__ to Globe! That's how I made my

liv - ing__ for ten long years or more, Was haul - ing coke for Lev - er-man, no

won - der I am poor. Then it's home, dear-est home,__ at home you'd bet - ter

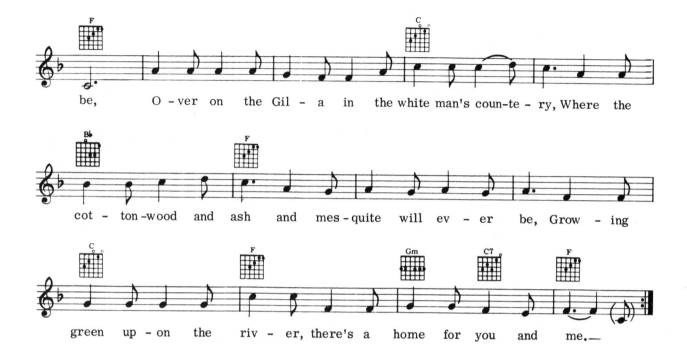

be, O-ver on the Gil - a in the white man's coun-te - ry, Where the

cot - ton -wood and ash and mes -quite will ev - er be, Grow - ing

green up - on the riv - er, there's a home for you and me.—

Come all you jolly freighters who travel upon the road,
That ever hauled a load of coke from Wilcox to Globe!
That's how I made my living for ten long years or more,
Was hauling coke for Leverman, no wonder I am poor.

Then it's home, dearest home, at home you'd better be,
Over on the Gila in the white man's coun-te-ry;
Where the cottonwood and ash and mesquite will ever be,
Growing green upon the river, there's a home for you and me.

In eighteen eighty-three I started with my team,
Chuck full of glee with that elusive dream.
But that first night out from Wilcox my best horse got stole
And it made me cuss a little when I came out in the hole.

That left me with but three, Kate, Molly, and Old Mike,
He being the best one, I put him out on spike;
I went the mountain road so the people wouldn't smile,
And it took me fifteen days to travel fourteen miles.

But I got there just the same with my little three-up spike,
But I had to go in debt again to get a mate for Mike.
And you all know how to pity me—when once you get behind
You never can get even, boys, unless you steal them blind.

I was an honest man when first I hit the road,
I wouldn't take a note nor I wouldn't tap a load.
But now you ought to see my mules when I begin to cuss,
They wiggle their tails and flop their ears and pull the load or bust.

Now I'm a freighter right and I'm up to all the tricks,
I can tap a whiskey barrel with nothing but a stick;
You never can detect it, I've got it down quite pat,
And fill it up with water again, sure there's no harm in that.

Barbed wire and bacon is all that they would pay;
We have to use our copper checks to buy our grain and hay.
When you ask them for five dollars, old Myers would scratch his pate,
And their clerks with paper collars will say, "Get down and pull your
    freight."

Our home is round the campfire where e'er we camp at night,
It's there we drink our coffee and pass around the pipe.
We sing our songs and spin our yarns and pass the bottle round,
And it's always filled with something good that some poor freighter
    found.

My clothes are rather rough and I know that they are not genteel,
But they are good enough till I can make another steal.
My boots are number ten, I stole them from a chaw,
And my coat cost "dorell-alles" * from a little Apache squaw.

---

* *Dos reales:* two bits.

I've traveled in the sunshine, I've traveled in the rain,
I've lost my wagons in the mud and dug them out again;
I've laid out in the snow till it's a wonder I'm not dead,
With a double "divil-a-bit" of cover but an Arizona bed.

We take our money minus Kellner's ten per cent,
And blow it in along the road until it is all spent.
And every town we come to, we have a jolly dance,
And try to kiss the pretty girls whenever we get the chance.

When we get to Pima the girls they are so fine
A fellow wants to treat them all to Uncle Moses' wine;
But Thatcher has the prettiest girls, it's where we stay all night,
But we have to go to Safford to get a little tight.

Another trip or two and Old Mike he will peg out,
As for Old Kate and Molly, they've gone up the spout.
Old Kate kicked out at Bailey's Wells and Moll lies at the Sub,
And if her bones could speak they'd say she died for want of grub.

Now I'll have to quit the road, before I do I'll tell
What I intend to do when I go down to hell;
'Tis there I'll meet old Leverman and Myers with his specs,
For the devil is sure to catch them both when they cash in their checks.

Then Leverman and Myers will be my peons, you see,
And I'll treat them like a yellow dog just like they treated me.
Hell fire and brimstone is all that I will pay,
They will have to use their copper checks to buy their grain and hay.

And when they ask for money, my clerk will make them wait,
And I'll pay them back in their own coin, "Get down and pull your
    freight!"

No. 21

Whoa! Ha! Buck and Jerry Boy

There were moments of lyrical gaiety on the treks west, as this song testifies. It is preserved in oral tradition among the descendants of the Mormon pioneers. (Melody and text: L. M. Hilton.)

WHOA! HA! BUCK AND JERRY BOY

With a mer-ry lit-tle jog and a gay lit-tle song, Whoa! Ha! Buck and Jer-ry Boy, We— trudge our way the whole day long, Whoa! Ha! Buck and Jer-ry Boy. What though we're cov-ered all o-ver with dust, It's bet-ter than stay-ing back home to rust, We'll reach Salt Lake some day or bust! Whoa! Ha! Buck and Jer-ry Boy.

With a merry little jog and a gay little song,
  Whoa! Ha! Buck and Jerry boy,
We trudge our way the whole day long,
  Whoa! Ha! Buck and Jerry boy.
What though we're covered all over with dust,
It is better than staying back home to rust,
We'll reach Salt Lake some day or bust!
  Whoa! Ha! Buck and Jerry boy.

There's a pretty little girl in the outfit ahead,
  Whoa! Ha! Buck and Jerry boy,
I wish she was by my side instead,
  Whoa! Ha! Buck and Jerry boy.
Look at her now with a pout on her lips
As daintily with her finger tips
She picks for the fire some buffalo chips.
  Whoa! Ha! Buck and Jerry boy.

Oh, tonight we'll dance by the light of the moon,
  Whoa! Ha! Buck and Jerry boy,
To the fiddler's best and only tune,
  Whoa! Ha! Buck and Jerry boy.
Holding her hand and stealing a kiss,
But never a step of the dance we miss,
Never did know a love like this!
  Whoa! Ha! Buck and Jerry boy.

Part Three

Frontier Realism

No. 22

The Lane County Bachelor

"The Lane County Bachelor," often known as "Government Claim," is probably the most widely sung of the "sodbuster" ballads. Bill Koch localizes its composition in Lane County, Kansas, in 1862. Its melody and basic ideas have been reused in a hundred different settings all the way from Canada to Arizona. The charm of the song is in the tone of rollicking human confrontation with the adversities of the frontier. Though the dirt farmer's pioneering experience lacked the glamour of the cattle range, it touched directly the lives of many more people, and probably left a more durable mark upon the human geography of the American West. (Melody: FAC I 531, sung by Bill Koch, formerly of Hecla, South Dakota, now of Manhattan, Kansas. Text: PC-F 116.)

THE LANE COUNTY BACHELOR

My name is Frank Bol - ar, an ol' bache - lor I am, I'm keep-ing ole bach on an el - e - gant plan;_ You'll find me out West in the coun - ty of Lane,_ Starv-ing to death on a gov - ern - ment claim._ _ My house it is built of the nat - u - ral soil, The

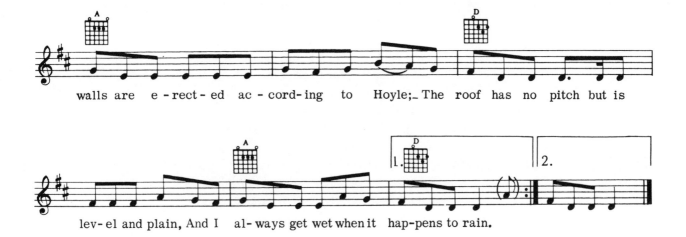

walls are e-rect-ed ac-cord-ing to Hoyle;_ The roof has no pitch but is

lev-el and plain, And I al-ways get wet when it hap-pens to rain.

My name is Frank Bolar, an ol' bachelor I am,
I'm keeping ol' bach on an elegant plan;
You'll find me out West in the County of Lane
Starving to death on a government claim.
My house it is built of the natural soil,
The walls are erected according to Hoyle;
The roof has no pitch but is level and plain,
And I always get wet when it happens to rain.

CHORUS NO. 1:
But hurrah for Lane County, the land of the free,
The home of the grasshopper, bedbug, and flea;
I'll sing loud her praises, and boast of her fame,
While starving to death on my government claim.

My clothes they are ragged, my language is rough,
My bread is case-hardened, both solid and tough;
The dough it is scattered all over the room,
And the floor would get scared at the sight of a broom.
My dishes are dirty and some in the bed,
Covered with sorghum and government bread;
But I have a good time, and live at my ease,
On common sap-sorghum, old bacon and grease.

CHORUS NO. 2:
 But hurray for Lane County, the land of the West,
 Where the farmers and laborers are always at rest;
 Where you've nothing to do but sweetly remain,
 And starve like a man on your government claim.

How happy am I when I crawl into bed
And a rattlesnake rattles his tail at my head;
And the gay little centipede, void of all fear,
Crawls over my pillow and into my ear;
And the nice little bedbug, so cheerful and bright,
Keeps me a-scratching full half of the night;
And the gay little flea with toes sharp as a tack,
Plays, "Why don't you catch me?" all over my back.

CHORUS NO. 3:
 But hurrah for Lane County, where blizzards arise,
 Where the winds never cease and the flea never dies;
 Where the sun is so hot if in it you remain
 'Twill burn you quite black on your government claim.

How happy am I on my government claim
Where I've nothing to lose and nothing to gain;
Nothing to eat, and nothing to wear,
Nothing from nothing is honest and square.
But here I am stuck, and here I must stay,
My money's all gone and I can't get away;
There's nothing will make a man hard and profane
Like starving to death on a government claim.

CHORUS NO. 4:
 Then come to Lane County, there's room for you all,
 Where the winds never cease and the rains never fall;
 Come join in the chorus and boast of her fame,
 While starving to death on your government claim.

Now don't get discouraged, you poor hungry men,
We're all here as free as a pig in a pen.
Just stick to your homestead and battle your fleas,
And look to your Maker to send you a breeze.
Now a word to claim-holders who are bound for to stay,
You may chew your hard-tack till you're toothless and gray;
But as for me, I'll no longer remain
And starve like a dog on my government claim.

CHORUS NO. 5:
    Then farewell to Lane County, farewell to the West,
    I'll travel back east to the girl I love best;
    I'll stop in Missouri and get me a wife,
    And live on corn dodgers the rest of my life.

No. 23

Dakota Land

"Dakota Land" is a classic among "sodbuster" songs. It has been localized in half the states from the Mississippi to the Pacific Coast. It served the first settler to relieve his soul concerning the hardships of subjecting virgin lands to the plow. Note that its melody is to be found in numerous other songs: "Beulah Land," "Maryland, My Maryland," "Sweet Genevieve," "Tannenbaum." (Melody: traditional. Text A: PNFQ 317. Text B: PNFQ 309. Text C: PNFQ 285.)

DAKOTA LAND

I have reached the land of drought and heat, Where noth-ing grows for a man to eat; The

wind that blows this aw - ful heat, In all this world is hard to beat. O Da-

ko - ta land, sweet Da - ko - ta land, As on the burn - ing soil I stand, And

look a-way a - cross the plains And won - der why it does-n't rain, Till

Gab - riel blows the trum-pet sound, And sad the rain has gone a-round.

Text A. O Dakota

I have reached the land of drought and heat,
Where nothing grows for a man to eat;
The wind that blows this awful heat,
In all this world is hard to beat.

CHORUS:
>O Dakota land, sweet Dakota land,
>As on the burning soil I stand,
>And look away across the plains
>And wonder why it doesn't rain,
>Till Gabriel blows the trumpet sound,
>And sad the rain has gone around.

The farmer goes out in his corn,
And there he stands and looks forlorn;
He stands and looks and is most shocked
To see the corn has missed the stock.

We have no wheat, we have no oats,
We have no corn to feed our shoats;
Our chickens are too poor to eat,
Our hogs go squealing down the street.

Our fuel is of the cheapest kind,
Our women are all of one mind;
With bag in hand and upturned nose,
They pick the chips of buffaloes.

Our horses are of broncho race,
Starvation stares them in the face;
We do not live, we only stay,
We are too poor to get away.

TEXT B. NEBRASKA LAND

I've reached the land of drouth and heat,
Where nothing grows for man to eat;
Our horses are the bronco race,
Starvation stares them in the face.

CHORUS:

Nebraska land, Nebraska land!
As on the burning soil I stand,
I look away across the plains
And wonder why it never rains.
Then Gabriel blows with trumpet sound
And says the rain has all gone round.

We have no wheat, we have no oats,
We have no corn to feed our shoats;
Our chickens are too poor to eat,
Our pigs go squealing down the street.

We do not live, we only stay,
We are too poor to get away;
Some day we'll reap more than we sow,
Then we'll have cash enough to go.

Our buildings here are made of sod,
Our hope and trust are still in God;
The schoolhouse here is made of turf,
The children all are full of mirth.

TEXT C. MISSOURI LAND

We're in a land of drouth and heat,
Where nothing grows for man to eat;
The wind it blows, this intense heat
Burns everything that man can eat.

CHORUS:

O, Missouri land, sweet Missouri land,
As on this burning soil I stand
I look away across the plains
And wonder why it never rains,
Till I heard the angel's trumpet sound
That all the rain has passed around.

We started in to raise our flock,
Our chickens were the Plymouth Rock,
Our cattle were the Jersey fine,
And Poland China were our swine.

We have no wheat, we have no oats,
We have no corn to feed our shoats;
Our chickens are too poor to eat
And the pigs go squealing through the street.

Our horses are the broncho race,
Starvation stares us in the face,
We do not live, we only stay,
We are too poor to move away.

The farmer goes into his corn
And there he stands and looks forlorn,
He kicks the clods with his old boots
And says, "This corn will turn to shoots."

64

No. 24
The Dreary Black Hills

Miners and adventurers poured into the Black Hills region in 1875 following an Army announcement that Custer's troops had discovered gold there. For most the only harvest was the suffering and exploitation described in the song. This blend of irony, social criticism, and humor is typical of many frontier songs. (Melody and text: FAC I 537, sung by Bill Koch, formerly of Hecla, South Dakota, now of Manhattan, Kansas.)

THE DREARY BLACK HILLS

Kind friends won't you lis - ten to my pit - i -ful tale, I'm an ob - ject of pit - y and look - ing quite stale, I gave up my job sell - ing Aire's Pat - ent Pills To pros - pect for gold in the Drear- y Black Hills.

Kind friends, won't you listen to my pitiful tale,
I'm an object of pity and looking quite stale,
I gave up my job selling Aire's Patent Pills
To prospect for gold in the Dreary Black Hills.

CHORUS:

Don't travel away, stay at home if you can,
Stay away from that city, they call it Cheyenne,
Where the blue waters roll and Comanche Bill
Will lift up your hair in the Dreary Black Hills.

The round house in Cheyenne is filled every night
With loafers and bummers of most every plight;
On their backs there's no clothes, in their pockets no bills,
Each night they keep leaving for the Dreary Black Hills.

I got to Cheyenne, no gold could I find,
And I thought of the maiden I'd left far behind;
The rain, hail and snow froze plumb to the gills,
They call me the orphan of the dreary Black Hills.

Kind friends, to conclude my advice I'll unfold,
Don't go to the Black Hills and search there for gold;
Railroad speculators their pockets you'll fill
By taking a trip to the Dreary Black Hills.

No. 25

The Little Old Sod Shanty

The family of songs sired by "The Little Old Sod Shanty" is as numerous and varied as the folks at a Mormon family reunion. There are little vine-clad cottages, little *adobe casas,* log cabins, and dugouts. There are answers to "The Little Old Sod Shanty," and answers to the answers. There is "The Little Red Caboose Behind the Train," with its answers, and its answers' answers. There is also a realistic song about the chuck wagon—heart and sinew for every roundup and trail drive, for on it converged all the cowboy's work, sustenance, and recreation. Nor should we forget "The Double-Breasted Mansion on the Square."

It all seems to have begun in 1871 when W. S. Hays came out with a popular song, "The Little Old Log Cabin in the Lane." It was imitated in 1879 by the poet-scout Jack Crawford in a song written and localized in Custer City in the Black Hills. Within five years new songs were appearing in a score of midwestern newspapers. To the eight songs we are giving here we might easily add a score more, not to mention innumerable variants. Nor have we mentioned less servile imitations of "The Little Old Log Cabin" such as "Little Joe, the Wrangler," which has, in turn, hatched its own nestlings. An epic poem in the making? The melody is given with Text F. (Text A: *Clark County Clipper,* September 25, 1884. Text B: *Thomas County Cat,* Colby, Kansas, December 3, 1885. Text C: JL 169. Text D: John W. Crawford, *The Poet Scout* [San Francisco: H. Keller and Co., 1879]. Text E: JL 44. Text F: Melody from Library of Congress #5383B2, recorded by Vance Randolph; text from JL 169. Text G: FAC II 641, from the collection of Alabama folklore made by Ray B. Browne, Bowling Green State University, Ohio. Text H: *The Lane County Herald,* Watson, Kansas, September 4, 1885 [The Kansas newspaper items are published through the courtesy of The Kansas State Historical Society].)

TEXT A. THE LITTLE OLD SOD SHANTY ON THE CLAIM

I am looking rather seedy now while holding down my claim,
   And my victuals are not always served the best,
And the mice play shyly round me as I nestle down to sleep
   In my little old sod shanty on the claim.

CHORUS:

     The hinges are of leather and the windows have no glass
       While the board roof lets the howling blizzard in,
     And I hear the hungry coyote as he sneaks up through the grass
       Round my little old sod shanty on the claim.

Yet I rather like the novelty of living in this way,
   Though my bill of fare is always rather tame,
But I'm happy as a clam on this land of Uncle Sam's
   In my little old sod shanty on the claim.

But when I left my eastern home, a bachelor so gay,
   To try to win my way to wealth and fame,
I little thought that I'd come down to burning twisted hay
   In my little old sod shanty on the claim.

My clothes are plastered o'er with dough and I'm looking like a fright,
   And everything is scattered round the room;
But I wouldn't give the freedom that I have out in the West
   For the bauble of an eastern mansard home.

Still I wish that some kind-hearted girl would pity on me take
   And relieve me from the mess that I am in,
The angel—how I'd bless her—if this her home she'd make
   In my little old sod shanty on the claim.

And when we've made our fortune on the prairies of the West
   Just as happy as two lovers we'd remain;
We'd forget the trials and troubles which we endured at first
   In our little old sod shanty on the claim.

And if the fates should bless us with now and then an heir
   To cheer our hearts with honest pride aflame,
Oh, then we'd be content for the toil that we had spent
   In our little old sod shanty on the claim.

When time enough had lapsed and all those little brats
   To man and modest womanhood has grown,
It won't seem half so lonely when around us we shall look
   And see other old sod shanties on the claim.

TEXT B. REPLY TO "THE LITTLE OLD SOD SHANTY ON THE CLAIM"

My Sam is getting seedy now while holding down his claim,
  And his flapjacks, so he writes, are not the best,
So I'll put my hair in papers ere I lay me down to rest,
  While my Sam is in his shanty on the claim.

Yet I rather like the novelty of living in this way,
  For such long engagements now are rather tame,
And I'm happy as a clam since I said good-bye to Sam
  When he went to seek his shanty on the claim.

CHORUS:
    The dances are so pleasant, so delightful I should say,
      Here I have as many beaus as I could name;
    Oh, the buggy rides I'll take while my Sam is far away
      In his little old sod shanty on the claim.

And since he left his eastern home I'm happy and I'm gay,
  For of course I've sought me out another flame;
No doubt he thought I'd come down to burning twisted hay
  In his filthy old sod shanty on the claim.

Oh, let him dabble in the dough, I'm sure it served him right
  For leaving me in the gutter for to roam;
Does he think me such a ninny as to marry such a fright,
  To be a slave in his dirty cabin home?

No doubt some tawny Indian miss will pity on him take
  And help extricate him from the mess he's in;
He ne d not think a city belle the sacrifice will make
  For there's many men to wed with lots of tin.

He says he'll make his fortune, but I fear he'll lose his hair
  'Way out among the wild Indians, frogs, and sloughs;
He'd better get some other lass as mother to his heir,
  For I'm determined some other man to choose.

He dreams his early bliss seen when in wedlock he is bound
  And is living with his fair and buxom dame;
But when his cash she's spent, until he's not a cent,
  She may leave him and his shanty on the claim.

And if she is a vixen she will make him toe the mark,
  And thresh and thump and pound him till he's lame;
I think I'll wed the owner of the stone front near the park,
  And leave Sam in his shanty on the claim.

Text C. The Little Vine-Clad Cottage

I am feeling sort of happy since I proved up on the farm,
  I have horses, sheep, and cattle not a few;
Pork and 'tatoes in the cellar, wheat and oats stored in the barn,
  And coal enough, I guess, to take us through.

CHORUS:

   The little old sod shanty where I nestled down to rest,
     Where the coyotes were howling round at night,
   Was changed in its appearance, like everything out West,
     To the little vine-clad cottage painted white.

I found that sweet kind-hearted girl of whom I used to dream
  When working hard to beautify the place;
She came just like an angel, as fair as any queen,
  And Belle and Beulah have their mother's face.

We have prayed and worked together for nearly twenty years,
  Have had our pleasures often mixed with pain;
But He in whom we trusted has wiped away our tears
  And blessed us in our cottage on the claim.

The good old home way back east, bright link in memory's chain,
  The joyous scenes, the friends that loved us best;
But I'd rather drink the balmy breeze that floats across the plain
  And watch the golden sunset of the West.

Dakota, fair Dakota, we love thy genial clime,
  The breezes filled with fragrance from the plain;
And on the broad prairie we'll live until we die
  In our little vine-clad cottage on the claim.

Text D. My Little New Log Cabin in the Hills

In my little new log cabin home my heart is light and free,
  While the boys around me gather every day,
And the sweetest hours I ever knew are those I'm passing now,
  While the banjo makes sweet music to my lay.

CHORUS:

   The scenes are changing every day, the snow is nearly gone,
     And there's music in the laughter of the rills;
   But the dearest spot of all the rest is where I love to dwell,
     In my little new log cabin in the Hills.

While the birds are sweetly singing to the coming of the spring,
  And the flow'rets peep their heads from out the sod,
We feel as gay and happy as the songsters on the wing
  Who are sending up sweet anthems to their God.

Then let us work with heart and hand, and help each other through
  In this pretty little world we call our own,
Whether building or prospecting—yes, or fighting with the Sioux,
  For 'tis hard sometimes to play your hand alone.

TEXT E. THE LITTLE 'DOBE CASA

It was just about a year ago I left my eastern home
  To try to make my way to wealth and fame,
But little did I think I'd turn up in Mexico
  In the little *'dobe casa* on the plain.

Oh, the roof is ocotillo, there are coyotes far and near,
  And the greasers roam about the place all day;
And at night when I lie down to sleep tarantulers around me creep,
  In my little *'dobe casa* on the plain.

There are cockroaches on the ceiling and *curocos* on the walls,
  And the bill of fare is always just the same—
'Tis *frijoles* and *tortillas,* all dressed up in chili sauce,
  In the little *'dobe casa* on the plain.

Oh, I wish that some kind-hearted girl would consent to be my wife,
  I would try to be content then to remain;
Or maybe I could find some better place to settle down
  Than the little *'dobe casa* on the plain.

THE LITTLE OLD SOD SHANTY

You may sing a-bout the lit-tle old log cab-in in the lane, Or of

lit-tle Ger-man homes a-cross the sea;___ But my lit-tle old sod

shan-ty that I built up-on my claim, Has be-come the dear-est

spot on earth to me.___ I built it in my pov-er-ty up-

on my prai-rie claim, And aft-er toil it gave me sweet-est

rest,___ Safe-ly shel-tered from the bliz-zards and all the storms that

came, In my lit-tle old sod shan-ty in the West.

You may sing about the little old log cabin in the lane,
   Or of little German homes across the sea;
But my little old sod shanty that I built upon my claim
   Has become the dearest spot on earth to me.
I built it in my poverty upon my prairie claim,
   And after toil it gave me sweetest rest;
Safely sheltered from the blizzards and all the storms that came
   In my little old sod shanty in the West.

CHORUS:
     It makes a pleasant memory that I shall not forget,
       Of all our western homes it suits me best;
     And often now I wish that I were living in it yet
       In my little old sod shanty in the West.

We had hungry wolves and coyotes for our nearest neighbors then,
   The buffalo and deer supplied our meat;
And when the black and prowling bear would fall before our men
   We would live like kings upon our game so sweet.
The only town we knew for miles by prairie dogs was made,
   They yelped and sported round our little nest;
And sometimes they took a tumble before the rifle's raid,
   And such we thought was sport out in the West.

Our path was full of troubles, nor were they little ones,
   For sure the pioneers were single boys;
Then every man's own bodyguard was two good shooting guns,
   With ropes and lariats to use as toys.
We sometimes hunted down the thief who stole from us a horse,
   A little neck-tie party did the rest;
The morning sun shone grimly as its rays fell on the corpse,
   Near my little old sod shanty in the West.

The miners built their cabins, the ranchers lived in shacks,
   And some were forced to make the log stockade;
For then the wildest redskins came down like wolves in packs
   To drive us from the home that we had made.
Ah, those were times that tried men's souls and sifted out the chaff,
   Each fight would mark the men we called the best;
And some proved weak and left us, it must be more than half,
   And others held their shanties in the West.

But all things change, those stirring times have long since passed away,
    And churches, schools, and cities followed on,
Along the trails we trecked upon all in that early day,
    And others hold the fields that we have won.
But we have saved a little cash, so we will not complain,
    Though others of our fruits shall reap the best;
But we hope they will remember not to treat us with disdain
    Because we built the shanties in the West.

Where once the cabin graced the gulch our shanties mark the plain,
    With signs of wealth the homes and mansions rise;
The wigwam, too, has passed away, the braves are with the slain,
    In the happy hunting grounds beyond the skies.
When round our winter fires we meet, not made of twisted hay,
    We recount the past before we seek our rest;
The stories of our struggles will hush the children's play,
    And their dreams will be of shanties in the West.

Text G. I Will Tell You My Troubles

I will tell you of my troubles, my ups and downs through life,
   And I'll tell to you a story rather strange;
I will tell you of my boardinghouse, a structure built on wheels,
   And it's drawn by four black horses 'cross the plains.

Oh, the wheels are made of black oak, the running gear white oak,
   And the bed is made to haul our bedding, chuck, and grain;
In the rear there is a chuck box where the cowboys get their chuck,
   It's the XIT chuck wagon on the plains.

As the old chuck wagon rolls on, you can hear the cowboys yell,
   You can hear the dogies bawling all around;
You can see the bronco pitching, trying to shake his rider off,
   But they seldom ever put one on the ground.

You can hear the howling coyotes, the barking prairie dog,
   You can see the bronco buster a-holding to his rein;
You can see a thousand white-face cattle grazing on the grass
   Round the XIT chuck wagon on the plains.

Oh, my life's a poor cow puncher's and I daily ride the range,
   While the iron's getting hot I ride my wild bronco;
When the rounding of the yearlings and the branding does begin,
   From my roping horse I throw my long lasso.

Oh, the boys go dog the yearlings to burn the XIT,
   While on guard the boys are holding to the reins;
When our day's work it is ended then we all go into camp
   To the XIT chuck wagon on the plains.

When the cook gets chuck all ready, and he hollers, "Here it is,"
   To the chuck box there's a rush by all the crew;
When our tins and cups are loaded with hot coffee, bread, and steak,
   Then we all sit down upon the grass to chew.

Oh, the beefsteak's brown and tender, the bread is sour dough,
   And the coffee's strong enough to float a barge of grain;
As we chew our floury greeting there's a loco weed in bloom,
   Round the XIT chuck wagon on the plains.

Oh, my buddies are cow punchers and their jewels are forty-fives,
   We're there with smoking rifles when trouble comes;
The only amusement is High Five and Seven Up,
   And the music is the rattle of the spurs.

Oh, our beds are made of tarpaulin, our blankets are Navajo,
   And we snap the tarp to keep out wind and rain;
When the boys are all through jesting then we all lie down to sleep,
   Round the XIT chuck wagon on the plains.

TEXT H. THE DOUBLE-BREASTED MANSION ON THE SQUARE

I once was young and gallant and drove a span of grays,
  I think about six-ninety was their pace,
I'd fifty thousand servant girls, but don't give this away,
  And a trotting cow I sent to every race.

I'd fifty thousand gold mines; I owned half of the world;
  No wonder that this statement makes you stare;
I'd fifty thousand dog puppies with their tails all turned up
  And my double-breasted mansion on the square.

CHORUS:

  The roof was copper-bottom, the chimney solid gold,
    An elevator placed at every stair;
  I lost a lot at "Keno" and I never shall forget
    My double-breasted mansion on the square.

One million head of cattle used to roam about my farm,
  And each it had a splendid feather bed;
There were male and female roosters and they took their whiskey warm,
  They were shanghai, shanghoop, pullin' China bred.

My peach trees yielded butter, my plum trees yielded cream;
  I used to sow and mow the yellow pear.
But alas, my wealth has vanished, and every night I dream
  Of my double-breasted mansion on the square.

Oh, well do I remember not many years ago
  The bummer used to hang around my door;
They got outside my whiskey, they smoked up my cigars,
  My servant girls and hash they did adore.

But scenes have changed since then, and I am poor myself,
  At a free lunch I can take quite a share;
I am thinking of the Switzer cheese that once I used to eat
  In my double-breasted mansion on the square.

No. 26
St. George and the Drag-On

In the 1860's a column of Mormon settlers made its way into the arid valley of the Virgin River in southwestern Utah. Their ultimate success proclaims itself by the vitality and prosperity evident to every tourist who passes through St. George along U.S. 91. But a century ago, witness the epic intensity of this song, it was touch-and-go between the colonists and malign nature. To make out of "Mesquite, soap root, prickly pear and briars" a refrain of the triumph of man over the wilderness is of Homeric proportions. (Melody and text: FMC I 641, sung by Rudger McArthur.)

ST. GEORGE AND THE DRAG-ON

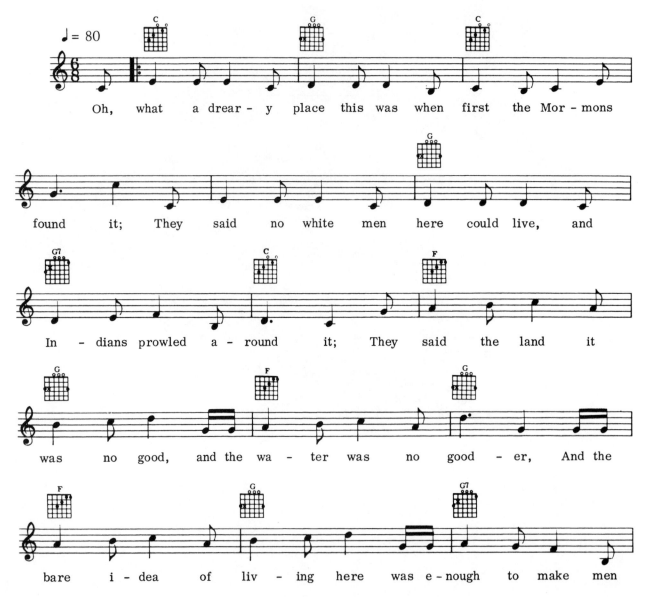

Oh, what a drear - y place this was when first the Mor - mons found it; They said no white men here could live, and In - dians prowled a - round it; They said the land it was no good, and the wa - ter was no good - er, And the bare i - dea of liv - ing here was e - nough to make men

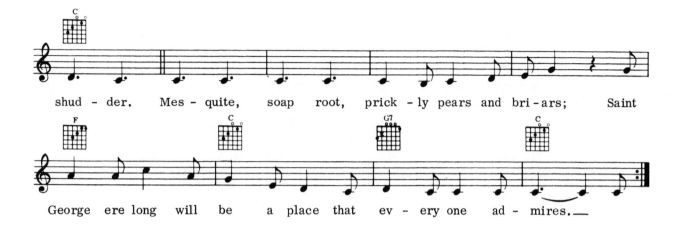

shud - der. Mes - quite, soap root, prick - ly pears and bri - ars; Saint

George ere long will be a place that ev - ery one ad - mires. ___

Oh, what a dreary place this was when first the Mormons found it;
They said no white men here could live, and Indians prowled around it;
They said the land it was no good, and the water was no gooder,
And the bare idea of living here was enough to make men shudder.

CHORUS:
    Mesquite, soap root, prickly pear and briars,
    St. George ere long will be a place that everyone admires.

Now green lucerne in verdant spots redeems our thriving city,
Whilst vines and fruit trees grace our lots with flowers sweet and pretty,
Where once the grass in single blades grew a mile apart in distance
And it kept the crickets on the hop to pick up their subsistence.

The sun it is so scorching hot it makes the water sizz, sir,
And the reason that it is so hot is just because it is, sir.
The wind with fury here doth blow, that when we plant or sow, sir,
We place one foot upon the seeds and hold them till they grow, sir.

No. 27
Hell in Texas

The physical and biologic environment of the great Southwest thrust images into American English that set it eternally apart from the language of our forebears. A cluster of songs, which we group under the rubric "Hell in Texas," accumulates a number of these images. These songs swept like a prairie fire through newspapers of the West in the '80's and '90's, and, with appropriate modifications to take care of local peculiarities, got applied to a dozen different regions, including Alaska. (Melody: George E. Hastings, "Hell in Texas," PTFLS IX [1931], p. 178 [published by permission of the Texas Folklore Society]. Text A: Gordon 876. Text B: FAC II 434, from Arizona Historical Library, Phoenix. Text C: PNFQ 2.)

HELL IN TEXAS

The dev-il, we're told,__ in Hell__ was chained, And a thou-sand years there he re-mained; He nev-er com-plained_nor did__ he groan, But de-ter-mined to start a Hell of his own, Where he could tor-ment__ the souls_ of men With-out be-ing chained in a

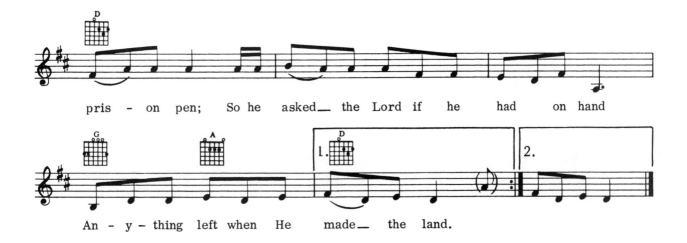

pris - on pen; So he asked— the Lord if he had on hand

An - y - thing left when He made— the land.

TEXT A. SONG OF THE BORDER

The devil, we're told, in Hell was chained,
And a thousand years there he remained;
He never complained nor did he groan,
But determined to start a Hell of his own,
Where he could torment the souls of men
Without being chained in a prison pen;
So he asked the Lord if he had on hand
Anything left when He made the land.

The Lord said, "Yes, I had plenty on hand,
But I left it down on the Rio Grande;
The fact is, old boy, the stuff is so poor
I don't think you could use it in Hell any more."
But the devil went down to look at the truck
And said if it came as a gift he was stuck;
For after examining it carefully and well
He concluded the place was too dry for Hell.

So in order to get it off his hands,
The Lord promised the devil to water the lands,
For he had some water, or rather the dregs,
A regular cathartic that smelled like bad eggs;
Hence the deal was closed and deed was given,
And the Lord went back to His home in Heaven;
And the devil then said, "I've all that is needed
To make a good Hell," and hence he succeeded.

He began to put thorns on all of the trees
And mixed up the sand with millions of fleas,
And scattered tarantulas along all the roads—
Put thorns on the cactus and horns on the toads;
He lengthened the horns of the Texas steers,
And put an addition on the rabbits' ears,
He put a little devil in the broncho,
And poisoned the feet of the centipede.

The rattlesnake bites you, the scorpion stings,
The mosquitoes delight you with buzzing wings;
The sand-burrs prevail and so do the ants,
And those who sit down need half-soles on their pants.
The devil then said that throughout the land
He'd managed to keep up the devil's own brand,
And all would be mavericks unless they bore
The marks of scratches and bites and thorns by the score.

The heat in the summer is one hundred and ten,
Too hot for the devil and too hot for men;
The wild boar roams through the wild chaparral,
It's a hell of a place he has for a hell;
The red pepper grows on the bank of the brook,
The Mexicans use it in all that they cook.
Just dine with a Greaser and then you'll shout,
"I've hell on the inside as well as without."

Text B. Someone's Opinion of Arizona

The devil was given permission one day
To select a land for his own special sway,
So he hunted around for a month or more
And fussed and fumed and terribly swore
But at last was delighted a country to view
Where the prickly pear and catclaw grew.

With a brief survey and without further excuse
He selected the land by the Santa Cruz;
He saw there were still improvements to make
For he felt his own reputation at stake.

An idea struck him, he swore by his horns
That he would make a complete vegetation of thorns.
So he studded the land with the prickly pear
And scattered the cacti everywhere,
The Spanish dagger, pointed and tall,
And at last the *cholla* to outstick them all.

He imported the Apache direct from hell
The size of the sweet-scented ranks to swell,
And legions of skunks whose loud, loud smell
Perfumed this bleak country he loved so well.

And for his life he couldn't see why
The river should any more water supply;
And he swore if they furnished another drop
You might use his head and horns for a mop.
He sanded the rivers till they were dry
And poisoned them all with alkali
And promised himself on this limey brink
The control of all who should from them drink.

He saw there was still one improvement to make
So imported the scorpion and rattlesnake,
That all who came to this country to dwell
Wouldn't fail to imagine a sure enough hell.
He fixed up the heat at one hundred and eleven
And banished forever the moisture of heaven,
And said as he heard the hot furnace roar
That the mercury might reach five hundred or more.
After fixing these things so thorny and well
He said, "I'll be damned if this don't beat hell."

Then he spread out his wings and away he flew
And vanished forever in a blaze of blue.
And now, no doubt, in some corner of hell
He gloats over the work he completed so well,
And vows Arizona can never be beat
For thorns, tarantulas, snakes, and heat.
For with all his plans carried out so well
He feels well assured Arizona is hell.

82

Text C. Alaska, or Hell of the Yukon

The devil in hell, we are told, was chained,
Thousands of years he there remained.
He did not complain nor did he groan,
But determined to have a hell of his own,
Where he could torment the souls of men
Without being chained in a solitary pen.

So he asked the Lord if he had any land
In a colder clime than a poor soul could stand.
The Lord said yes, but it's not much use,
It's cold Alaska, and it is cold as the deuce.
In fact, old boy, the place is bare,
I don't think you could make a good hell there.

The devil said he couldn't see why,
For he sure knew his business and would like to try.
So the bargain was made and the deed was given
And the devil quickly departed from heaven.
We next see the devil far up in the north
Examining Alaska, to see what it is worth.

From the top of McKinley he looked at the truck,
And said, "If I get this for nothing I still am stuck."
But, oh, it was fine to be out in the cold.
The wind blew a gale and the devil grew bold,
And there on the height of the mountain he planned
To make of Alaska the home of the damned—
A different place from the old-fashioned hell
Where each soul burned in an awful hot cell.

He used every means that a wise devil needed
To make a good hell, and he sure succeeded.
He filled the air with millions of gnats
And spread the Yukon over the flats,
And set a line of volcanoes in Yawnamice Pass,
And bred mosquitoes in the dungre grass.

And made six months' night where it's sixty below,
A howling wind and a pelting snow;
Six months' day with a spell now and then
Too hot for the devil, too hot for his men;
Hungry dogs and wolves by the pack
That when they yell send chills down your back.
And when you mush o'er the barren expanse,
The wind blows wicked holes in your pants.

But of all the pests the imps could devise,
The Yukon mosquitoes were the devil's pride.
They're like the rattlesnake's bite or scorpion's sting,
And they measure six inches from wing to wing.
And the devil said when he fashioned these,
"Each one will be worth a million fleas."

And over the mountains, valleys and plains,
Where the dew falls heavy and sometimes rains,
He grew a few flowers and berries, just for a bluff,
For the devil sure knew how to peddle his stuff.

To show how well he knew his game,
The devil next salted his new hell claim,
Put gold nuggets in some of his streams
To lure men on in their hopes and dreams.

He hid them deep in the glacial ice
Like a reformed city hides its vice,
And bid Dame Rumor to spread the news
To all the world and its holy crews
That there was gold in heaps and piles
In all the colors and all the styles.

He grinned a grin, a satisfied grin,
And said, "Now watch the fools rush in.
They will fight for gold and steal and slay,
But in the end it's me they will pay."

Oh, what a fine hell this that the devil owns,
His trails are marked by frozen bones;
The wild wind moans o'er plain, hill and dell,
It's a hell of a place he has his hell.
Now you know, should any one ask you,
What kind of a place is our own Alaska.

No. 28

Idyl of the Plains

This song gives room for speculation concerning the transcendence of the cowboy into a hero-image. The 1884 view of the cowboy is realistic and less than complimentary: a penchant for violence, scornful of life and defiant of death, unremorseful addiction to the trinity of vices—drink, women, and cards—and above all, defiance of the law. Are these the values that form the inner core of the American culture? (Melody: Hugo Frey, *American Cowboy Songs* [New York: Robbins Music Corp., 1936], p. 31. Text: *Kansas Cowboy,* Dodge City, June 28, 1884.)

IDYL OF THE PLAINS

A man there lives on the West-ern plain, With a
ton of ___ fight and an ounce of brain, Who
herds the cat-tle and rides the train, And
goes by the name of cow-boy.

A man there lives on the Western plain,
With a ton of fight and an ounce of brain,
Who herds the cattle and rides the train
   And goes by the name of cowboy.

He shoots with pistol and carves with knife,
He feels unwell unless in strife,
He laughs at death and mocks at life,
   For he is the terrible cowboy.

He snuffs out candles with pistol balls,
He snuffs out lives in drunken brawls,
He gets snuffed out in gambling halls,
   This wayward, frolicsome cowboy.

He riots in cities and towns, and browbeats;
He drives policemen off the streets,
He fills with terror all he meets,
   For all give way to the cowboy.

Ten cowboys drunk near a small station,
Ten pistols ring in sepulchral tune,
Ten corpses stare at the big white moon,
   And where, oh, where is the cowboy?

No. 29
When I Was a Cowboy

The mood and structure of the blues permeates this southern prison camp treatment of a cowboy theme, a fact which should not be surprising if we recall that what we know as "western," "hillbilly," and "blues" belong to the same moments in our history and to folk environments that had close ties with one another. Negro hands were full participants in all of the activities of the cowboy culture. (Melody: collected, adapted and arranged by John A. Lomax and Alan Lomax, *Cowboy Songs and Other Frontier Ballads* [New York: The Macmillan Company, 1957], p. 39 [© Copyright 1934 and renewed 1962 Ludlow Music, Inc., New York, N.Y. Used by permission]. Text A: Hendren 117. Text B: FAC II 658, Library of Congress, Lomax manuscript file.)

WHEN I WAS A COWBOY

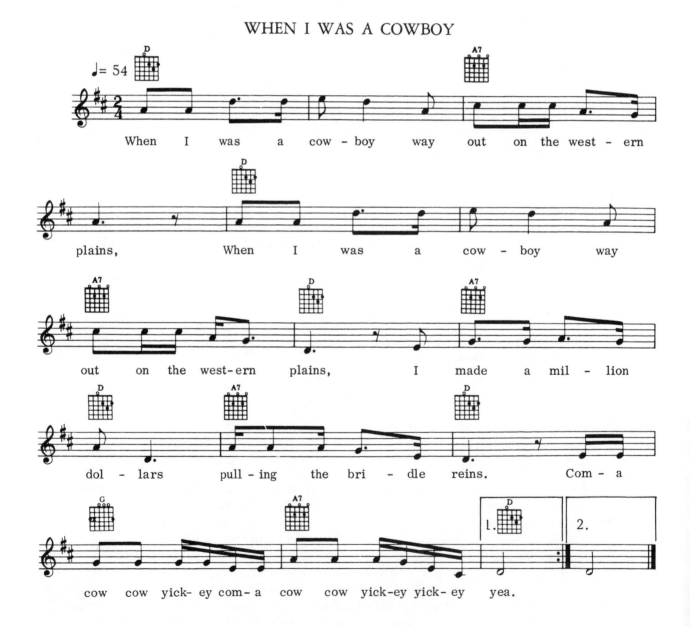

When I was a cow-boy way out on the west-ern plains, When I was a cow-boy way out on the west-ern plains, I made a mil-lion dol-lars pull-ing the bri-dle reins. Com-a cow cow yick-ey com-a cow cow yick-ey yick-ey yea.

TEXT A. WHEN I WAS A COWBOY

When I was a cowboy, way out on the western plains,
When I was a cowboy, way out on the western plains;
I made a million dollars pulling the bridle reins.

CHORUS:
    Coma cow cow yickey, coma cow cow yickey yickey yea.

I went to my girl's house and was sitting there alone,
I went to my girl's house, she was sitting there alone,
I'm a poor lonesome cowboy, and a long way from home.

When I left my girl's house she was sitting in a rocking chair,
When I left my girl's house she was sitting in a rocking chair,
Oh wild western cowboy, oh please don't leave me here.

Feet in my stirrups, sitting deep down in my saddle,
Feet in my stirrups, sitting deep down in my saddle;
I'm the best cowboy that ever herded cattle.

Oh, the hardest battle was ever on a Bunker Hill,
Oh, the hardest battle was ever on a Bunker Hill,
When me and a bunch of cowboys run into Buffalo Bill.

Oh, the hardest battle was ever on the western plains,
Oh, the hardest battle was ever on the western plains,
When me and a bunch of cowboys run into Jesse James.

When me and a bunch of cowboys run into Jesse James,
When me and a bunch of cowboys run into Jesse James,
The bullets was a-falling just like a shower of rain.

Your house catch afire and there ain't no water round,
Your house catch afire and there ain't no water round,
Throw your baby out the window, let the doggone shack burn down.

TEXT B. WESTERN COWBOY

When I was a cowboy out on the Western plains,
When I was a cowboy out on the Western plains,
I made a half a million, snatching bridle reins.

I'm goin' out in West Texas, out on the Western plains,
I'm goin' out in West Texas, out on the Western plains,
I can make a half a million that'll be added to my name.

Early one frosty morning, come knocking at my door,
Early one frosty morning, come knocking at my door,
Shoes and stockings in her hand and she was shivering cold.

I picked her up, I slyly laid her down,
I picked her up, I slyly laid her down,
I hugged her real close and you ought to heard her whine.

Says, "If it be a boy child, please name him after me,"
Says, "If it be a boy child, please name him after me,
Let him be a cowboy like his daddy used to be."

"If it be a girl child, name it Margery;
If it be a girl child, name it Margery,
Let it be a streetwalker like its mama used to be."

Says, "I had a little woman and she was hard to please."
Says, "I had a little woman and she was hard to please."
Says, "I roped a hard streak of lightning and drug it to my knees."

I rode around them longhorn cattle until I got to be old,
I rode around them longhorn cattle until I got to be old,
Now I'm drawing my salary, getting my room and board.

"Good morning, young fellow, where would you like to go?
Good morning, young fellow, where would you like to go?
I got a whole lot of land and cattle way down in Mexico."

No. 30
The Hills of Mexico

This parody of the universal "Buffalo Skinners" was known everywhere in the West, and is itself a parody of a lumberjack song known, sung, and loved from Maine to Vancouver Island. The song attains classic greatness in the rare balance achieved between realistic, ironic, and humorous elements, not unlike the tense moments in a Molière comedy. (Melody: Library of Congress #2075A, recorded by John A. Lomax. Text: FAC I 51, recited by Bye Hutchins.)

THE HILLS OF MEXICO

Well, I land - ed in old San - ta Fe in nine - teen hun - dred and three.____ Ben John - son there, by name sir,____ stepped up and said to me,____ "How do you do, young fel - low,____ how'd you like to go____ And spend one sum - mer punch - in' in the hills of New Mex - i - co."____

Well, I landed in old Santa Fe in nineteen hundred and three.
Ben Johnson there, by name sir, stepped up and says to me,
"How do you do, young fellow, how'd you like to go
And spend one summer punchin' in the hills of New Mexico?"

Well, me being out of employment, to Ben Johnson I did say,
"As for me going with you, it depends upon the pay;
If you pay good wages and a pretty good mount too,
I really think that I will go and spend one summer through."

With all of his flattering talk he enlisted quite a train,
About twenty of us in number, all able-bodied men.
The trip it was a pleasant one, the way we had to go,
Till we crossed the Rio Grande in the hills of New Mexico.

The Rio Grande was salty as brine—and alkali too,
Ben Johnson led the way, and you bet he put us through.
The way the mosquitoes and buffalo gnats did work, it was not slow,
There is no worse hell upon earth than the hills of New Mexico.

Well, now the trip is ended and we reached Ben Johnson's farm,
The first old bronco I tried to break, by God, he broke my arm.
While punchin' the damned old longhorns, our lives, we had no show,
There was Indians to pick us off in the hills of New Mexico.

Now the round-up's over and Ben Johnson would not pay,
He said we'd been so extravagant that he was in debt that day.
But we showed him about the punchers, that old bankrupt would not go,
So we left Ben Johnson's bones to bleach in the hills of New Mexico.

Now the summer's ended and homeward we are bound
And in this cursed country we will never more be found;
Go home to our wives and sweethearts and tell others not to go
To that God-forsaken country in the hills of New Mexico.

No. 31
The Texas Cowboy

Many of the cowboys were floaters; they drifted from ranch to ranch, taking work where and when it was offered. Between jobs they "rode the chuck line," i.e., enjoyed the hospitality of ranchers encountered in their wanderings until their welcome wore thin. Then they set out once more, their only possessions being a horse, saddle, and "hot roll" containing bedding and a few personal effects. "The Texas Cowboy" is one of the best of several songs that capture the realism and pathos of the chuck-line riders. (Melody and text A: FAC I 508, sung by Kathy Dagel. Text B: JL 228. Text C: *The Glendive Independent,* Montana, March 31, 1888.)

THE TEXAS COWBOY

I am a Tex-as cow-boy and I am far a-way from home. If I ev-er get back to Tex-as I never more will roam. Mon-tan-a is too cold for me and the win-ters are too long, Be-fore the round-ups do be-gin my mon-ey is all gone.

Oh, I'm a Texas cowboy and far away from home,
If ever I get back to Texas I never more will roam.

Montana is too cold for me and the winters are too long,
Before the roundups do begin, my money is all gone.

I worked out in Nebraska where the grass grows ten feet high,
And the cattle are such rustlers that they seldom ever die.

I've worked up in the sand hills and down along the Platte
Where the cowboys are good fellows and the dogies all are fat.

I've traveled lots of country, Nebraska's hills of sand,
Down through the Indian nation and up the Rio Grande;

But the badlands of Montana are the worst I ever seen,
The cowboys all are tenderfeet and the dogies all are lean.

All along the Yellowstone it's cold all year round,
You'll surely get consumption from a-sleeping on the ground.

Work in Montana lasts six months in the year,
When all your bills are settled, there's nothing left for beer.

Work down in Texas lasts all the year around,
You'll never get consumption from sleeping on the ground.

Come all you Texas cowboys and a warning take from me,
And do not go to Montana to spend your money free;

But stay at home in Texas where the work lasts all year round,
And you'll never get consumption from the sleeping on the ground.

Text B

Come all you Texas cowboys, and warning take of me,
Don't go out in Montana for wealth or liberty.

But stay home here in Texas where they work the year around,
And where you'll not get consumption from sleeping on the ground.

Montana is too cold for me and the winters are too long,
Before the roundups have begun your money all is gone.

For in Montana the boys get work but six months in the year,
And they charge for things three prices, in that land so bleak and drear.

This thin old hen skin bedding, 'tis not enough to shield my form,
For I almost freeze to death whenever there comes a storm.

I've an outfit on the Muscle Shell which I expect I'll never see,
Unless by chance I'm sent to represent that A R and P T.

All along these badlands, and down upon the Dry,
Where the canyons have no bottoms and the mountains reach the sky,

Your chuck is bread and bacon, and coffee black as ink,
And hard old alkali water that's scarcely fit to drink.

They'll wake you in the morning before the break of day,
And send you out on circle full twenty miles away.

With a tenderfoot to lead you who never knows the way,
You're pegging in the best of luck if you get two meals a day.

I've been over in Colorado, and down upon the Platte,
Where the cowboys work in pastures and the cattle all are fat;

Where they ride silver mounted saddles, and spurs and leggings too,
And the horses are all Normans and only fit to plow.

Yes, I've travelled lots of country, Arizona's hills of sand,
Down through the Indian nation plumb to the Rio Grande.

Montana is the badland, the worst I've ever seen,
Where the cowboys are all tenderfeet and the dogies are all lean.

Text C

I am a Texas cowboy, and I am far away from home,
If I ever get back to Texas, I never more will roam.
Montana is too cold for me, and the winters are too long,
Before the roundups do begin your money is all gone.

Now, to win these fancy leggings you will have enough to do;
They cost me fourteen dollars the day that they were new.
And this old hen skin bedding too thin to keep me warm,
I nearly freeze to death my boys, whenever there comes a storm.

I have worked down in Nebraska, where the grass grows ten feet high;
Where the cattle are such rustlers they hardly ever die.
I have been up in the sand hills, and down upon the Platte,
Where the punchers are good fellows and the cattle always fat.

I have traveled lots of country, from Nebraska's hills of sand,
Down through the Indian Nation and up the Rio Grande.
But the Bad Lands of Montana are the worst I ever seen,
Where the punchers are all tenderfeet and the doggies are so lean.

They will wake you in the morning before the break of day,
And send you on a circle a hundred miles away.
Your grub is bread and bacon, with coffee black as ink,
And the water so full of alkali that it isn't fit to drink.

If you want to see some Bad Lands just go over on the Dry,
Where you'll bog down in the coulies and the mountains touch the sky,
With a tenderfoot to guide you who never knows the way,
And you are playing in the best of luck if you eat three times a day.

Up along the Yellowstone it is cold the year around,
You will surely get consumption if you sleep upon the ground.
And the wages almost nothing for six months in the year,
When you pay up all your outside debts you have nothing left for beer.

Now all you Texas cowboys this warning take by me,
Don't come up to Montana to spend your money free,
But stay at home in Texas where there is work all the year around,
And you will never get consumption by sleeping on the ground.

Part Four

Boasting, Humor, and Western Primitive

No. 32
In Kansas

Frontiersmen loved to create and sing satirical and humorous doggerel about the uncouth habits of their neighbors. "In Kansas" is a good example: it appears with numerous variant stanzas at least since the 1840's. "Way Out West in Kansas" expands the theme into a full-blown ballad. (Melody and Text A: FAC I 99, sung by Joan O'Bryant. Text B: Hendren 158.)

IN KANSAS

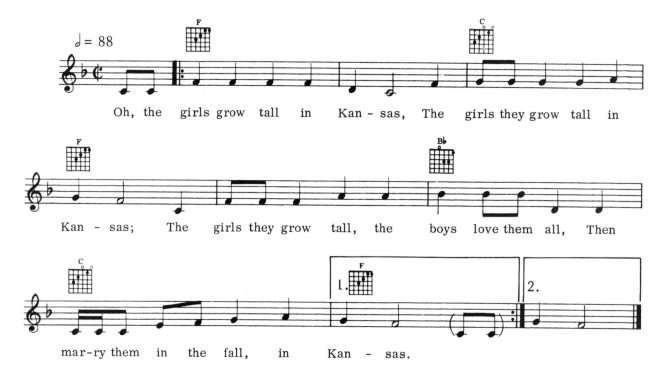

Oh, the girls grow tall in Kan - sas, The girls they grow tall in Kan - sas; The girls they grow tall, the boys love them all, Then mar-ry them in the fall, in Kan - sas.

TEXT A. IN KANSAS

Oh, the girls grow tall in Kansas,
The girls they grow tall in Kansas;
  The girls they grow tall, the boys love them all,
Then marry them in the fall, in Kansas.

Now potatoes they grow small in Kansas,
Potatoes they grow small in Kansas;
  Potatoes they grow small, they dig them in the fall,
And eat them hide and all, in Kansas.

Now they say to drink's a sin in Kansas,
They say to drink's a sin in Kansas;
  They say to drink's a sin so they guzzle all they kin,
Though the dries are voted in, in Kansas.

Oh, they chaw tobacco thin in Kansas,
They chaw tobacco thin in Kansas;
  They chaw tobacco thin, they spit it on their chin,
And lap it up again, in Kansas.

So come all who want to roam to Kansas,
Come all who want to roam to Kansas;
  Come all who want to roam and seek a prairie home,
And be happy with your doom, in Kansas.

TEXT B. WAY OUT WEST IN KANSAS

The sun's so hot that eggs will hatch
  Way out west in Kansas,
It'll pop the corn in a popcorn patch
  Way out west in Kansas.
An old mule coming down the path
Saw the corn and lost his breath,
He thought it was snow and froze to death,
  Way out west in Kansas.

There's a man who loved his wife
  Way out west in Kansas,
They must live a peaceful life
  Way out west in Kansas.
There's a reason why each night
They hold each other's hands so tight,
If one turns loose it starts a fight,
  Way out west in Kansas.

Folks don't stay out very late
  Way out west in Kansas,
They take the sidewalks in at eight
  Way out west in Kansas.
It's some town by heck I'll swear,
You can stand in the old town square
And knock on every front door there,
  Way out west in Kansas.

There's a gal in Abiline
  Way out west in Kansas,
Says she's just turned seventeen
  Way out west in Kansas.
But she's so old she's muscle bound,
Folks all say she built the town,
For she's turned seventeen around,
  Way out west in Kansas.

There's a man that grew so tall
  Way out west in Kansas,
If he'd ever start to fall
  He'd be out of Kansas.
He grew so tall, I do repeat,
He'd be as long as our main street,
But there's a lot turned down for feet,
  Way out west in Kansas.

There's a man named Cross-eyed Pat
  Way out west in Kansas,
You can't tell who he's looking at
  Way out west in Kansas.
He cried because he's such a wreck,
The tears ran down the back of his neck,
He don't look straight to me, by heck,
  Way out west in Kansas.

No. 33

My Ma Was Born in Texas

Cowboy values presume difficult relations between the sexes. The cowboy felt comfortable with mother, sister, and sweetheart, but these represented only three from among all the women in a man's life: the others were more often than not a source of shame or distress. Scores of songs popular on the frontier treat this perennial battle of the sexes in dead seriousness, or with comic relief, as in this song. (Melody and text: FAC I 493, collected by Edith Fowke from Mrs. Tom Sullivan, Lakefield, Ontario, Canada.)

MY MA WAS BORN IN TEXAS

My ma was born in Tex - as, my pa in Ten - nes - see, They were mar - ried in the sum - mer of eigh - teen nine - ty three. They moved to Cal - i - for - ni - a and that's where I was born, In a roll - in' cov - ered wag - on on a bright Sep - tem - ber morn.

My ma was born in Texas, my pa in Tennessee,
They were married in the summer of eighteen ninety-three.
They moved to California and that's where I was born,
In a rollin' covered wagon on a bright September morn.

I grew up in my saddle, my play toy was a gun,
Shooting at the rattlesnakes was my idea of fun.
'Twas at the age of seventeen I left my happy home,
The open range was calling and my time had come to roam.

I met a fair young maiden, she's the flower of the plains,
I married her one morning, which showed I had no brains.
She said she was a maiden, but oh, how she had lied,
When the honeymoon was over, seven kids were by her side.

Oh, I was disappointed, but I said I didn't mind,
I remained her husband, honest, true and kind,
Until one night I found her upon a stranger's knee,
To be her long-lost cousin he was introduced to me.

I knew that she was lying, so I pulled my gun and said,
"You're a low down, sneakin' coward," and I filled him full of lead.
The jury found me guilty and they sentenced me for life,
But I'm better off in prison than to live with such a wife.

No. 34
Clementine

"Clementine" is a humorous ballad on the ancient theme of the supremely ugly woman. In its most typical form it is a '49er ballad. The oldest text we have encountered (1864) shows no Gold Rush influence. (Melody: traditional. Text: *Billy Morris' Songs* [Boston, 1864], pp. 26–27.)

CLEMENTINE

Down by the riv - er there lived a maid - en in a cot - tage built just sev - en by nine, And all a - round this love - ly bow - er the sun-flower blos - soms used to twine. Oh my Clem - a, oh my Clem - a, Oh my dar - ling Clem - en - tine, Now you are lost and gone for - ev - er, I'm dread-ful sor - ry, Clem - en - tine.

Down by the river there lived a maiden
  In a cottage built just seven by nine,
And all around this lovely bower
  The sunflower blossoms used to twine.

CHORUS:
    Oh my Clema, oh my Clema, oh my darling Clementine,
      Now you are lost and gone forever,
        I'm dreadful sorry, Clementine.

Her lips were like two luscious beef steaks
  Dipped in tomato sass and wine,
And like the Cashmere goat's covering
  Was the fine wool of Clementine.

Her foot, oh golly, 'twas a beauty,
  Her shoes was made of Digby pine;
Two herring boxes without the tops on
  Just made the sandals for Clementine.

One day the wind was just blowing awful,
  I took her down some old rye wine
And listened to the flute-like ravings
  Of my sweet sunflower, Clementine.

The ducks had gone down to the river
  To drive them back she did incline,
She stubbed her toe on an oaken sliver,
  She fell into the foamy brine.

I see'd her lips above the water
  A-blowing bubbles very fine,
But 'twasn't no use, I wasn't no swimmer
  And so I lost my Clementine.

Now every night down by the river
  Her ghostus walks 'bout half-past nine;
I know 'tis hers a-kase I've tracked her,
  And by the smell 'tis Clementine.

Now all young men, by this take warning,
  Don't give your ladies too much wine,
'Kase like as not in this wet weather
  She'll share the fate of Clementine.

No. 35
Cowboy Boasters

Cowboy boasting songs are so numerous and varied that they seem symptomatic. Even as humor (which is born of the ironical disparity between utterance and reality) they evoke the unequal battle between man and raw nature. Still, laughter and defiance—awareness, that is, of the existential facts—are far better than withdrawal into a world of comfortable fantasy. In these songs there is more artistry than meets the ear. Rich internal rhymes and highly imaginative imagery suggest a good deal of poetic sophistication. (Melody A: Sterling Sherwin and Harry A. Powell, *Bad Man Songs of the Wild and Woolly West* [Copyright (©) MCMXXXIII by Sam Fox Publishing Company, Inc., New York, N.Y. International copyright secured. Used by special permission], pp. 14-15. Text A: Library of Congress #5643A3, recorded by John A. Lomax. Text B: *Kansas Cowboy,* Dodge City, July 12, 1884. Melody C: Library of Congress #671A2, recorded by John A. Lomax. Text C: PNFQ 520 (written by Curley Fletcher). Text D: FAC III 100, from broadside dated 1884. Text E: *Hoofs and Horns,* July 1935, p. 12.)

COWBOY BOASTERS

I'm a howl-er from the prai-ries of the West. __ If you want to die with ter-ror look at me. __ I'm chain light-ning, if I ain't, may I be blessed, __ I'm the

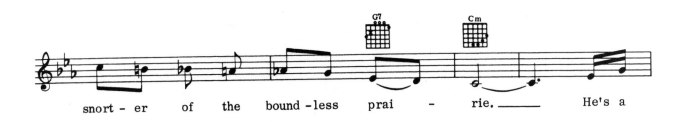

snort - er   of   the   bound - less   prai   -   rie._____   He's   a

CHORUS

kill - er   and   a   hat - er!   He's   the   great   an - ni - hi -

la - tor!   He's   a   ter - ror   of   the   bound - less   prai   -   rie.____

____   He's   a   kill - er   and   a   hat - er!   He's   the   great   an - ni - hi -

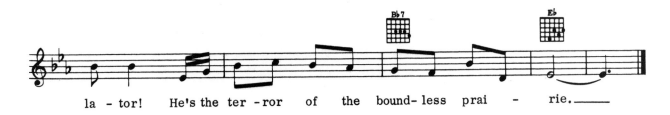

la - tor!   He's   the   ter - ror   of   the   bound - less   prai   -   rie._____

TEXT AND MELODY A. THE FIGHTIN' BOOZE FIGHTER

I'm a howler from the prairies of the West.
  If you want to die with terror, look at me—
I'm chain light'ning, if I ain't, may I be blessed,
  I'm the snorter of the boundless prairie.

    He's a killer and a hater!
    He's the great annihilator!
    He's a terror of the boundless prairie.

I'm the snoozer from the steepest upper trail!
  I'm the reveler in murder and in gore!
I can bust more Pullman coaches on the rail—
  Than anybody who has worked the job before.

    He's a snorter and a snoozer!
    He's the great trunk line abuser!
    He's the man who puts the sleeper on the rail.

I'm the double-jawed hyena from the East.
  I'm the blazing bloody blizzard of the States.
I'm the celebrated slugger; I'm the Beast—
  I can snatch a man bald-headed while he waits.

    He's a double-jawed hyena!
    He's the villain of the scena!
    He can snatch a man bald-headed while he waits.

TEXT B. A TEXAS IDOL

I'm a buzzard from the Brazos on a tear, hear me toot!
I'm a lifter of the flowing locks of hair, hear me hoot!
  I'm a racker from the Rockies
  And of all the town the talk is
"He's a pirate from the pampas," on the shoot.

Those who love me call me Little Dynamite. I'm a pet.
I'm a walking, stalking terror of the night, you can bet.
  By my nickel plated teasers
Many a rusty featured Greaser's sun has set.

Sometimes I strike an unprotected town, paint it red.
Choke the sheriff, turn the marshall upside down, on his head.
  Call for drinks for all the party
And if chinned by any smarty, pay in lead.

I'm a coyote of the sunset, "Pirate Dude!" Hear me zip.
In the company of gentlemen I'm rude, with my lip.
  Down in front remove that nigger
  Or I'll perforate his figger,
I am fly, I am fighter, I am flip.

I've been ridin' for cattle for the most of my life;
I ain't got no family and I ain't got no wife;
I ain't got no kith and I ain't got no kin;
I never will finish and I ne'er did begin.
I've rode down in Texas where the cowboys are tall,
The state's pretty big, but the horses are small.
When it comes to cowpunchin' I'm hard to out-do—
I'm a high-loping cowboy and a wild buckaroo.

I have rode up in Montana and I've rode in Idaho,
I have rode for old Terasus down in old Mexico.
I have roped a mountain lion and a she grizzly bear;
I have used a choya cactus fer to comb my hair.
I have rode across the desert with the water far between,
And I've crossed Death Valley without a canteen.
When it comes to crossin' deserts, I'm hard to out-do—
I'm a high-loping cowboy and a wild buckaroo.

I talk a lot of Spanish and I talk Piute,
Oh, I pack a long knife and a pistol to shoot.
I got no *señorita,* and I got no squaw,
I got no sweetheart nor no mother-in-law.
I have never been tied to no apron strings,
Oh, I ain't no devil, but I got no wings.
When it comes to dodgin' women, I'm hard to out-do—
I'm a high-loping cowboy and a wild buckaroo.

Oh, I don't like whiskey, but I do like my beer.
Oh, I don't like mutton, but I do like steer.
I will let you alone if you'll let me be,
But don't you think you can crawl on me.
I will fight anybody at the drop of a hat
And he'll think he's in a sack with a panther cat.
When it comes to whipping bad men, I'm hard to out-do—
I'm a high-loping cowboy and a wild buckaroo.

TEXT D. THE TEXAS COWBOY

With a sort of careless swagger,
And a movement half a stagger,
With now and then a kind of angry frown;
With an air that's free and easy,
And "I don't care if I please ye,"
Is the way the Texas cowboy seems in town.

His chappies, made of leather,
Art good for any weather,
His wide-brimmed hat he wears with manly pride;
His spurs they drag and rattle
And remind of running cattle,
His faithful gun hangs ready at his side.

He loves to talk of "trailing,"
With one foot on the railing,
And watch the gentle bar-keep smile and wait;
When he calls for "good, red licker,"
He pours a man's size "kicker,"
And cowboys like him take that licker straight.

He can ride a bucking broncho,
From Austin to the Concho
And never once be pitched into the air;
He will rope a cow or rabbit,
From the force of early habit,
And when he works he never has a care.

But to see him in his glory,
This hero of my story,
Just watch him in a round-up on the plain;
When he's cutting out a "stranger,"
He never thinks of danger,
Nor does he seem to feel the constant strain.

If night should overtake him
It does not move or shake him,
Just so his horse can find a place to graze;
With his saddle for his pillow
He dreams of some fond willow
Where he sat with one he loved in other days.

He can dance the gay *bolero,*
And make himself a hero,
In the eyes of any *señorita* fair;
He will meet a girl and love her,
And his pleadings soon will move her,
For he's the boy that anything will dare.

He can take a joke or give it;
His life, 'tis his to live it,
And little does he care for worldly gains;
And as we have his measure,
Let us drink a toast with pleasure
To this daring Texas cowboy of the plains.

TEXT E. AN AFTERNOON LIKE THIS

An afternoon like this it was in tough old Cherokee,
An outlaw come a-hornin' in an' ask who I might be.

He spun around his finger joint a six-gun primed with lead,
He yelled, "By Judas, answer quick!" And this is what I said.

"My Uncle Jess was Jesse James, my ma was Chuck-taw-said.
Black Jack Catch-um was my paw, Sam Bass my cradle maid.

"They fed me first on she-wolf's milk, and while my teeth was cuttin'
My rattle was a diamond-back with twenty-seven button.

"I learned to bark before I talked, before I talked, to swear.
I always use tarantulas to comb my shinin' hair.

"Where ere I make my bed at night, the grass it fades and dies,
And when I'm ridin' in the rain the fearful lightnin' shies."

107

No. 36
Life in a Prairie Shack

Seasoned frontiersmen took great delight in the foibles and misapprehensions of the tenderfoot, measuring thus their own fortitude against the weakness of the uninitiated. (Melody and text: FAC I 487, collected by Edith Fowke from Captain Charles Cates, North Vancouver, B.C.)

LIFE IN A PRAIRIE SHACK

Oh, a life in the prai-rie shack __ when the rain be-gins to pour, __ Drip, dri p it comes through the roof, __ and some comes through__ the door. __ The ten-der-foot curs-es his fate, __ and faint-ly mut-ters "Ah, __ This bloom-in' coun-try's a fraud, __ and I want to go home to my ma. __ Ma __ Ma __ I want to go home to my ma. __ This bloom-in' coun-try's a fraud, __ And I want to go home to my ma." __

Oh, a life in the prairie shack when the rain begins to pour,
Drip, drip it comes through the roof, and some comes through the door.
The tenderfoot curses his fate, and faintly mutters, "Ah,
This bloomin' country's a fraud, and I want to go home to my ma."

CHORUS:
    Ma! Ma! I want to go home to my ma.
    This bloomin' country's a fraud,
    And I want to go home to my ma.

Oh, he saddled his fiery cayuse, determined to flourish 'round,
The critter began to buck and threw him off on the ground.
And as he picked himself up, he was heard to mutter, "Ah,
This bloomin' country's a fraud, and I want to go home to my ma."

Oh, he tried to light a fire at twenty degrees below,
He made a lick at the stick and he amputated his toe;
And as he crawled to his shack he was heard to mutter, "Ah,
This bloomin' country's a fraud, and I want to go home to my ma."

Now all you tenderfeet, list before you go too far,
If you haven't a government site, you'd better stay where you are,
And if you take my advice, then you will not mutter, "Ah,
This bloomin' country's a fraud, and I want to go home to my ma."

No. 37
Punchin' Dough

Social life on a roundup or cattle drive, such as it was, revolved around the chuck wagon. The camp cook was typically a stove-up cowpuncher whose store of songs and reminiscences could be even more salty than his fare. His prestige in the outfit was just a little below that of foreman or trail boss, and he used his command over the chuck to keep the hands in line. (Melody: FAC I 183, reproduced with permission of the collector, Dean Emeritus John Donald Robb of the University of New Mexico. Text: Henry Herbert Knibbs, *Saddle Songs and Other Verse* [Boston and New York: Houghton Mifflin Company, 1922], pp. 19–20 [by permission].)

PUNCHIN' DOUGH

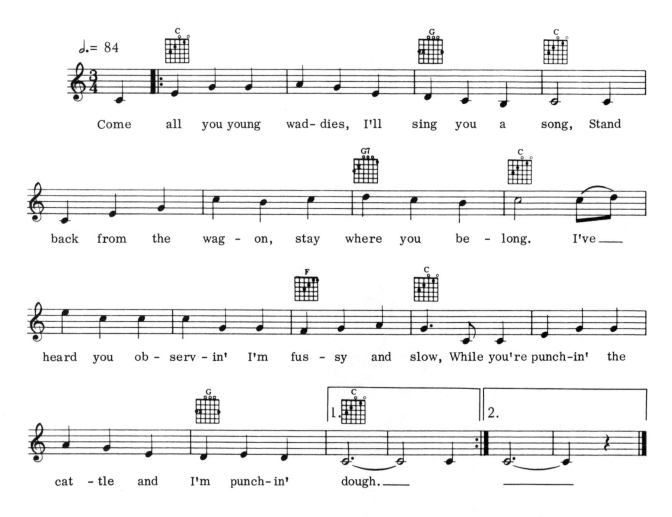

Come all you young wad-dies, I'll sing you a song, Stand back from the wag-on, stay where you be-long. I've heard you ob-serv-in' I'm fus-sy and slow, While you're punch-in' the cat-tle and I'm punch-in' dough.

Come, all you young waddies, I'll sing you a song,
Stand back from the wagon, stay where you belong:
I've heard you observin' I'm fussy and slow,
While you're punchin' the cattle and I'm punchin' dough.

Now I reckon your stomach would grow to your back
If it wa'n't for the cook that keeps fillin' the slack:
With the beans in the box and the pork in the tub,
I'm a-wonderin' now, who would fill you with grub?

You think you're right handy with gun and with rope,
But I've noticed you're bashful when usin' the soap:
When you're rollin' your Bull for your brown cigarette
I been rollin' the dough for them biscuits you et.

When you're cuttin' stock, then I'm cuttin' a steak:
When you're wranglin' hosses, I'm wranglin' a cake:
When you're hazin' the dogies and battin' your eyes,
I'm hazin' dried apples that aim to be pies.

You brag about shootin' up windows and lights,
But try shootin' biscuits for twelve appetites:
When you crawl from your roll and the ground it is froze,
Then who biles the coffee that thaws out your nose?

In the old days the punchers took just what they got:
It was sow-belly, beans, and the old coffee pot;
But now you come howlin' for pie and for cake,
Then you cuss at the cook for a good bellyache.

You say that I'm old, with my feet on the skids;
Well, I'm tellin' you now that you're nothin' but kids;
If you reckon your mounts are some snaky and raw,
Just try ridin' herd on a stove that won't draw.

When you look at my apron, you're readin' my brand,
Four-X, which is sign for the best in the land:
On bottle or sack it sure stands for good luck,
So line up, you waddies, and wrangle your chuck.

No use of your snortin' and fightin' your head;
If you like it with chili, just eat what I said:
For I aim to be boss of this end of the show
While you're punchin' cattle, and I'm punchin' dough.

No. 38

Blood on the Saddle

"Blood on the Saddle" is known to thousands as a college favorite—hilariously funny because of the gory images it contains. Kathy Dagel, unspoiled by collegiate superciliousness, sang it with a mood of tragedy and pathos. Melody and basic imagery are traceable to "Halbert the Grim," a stark romantic ballad of the early 1800's. (Melody and Text A: FAC I 511, sung by Kathy Dagel. Text B: FAC II 189, from Western Kentucky Folklore Archive at the University of California at Los Angeles.)

BLOOD ON THE SADDLE

There's blood on the sad - dle and blood on the ground, And a great big pud - dle of blood all a - round; A cow - boy lay in —— it all cov - ered with gore, And he nev - er will ride an - y bron - cos no more. ——

TEXT A. BLOOD ON THE SADDLE

There's blood on the saddle and blood on the ground,
And a great big puddle of blood all around;
A cowboy lay in it all covered with gore
And he never will ride any broncos no more.

Oh, pity the cowboy all gory and red,
A bronco fell on him and bashed in his head.
There was blood on the saddle and blood on the ground,
And a great big puddle of blood all around.

TEXT B. THE BLOODY COWBOY

Pity the cowboy all bloody and dead,
His horse fell upon him and bashed in his head.
Blood on the saddle and blood on the ground,
Puddles and puddles of blood all around.

    Blood on the saddle, drip;
    Blood upon the ground, splash;
    Great big puddles of blood all around.

    Horse's a crying, eeeee,
    Cowboy's a dying, ugh,
    This is the end of my tail, swish.

No. 39

The Lavender Cowboy

The title alone suggests a spoof on the tough hombres that myth insists the cowboys were: this, plus the dream symbolism, suggests that it is a latecomer among cowboy songs. (Melody: FAC I 220, reproduced with permission of the collector, Dean Emeritus John Donald Robb of the University of New Mexico. Text: Bluebird B-8229A, Vernon Dalhart and His Big Cypress Boys.)

THE LAVENDER COWBOY

He was on - ly a lav - en - der cow - boy, _____ The hairs on his chest ___ were two, _____ But he wished to fol - low the he - roes _____ And fight like the he - men ___ do.

He was only a lavender cowboy
  The hairs on his chest were two,
But he wished to follow the heroes
  And fight like the he-men do.

But he was inwardly troubled
  By a dream that gave him no rest,
That he'd go with heroes in action
  With only two hairs on his chest.

First he tried many a hair tonic,
  'Twar rubbed in on him each night,
But still when he looked in the mirror
  Those two hairs were ever in sight.

But with a spirit undaunted
  He wandered out to fight,
Just like an old-time knight errant
  To win combat for the right.

He battled for Red Nellie's honor
And cleaned out a holdup's nest,
He died with his six guns a-smoking
With only two hairs on his chest.

114

Part Five

Red Men and White

No. 40
The Indian's Death Song

From the first moments of colonization Anglo-Americans have had prickings of conscience concerning their behavior toward the Indian, and, despite all the conflict, have eulogized his proud resistance to white aggressions. Alknomook is one of these perennial noble savages sung about on the frontier since the first years of American independence. It was composed by Mrs. John Hunter, British lyricist, the theme suggested by an account of Indian death chants brought to her by a gentleman who had resided many years in the colonies. (Melody and text: W. O. Hickok, *The Social Lyrist* [Harrisburg, Pa. 1840], pp. 55–56.)

THE INDIAN'S DEATH SONG

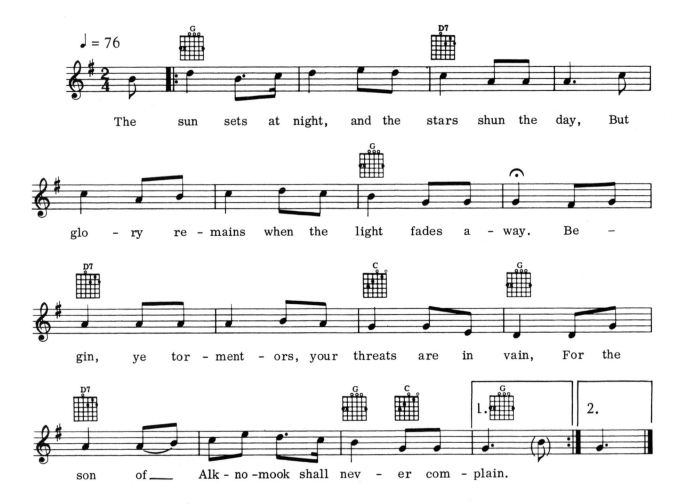

The sun sets at night, and the stars shun the day, But glo - ry re - mains when the light fades a - way. Be - gin, ye tor - ment - ors, your threats are in vain, For the son of __ Alk - no -mook shall nev - er com - plain.

The sun sets at night, and the stars shun the day,
But glory remains when the light fades away.
Begin, ye tormentors, your threats are in vain,
For the son of Alknomook shall never complain.

Remember the arrows he shot from his bow;
Remember your chiefs by his hatchet laid low;
Why so slow? Do you wait till I shrink from my pain?
No! The son of Alknomook shall never complain.

Remember the wood where in ambush we lay,
And the scalps which we bore from your nation away;
Now the flame rises fast, you exult in my pain,
But the son of Alknomook shall never complain.

I'll go to the land where my father is gone;
His ghost shall rejoice in the fame of his son;
Death comes like a friend to relieve me from pain;
And thy son, oh! Alknomook, has scorn'd to complain.

No. 41
Haunted Wood

"Haunted Wood" is the grim account of revengeful murder wrought by Indians upon the wife and children of a frontier settler. It moves with romantic impetuousness from a description of the cavernous valley to the departure of the frontiersman, the arrival of the Indians, their savage crime, and the frontiersman's return to the carnage which had been his home. It stands comparison, we think, with the greatest ballads of English and Scottish tradition. (Melody: FMC I 581, sung by Buck Lee. Text: PNFQ 510.)

HAUNTED WOOD

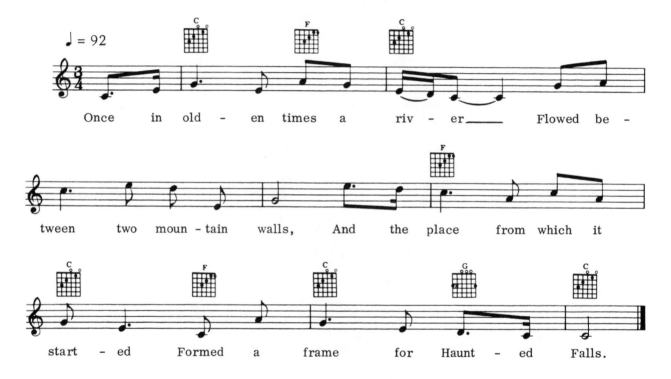

Once in olden times a river
   Flowed between two mountain walls,
And the place from which it started
   Formed a frame for Haunted Falls.

Rugged rocks well they had risen
   Far upon either side;
And its powerful base been washed there
   By many an incoming tide.

On the bosom of this river
   Launched many a light canoe,
While the winds were softly sighing
   And the summer skies were blue.

On the banks there lived a white man,
   Wife, and children, he had two.
While the winds were softly sighing,
   And the summer skies were blue.

One quiet day the father
   To a little town for the mail had gone,
Left his wife and little babies
   Just a few quiet hours alone.

Hark! she heard the tramp of horses
   And then she turned in fright
Just in time to draw the door bolt
   As some Indians rode in sight.

Then she seized and kissed her babies,
   Bid them neither speak or cry;
Cast them in a secret closet,
   Then she nerved herself to die.

With an angry push, the chieftain
   Tore the bolt from off the door,
There he saw this weeping woman
   Lying there upon the floor.

"Come, let's drown this weeping woman,"
   And he raised his heavy stick.
"Come, let's drown this weeping woman,
   Lose no time, I say, be quick."

Then they seized this weeping woman,
   Roughly raised her from the floor,
Took her by her dark brown tresses,
   Roughly dragged her to the shore.

Then they sang and danced around her,
   Heeding not her piteous cries,
Cast her on the rocks below them,
   And in agony she died.

"Come, let's burn this little dwelling,"
   And then they circled 'round,
Then they burned the little babies,
   And the dwelling to the ground.

Now this old man wanders lonely
   Round the place where the dwelling stood,
And the people of this village
   Call this place the Haunted Wood.

No. 42

Fair Lady of the Plains

"Fair Lady of the Plains" gives us one of the most haunting female images offered by frontier literature—a complete acceptance of the rough-and-tumble life to which she is committed. Her fortuitous death comes as a stark reminder that the malignancies of frontier life could cut man down to size whenever and wherever they chose. What a spectrum of human behavior is suggested by this image of "a fair lady as white as the snow" who "drank the red liquor that affects a man's soul"! (Melody: FAC I 97, sung by Joan O'Bryant. Text A: FAC I 100, recorded by Kathy Dagel. Text B: PC-F 35.)

FAIR LADY OF THE PLAINS

I once knew a maid-en who lived on the plains, She
helped me to herd cat-tle through slow,— stead-y rains, She
helped me one sea-son, one whole year's round-up, But
she would drink red liq-uor from a cold— bit-ter cup.

TEXT A. MAIDEN OF THE PLAINS

I once knew a maiden who lived on the plains,
She helped me to herd cattle through slow, steady rains,
She helped me one season, one whole year's roundup,
But she would drink red liquor from a cold bitter cup.

She would drink red liquor, that affects a man's soul,
But she was a fair maiden and as white as the snow.
I learned her the cow trade, the ranger's command,
I learned her to handle a six-shooter in right or left hand.

I learned her to handle a six-shooter and never to run,
Never fear danger while a bullet's in a gun.
We camped in a canyon in the fall of the year,
We camped in a canyon with a bunch of fat steers.

The Indians broke in on us at the dead hours of night,
She had rose from her warm bed a battle to fight.
Then out roared the thunder and down come the rain,
Along come a bullet and crushed out her brain.

Now arise all you cowboys, let's fight for our life
For these wretched redskins have murdered my wife.

TEXT B. FAIR LADY OF THE PLAINS

There was a fair lady who lived on the plains,
She stayed with me through the long steady rains;
She stayed with me through long roundup
And drank with me from the poor bitter cup.
She drank the red liquor that affects a man's soul,
She was a fair lady, just white as the snow.

I taught her the tricks at the cowboy's command,
To use a six-shooter in each one of her hands,
To use a six-shooter and never to run
As long as there was a load left in her gun.

We camped in the canyon the following year,
We stayed there that summer with a herd of fat steer;
'Til the Indians came in on us at the dead hour of night,
She arose from her pillow all ready to fight;
She arose from her pillow with a gun in each hand
Saying, "Come all you brave cowboys, we must win this fair land!"

So loud rolled the thunder and down came the rain
And in came a bullet that dashed out her brain.
I jumped in my saddle to battle, to fight,
For the Indians had murdered my dear loving wife.

No. 43
Sioux Indians

This overlander's ballad vibrates with epic realism and directness: not a spare word, and no image that departs from the bitter reality of the moment. It is sung in the West wherever pioneer memories linger. Text B has a Northwestern locale. The song also appears as a California gold digger's ballad. (Melody: FAC I 198, reproduced with permission of the collector, Dean Emeritus John Donald Robb of the University of New Mexico. Text A: PNFQ 426. Text B: Gordon 1527.)

SIOUX INDIANS

I'll sing you a song though it may be a sad one,_____ Of trials and troub - les and where they first be - gun _____ I left my dear kin - dred, my friends and my home, A - cross the wild des - erts and moun - tains to roam._____

Text A. Sioux Indians

I'll sing you a song though it may be a sad one,
Of trials and troubles and where they first begun;
I left my dear kindred, my friends and my home,
Across the wild deserts and mountains to roam.

I crossed the Missouri and joined a large train,
Which bore us over mountain and valley and plain;
And often of evenings out hunting we'd go,
To shoot the fleet antelope and wild buffalo.

We heard of Sioux Indians all out on the plains,
A-killing poor drivers and burning their trains;
A-killing poor drivers with arrows and bow,
When captured by Indians no mercy they show.

We traveled three weeks till we came to the Platte,
And pitched out our tents at the end of the flat;
We spread down our blankets on the green, grassy ground,
While our horses and mules were grazing around.

While taking refreshment we heard a low yell,
The whoop of Sioux Indians coming up from the dell;
We sprang to our rifles with a flash in each eye,
"Boys," says our brave leader, "we'll fight till we die."

They made a bold dash and came near to our train,
And arrows fell around us like hail and like rain;
But with our long rifles we fed them cold lead,
Till many a brave warrior around us lay dead.

We shot their bold chief at the head of his band,
He died like a warrior with a gun in his hand;
When they saw their bold chief lying dead in his gore,
They whooped and they yelled and we saw them no more.

With our small band—there were just twenty-four—
And of the Sioux Indians five hundred or more—
We fought them with courage; we spoke not a word,
Till the end of the battle was all that was heard.

We hitched up our horses and we started our train;
Three more savage battles this trip on the plains;
And in our last battle, three of our brave boys fell,
And we left them to rest in a green, shady dell.

B. Song of the Emigrant Trail

I will sing you a song, e'en though a sad tale,
Of hardships we met on the emigrant trail;
When parting from kindred, from friends and our home,
We westward o'er valleys and mountains did roam.

They told us of Indians who harassed the plains,
The killing of drivers and burning of trains;
Of people they'd slaughtered with arrows and bow,
Of cruelties practiced when striking the blow.

We crossed the Missouri and joined a long train
Which crawled slowly onward o'er boundless wide plain;
While rambling and traveling we oft times would go
To hunt antelope or the wild buffalo.

By short daily marches we reached the North Platte,
Made camp by its waters, a green shady flat;
There circled our wagons 'mid trees on a mound
And herded our oxen and horses around.

In midst of our labor we heard a low wail,
The war cry of Indians who followed our trail;
Men sprung to their rifles in the flash of an eye.
Exclaimed our bold leader: "We'll fight till we die!"

We drove in our cattle, made ready to fight,
As painted red devils dashed plainly in sight;
They charged on our wagons with fierce whoop and yell;
At crack of our rifles six red warriors fell.

We killed their bold leader at the head of his band;
He died like a warrior, his bow in his hand.
A moment they halted when he fell to the ground,
Then screeching with hatred they circled us 'round.

With trusty long rifles we gave them cold lead
Till many Sioux warriors lay on the ground dead;
They whooped and they hollered, then fled in dismay
With their chieftain's body when we won the day.

We had other combats, three brave men were slain
Defending their loved ones while crossing the plain;
We laid them at rest in a green shady dell.
Fond mem'ries there guard them—they fought true and well.

We traveled by day, guarded camp during night
Till Oregon's mountains loomed high in their might;
Now at Pocahontas beside a clear stream
Our journey is ended in the land of our dream.

No. 44
Texas Jack

In "Texas Jack" we see the rugged life of the first overlanders ampli-
fied into mythic proportions: the Indians' rape of the pioneer children
is viewed through the telescope of time, and the hero-that-was is glorified
by a cowboy in his declining years. (Melody: FAC I 565, as sung by
Ezra Barhight, collected by Ellen J. Stekert. Text: Clark Stanley, *The
Life and Adventures of the American Cowboy* [Providence, R. I., c.
1905], p. 37.)

TEXAS JACK

Come, give me your at-ten-tion, and see the right and wrong,— It
is a sim-ple sto-ry and won't de-tain— you long;— I'll
try to tell— the rea-son why we are bound to roam,— And
why— we are so friend-less and nev-er have a home.

Come, give me your attention, and see the right and wrong,
It is a simple story and won't detain you long;
I'll try to tell the reason why we are bound to roam,
And why we are so friendless and never have a home.

My home is in the saddle, upon a pony's back,
I am a roving Cow-boy and find the hostile track;
They say I am a sure shot, and danger I never knew;
But I have often heard the story that now I'll tell to you.

In eighteen hundred and sixty-three a little emigrant band
Was massacred by Indians, bound West by overland;
They scalped our noble soldiers, and the emigrants had to die,
And the only living captives were two small girls and I.

I was rescued from the Indians by a brave and noble man,
Who trailed the thieving Indians and fought them hand to hand;
He was noted for his bravery while on an enemy's track;
He has a noble history and his name is Texas Jack.

Old Jack could tell a story if he was only here,
Of the trouble and the hardships of the Western pioneer;
He would tell you how the mothers and comrades lost their lives,
And how the noble fathers were scalped before our eyes.

I was raised among the Cow-boys, my saddle is my home,
And I'll always be a Cow-boy, no difference where I roam;
And like our noble heroes my help I volunteer,
And try to be of service to the Western pioneer.

I am a roving Cow-boy, I've worked upon the trail,
I've shot the shaggy buffalo and heard the coyote's wail;
I have slept upon my saddle, and covered by the moon;
I expect to keep it up, dear friends, until I meet my doom.

No. 45
Custer's Last Charge

The Custer tragedy produced or attracted a dozen or more ballads. This one, for example, derives from a favorite Civil War song about comrades-in-arms, each of whom vows to take the message of his friend's death back to sweetheart or mother. Both are killed, and the real tragedy seems to lie not in the soldiers' demise but in anticipated bereavement of the womenfolk. (Melody and text: FAC I 103, recorded by Kathy Dagel.)

CUSTER'S LAST CHARGE

Just be-fore brave Cust-er's charge, Two sol-diers drew their reins, ___ With part-ing words and clasp-ing hands That they might nev-er meet a-gain. One was a tall and a slen-der-y lad, And had trust-ed in the one ___ That he loved so best, so well, For she's all ___ this world to him.

Just before brave Custer's charge
  Two soldiers drew their reins,
With parting words and clasping hands
  That they might never meet again.
One was a tall and a slendery lad,
  And had trusted in the one
That he loved so best, so well,
  For she's all this world to him.

"Upon my breast I have a face,
  I'll wear it in a fight;
A face that is all this world to me
  And it shines like a morning light.
Like a morning light was her love to me
  For she cherished a lovely smile,
And little have I cared for another face
  Since she promised to be my wife.

"Will you write to her, Charlie, when I am gone,
  Send back that fair fond face,
And tell her gently how I died
  And where was my resting place."
Tears filled the eyes of the blue-eyed boy
  And his sad heart filled with pain.
"I'll do your bidding, brave comrade mine,
  If I never do meet again.

"But if I get killed will you ride back
  And do as much for me?
I have a mother who's waiting at home
  And she's all this world to me.
One by one she lost us all,
  She lost both husband and son,
And I was the last that our country called
  And she kissed me and sent me on."

Just then the order came to charge,
  With an instant clasp of hands,
And on and on they rode,
  This brave and devoted band.
They returned from the hill but they could not gain
For out of the gathering doom
  Where the Indians shot like hail
And they poured out death on Custer's ranks
  And scalped them as they fell.

Among the dead who were left behind
  Was a boy with curly hair,
And the cold dark form that rode by his side
  Lay dead beside him there.
No one left to tell the blue-eyed girl
  The last words that her lover had said,
But the aged mother who's waiting at home
  Will learn that her boy is dead.

No. 46
Billy Veniro

Billy Veniro's ride to warn the dwellers at an isolated ranch (especially his beloved Bess) of an impending Indian raid is a classic of frontier heroism. The song oozes with the sentimentality, the cult of service to woman, the throbbing tempo, the forebodings, and the melodrama that make the cowboy image vie with those of the gallant knights and courtly ladies of medieval times. We are told that Billy's grave is located near the town of Payson in northeastern Arizona. (Melody: FAC I 190, reproduced with permission of the collector, Dean Emeritus John Donald Robb of the University of New Mexico. Text: FMC I 804, sung by Buck Lee.)

BILLY VENIRO

Bil-ly Ve-nir-o heard them say In an Ar-i-zo-na town one day, That a band of A-pach-e In-dians Were up-on the trail of death. Heard them tell of mur-der done, Men been killed at Rock-y Run; "They're in dan-ger at the cow ranch," Said Ve-nir-o un-der breath.

Billy Veniro heard them say
In an Arizona town one day
That a band of Apache Indians
Were upon the trail of death.

Heard them tell of murder done,
Men been killed at Rocky Run.
"They're in danger at the cow ranch,"
Said Veniro under breath.

Cow ranch forty miles away
Was a little place that lay
In a green and shady valley
Of a mighty wilderness.

Half a score of homes were there,
And in one a maiden fair
Held the heart of Billy Veniro,
Billy Veniro's little Bess.

So no wonder he grew pale
When he heard the cowboy's tale
Of the men that he'd seen murdered
The day before at Rocky Run.

"If there is a God above
I will save the girl I love,
For my love for little Bessie
I will see that something's done."

Not a moment he delayed
When his brave resolve was made,
And his many comrades told him
When they heard his daring plan:

"You are riding straight to death."
But he answered, "Save your breath.
I may never reach the cow ranch
But I'll do the best I can."

As across the alkali he sped
All his thoughts raced on ahead
To the little band at the cow ranch,
Never thinking of danger near.

With his quirt's unceasing whirl
And the jingle of his spurs
Little brown Chappo bore the cowboy
O'er the far away frontier.

Lower and lower sank the sun,
He drew rein at Rocky Run,
"Here the men met death, my Chappo,"
When he stroked his horse's mane.

"So will those we go to warn
Ere the coming of the morn.
If I fail God bless my Bessie,"
And he started on again.

Keen and clear a rifle shot
Woke the echoes of the spot,
"I am wounded," cried Veniro,
And he swayed from side to side.

"While there's life there's always hope,
Slowly onward I will lope,
If I never reach the cow ranch
Little Bess will know I tried.

"I will save her yet," he cried,
"Bessie Lee shall know I tried,"
Then for her sake he halted
In the shadow of a hill.

From his *chaparajos* he took
With weak hand a little book,
Tore a blank leaf from its pages
Saying, "This shall be my will."

From a limb a bow he broke,
Dipped his little pen of oak
In the warm blood that was spurting
From the wound above his heart.

Then he wrote before too late:
"Apache warriors lie in wait,
Goodbye, Bess, God bless you, darling,"
And he felt the cold fear start.

Then he made his message fast,
Love's first letter and its last,
And he tied it to the saddle
And he gave his horse the rein.

"Take this message if not me
To my little Bessie Lee."
Then he tied himself to the saddle
And his lips were white with pain.

Just at dusk the horse of brown
Wet with sweat came padding down,
Down the little lane at the cow ranch
And he stopped at Bessie's door.

But the cowboy was asleep
And his slumbers were so deep
That little Bess ne'er could wake him
Though she tried forever more.

Now you've heard the story told
By the young and by the old
Of how the Apache warriors
To the little cow ranch came.

Of the sharp and bloody fight,
How the chief fell in the fight,
And the panic-stricken warriors
When they heard Veniro's name.

Many a day has passed away,
And the maiden's hair turned gray,
But still she plants the roses
On Billy Veniro's grave.

Part Six

Love Across Cultures

No. 47
Little Mohea

The West has no monopoly on "Little Mohea," an Indian maiden wooed, won, and abandoned by sailors, adventurers, trappers, soldiers, cowboys, and sundry other virile types since the early decades of European men's ventures into the New World. Hundreds of texts could be assembled with untold variation in content and melodic shape. In some texts the ballad ends with the lovers' parting; in others it goes on to tell how the cruel lover himself returns to the Old Country to find his own true love has abandoned him—a deserved if sad retribution. (Melody and Text A: FAC I 14, recorded by Rosalie Sorrels. Text B: PNFQ 371.)

LITTLE MOHEA

As I was out walk-ing for pleas-ure one day, Or to seek rec-re-a-tion, I scarce-ly can say, As I was a-mus-ing my-self in the shade, Who chanced to come by me but a fair In-dian maid.

Text A. Little Mohea

As I was out walking for pleasure one day,
Or to seek recreation, I scarcely can say,
As I was amusing myself in the shade
Who chanced to come by me but a fair Indian maid.

She sat down beside me, and taking my hand,
Said, "You look like a stranger, not one of my band.
But if you are willing you're welcome to come,
And share with myself a snug little home.
But if you are willing you're welcome to come,
And share with myself a snug little home."

Together we wandered, together we roamed,
Till we came to a log hut in a coconut grove.
As we came to the log hut she turned unto me,
Saying, "Go no more roaming far across the blue sea."
Saying, "Go no more roving but stay here with me,
And I'll teach you the language of the little Mohea."

"Oh, no, my fair maiden, that never could be
For I have my own true love far across the blue sea.
And if I bereave her, why lonely she'd be,
For her heart beats as truly as the little Mohea."

Oh, now I've safe landed on my own native shore,
My friends and companions all around me once more.
I look all about me but none do I see
With lips to compare with the little Mohea.
I look all about me but none do I see
With lips to compare with the little Mohea.

Text B. The Pretty Mohea

As I went out walking for pleasure one day,
In sweet recreation to while time away;
As I sat amusing myself on the grass,
Oh, who should I spy but a fair Indian lass.

She sat down beside me and, taking my hand,
Said, "You are a stranger and in a strange land;
But if you will follow you're welcome to come
And dwell in the cottage that I call my home."

The sun was fast sinking far o'er the blue sea
When I wandered alone with my pretty Mohea.
Together we wandered, together did rove,
Till we came to the cot in the coconut grove.

Then this kind expression she made unto me:
"If you will consent, sir, to stay here with me
And go no more roving upon the salt sea,
I'll teach you the language of the lass of Mohea!"

"Oh, no! my dear maiden, that never could be;
For I have a true love in my own country;
And I'll not forsake her, for I know she loves me,
And her heart is as true as the pretty Mohea."

'Twas early one morning, a morning in May,
That to this fair maiden these words I did say:
"I'm going to leave you, so farewell, my dear;
My ship's sails are spreading, and home I must steer."

The last time I saw her she stood on the strand;
And as my boat passed her she waved me her hand,
Saying, "When you have landed with the girl that you love,
Think of little Mohea in the coconut grove."

And then when I landed on my own native shore,
With friends and relations around me once more,
I gazed all about me, no one could I see
That was fit to compare with the pretty Mohea.

And the girl that I trusted proved untrue to me;
So I'll turn my course backward, far o'er the deep sea,
I'll turn my course backward, from this land I'll flee;
I'll go spend my days with my pretty Mohea.

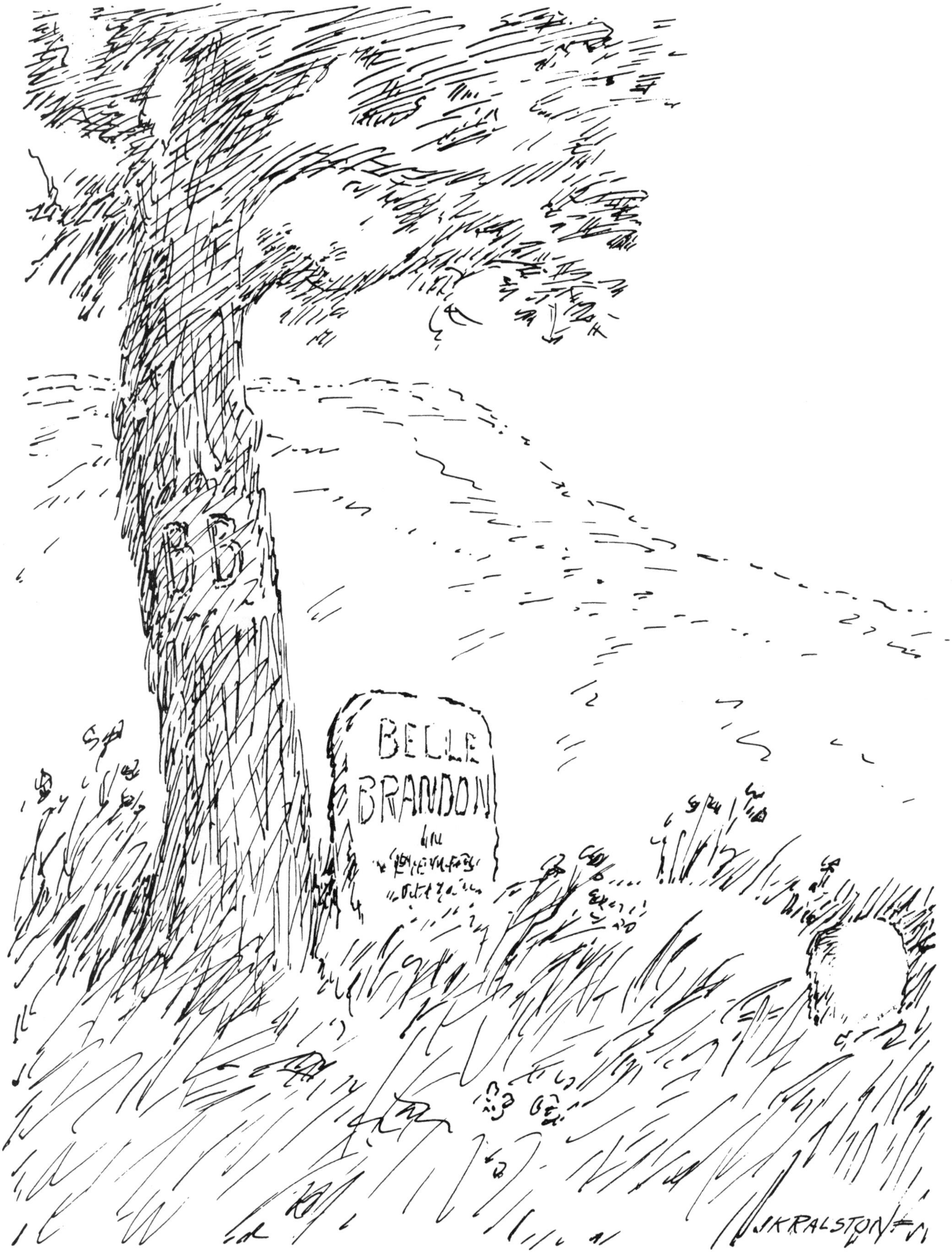
BB
BELLE
BRANDON
J.K. RALSTON

No. 48
Belle Brandon

"Belle Brandon" illuminates some of the enduring clichés of frontier life—the titillation of a damsel whose veins are "tinged with the life current of the Redman" . . . love's rewards gathered beneath the old arbor tree and witness thereof carved into its aged bark . . . separation through death, burial at the site of ecstasy—more than enough, indeed, to guarantee any song a long life in the lore of the folk. (Melody: FMC I 725, sung by Fletcher Bronson. Text: *Beadle's Dime Song Books,* No. 1 [New York, 1859], p. 46.)

BELLE BRANDON

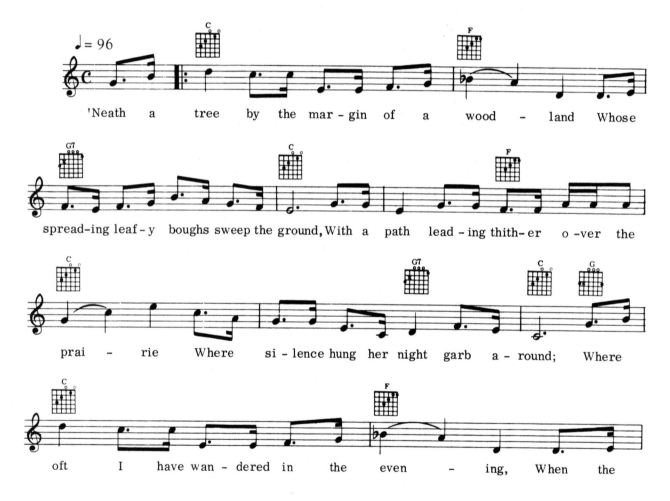

'Neath a tree by the mar-gin of a wood – land Whose spread-ing leaf-y boughs sweep the ground, With a path lead-ing thith-er o-ver the prai – rie Where si-lence hung her night garb a-round; Where oft I have wan-dered in the even – ing, When the

sum - mer winds were fra - grant on the leaves, There I saw the lit - tle beau - ty Belle Bran - don, And we met 'neath the old ar - bor tree. There I saw the lit - tle beau - ty Belle Bran - don, And we met 'neath the old ar - bor tree.

'Neath a tree by the margin of a woodland
  Whose spreading leafy boughs sweep the ground,
With a path leading thither over the prairie
  Where silence hung her night garb around;
Where oft I have wandered in the evening
  When the summer winds were fragrant on the leaves,
There I saw the little beauty Belle Brandon,
  And we met 'neath the old arbor tree.
There I saw the little beauty Belle Brandon,
  And we met 'neath the old arbor tree.

Belle Brandon was a birdling of the mountain,
  In freedom she sported on the lea,
And they said the life current of the Redman
  Tinged her veins from a far distant sea.
And she loved her humble dwelling on the prairie,
  And her guileless happy heart clung to me,
And I loved the little beauty Belle Brandon,
  And we both loved the old arbor tree,
And I loved the little beauty Belle Brandon,
  And we both loved the old arbor tree.

On the trunk of an aged tree I carved them,
  And our names on the sturdy oak remain,
But I now repair in sorrow to its shelter
  And murmur to the wild winds my pain.
And I sat there in solitude repining
  For the beauty dream night brought to me,
Death has wed the little beauty Belle Brandon
  And she sleeps 'neath the old arbor tree.
Death has wed the little beauty Belle Brandon
  And she sleeps 'neath the old arbor tree.

No. 49
Mustang Gray

Ever since ancient times when women intervened in the war between the Sabines and the warriors of Latium, ballads have been written about heroic maidens who have befriended the wounded on the field of battle: here it is a Mexican *señorita* who arranges the escape of Mustang Gray on her father's favorite mount. The song derives through oral tradition from a "ballad opera" composed by John Hill (1801–1890) in 1848. (Melody: Varsity 5135. Text: Everett Dick, "The Long Drive," *Kansas Historical Collections* [Vol. XVII, 1926–1928], pp. 93–94.)

MUSTANG GRAY

There was once a no-ble ran-ger, they called him Mus-tang Gray; He left his home when but a youth, went rang-ing far a-way. But he'll go no more a-rang-ing the sav-age to a-fright; He has heard his last war-whoop, and fought his last fight.

There was once a noble ranger,
  They called him Mustang Gray;
He left his home when but a youth,
  Went ranging far away.

CHORUS:
    But he'll go no more a-ranging
      The savage to affright;
    He has heard his last war whoop,
      And fought his last fight.

He ne'er would sleep within a tent,
  No comforts would he know;
But like a brave old Tex-i-an,
  A-ranging he did go.

Once he was taken prisoner,
  Bound in chains upon the way;
He wore a yoke of bondage
  Through the streets of Monterey.

A *señorita* loved him
  And followed by his side;
She opened the gates and gave to him
  Her father's steed to ride.

God bless the *señorita,*
  The belle of Monterey;
She opened wide the prison door
  And let him ride away.

And when this veteran's life was spent.
  It was his last command
To bury him on Texas soil
  On the banks of the Rio Grande.

And there the lonely traveler,
  When passing by his grave,
Will shed a farewell tear
  O'er the bravest of the brave.

No. 50
Red Wing

Everyone in the West in the '20's seemed to know the tear-jerking bit of doggerel about Red Wing, who fretted her poor heart away for a warrior who never returned. The simple repetitive motifs of its melody have been used to produce dozens of parodies: cowboy, bawdy, military, even lullabies. (Melody: FMC I 580, sung by Albert R. Lyman. Text: FMC II 557, album of Verona Stocks.)

RED WING

There once was an In-dian maid, A shy lit-tle prai-rie maid, She sang a-way a love song gay, As out on the prai-rie she whiled a-way the day. She loved a war-rior bold, This shy lit-tle maid of old. Brave and gay he rode one day To a bat-tle far a-way.

CHORUS

Now the moon shines to-night on pret-ty Red Wing,—

The breez - es sigh - ing, ___ the night birds cry - ing. ___

So ___ far be - neath the stars her brave is sleep - ing, ___

While Red Wing's weep - ing ___ her heart a - way.

There once lived an Indian maid,
A shy little prairie maid,
She sang away a love song gay
As out on the prairie she whiled away the day.
She loved a warrior bold,
This shy little maid of old.
Brave and gay he rode one day
To a battle far away.

CHORUS:

    Now the moon shines tonight on pretty Red Wing,
    The breezes sighing, the night birds crying.
    So far beneath the stars her brave is sleeping,
    While Red Wing's weeping her heart away.

She watched for him night and day
And kept all the campfires bright.
Each night she would lie in under the sky
And dream of his coming bye and bye.
When all the braves returned
The heart of Red Wing yearned,
Far, far away her warrior gay
Fell bravely in the fray.

No. 51
Juanita

In "Juanita" a cowboy who has loved and abandoned a Mexican beauty doesn't live to regret the deed: the maiden plants a dagger in his heart. The tragic parting of the lovers comes off in a dialogue of rare directness and intensity. (Melody: FAC I 352, sung by Nadine Blau. Text: FMC I 797, sung by Buck Lee.)

JUANITA

"Juan - i - ta, I must leave you. I have come to say fare-

well." They were stand - ing near the ru - ins

Where the am - ber shad - ows fell. "Cry - ing, why my brave Juan-

i - ta? Do not grieve be-cause I go." "But, *Se - ñor,* if you

love me You would nev - er, nev - er go."

"Juanita, I must leave you.
　　I have come to say farewell."
They were standing near the ruins
　　Where the amber shadows fell.

"Crying, why my brave Juanita?
　　Do not grieve because I go."
"But, *señor,* if you love me
　　You would never, never go."

"I did not think that my flirtations
　　Would leave an impress on your heart.
When I return to wed a maiden
　　Of my country, we must part.

"One more kiss? I'll give you fifty."
　　Round her form his arms entwined.
They were standing near the ruins
　　Almost hid by clustering vines.

"Crying? Why, my brave Juanita?
　　Do not grieve because I go,
For your bright eyes flash like jewels,
　　Fairest maid in Mexico.

"Love you? Yes, of course, Juanita,
　　And my love, you do not grieve."
"But, *señor,* if you loved me,
　　You would never, never leave."

In the morning two *vaqueros*
　　Chanced to rest beneath the shade,
For siesta's softest shelter
　　Close beside the foliage made.

"Por Dios!" cried *un vaquero*
　　As he pulled the vines apart.
"Here lies *un americano*
　　With a dagger in his heart."

Memories haunt the crumbling ruins,
　　Juanita lives here all alone.
In her eyes no teardrops glisten,
　　From her heart the love has flown.

No. 52
Border Affair

Love between the sexes was never easy in frontier days—or now, for that matter. It was further complicated when cross-cultural attachments were involved, as in this elegy to the greener pastures symbolized by the *señoritas* from across the Mexican border. We give two texts: the original Charles Badger Clark poem, and another, encountered in Idaho, which shows what can happen to a song when it floats in oral tradition. (Melody: FAC I 67, sung by Billy Simon. Text A: Charles Badger Clark, *Sun and Saddle Leather* [Boston: Richard G. Badger, 1920], pp. 42–44. Text B: Hendren 131.)

BORDER AFFAIR

Span - ish is the lov - in' tongue, Soft as mu - sic, light as spray. 'Twas a girl I learnt it from, Liv - in' down So - no - ra way.___ I don't look much like a lov - er, Yet I say her love words o - ver Of - ten when I'm all a - lone_ "Mi a - mor, mi cor - a - zōn."

Text A

Spanish is the lovin' tongue,
  Soft as music, light as spray.
'Twas a girl I learnt it from,
  Livin' down Sonora way.
I don't look much like a lover,
Yet I say her love words over
  Often when I'm all alone—
  "Mi amor, mi corazón."

Nights when she knew where I'd ride
  She would listen for my spurs,
Fling the big door open wide,
  Raise them laughin' eyes of hers.
And my heart would nigh stop beatin'
When I heard her tender greetin',
  Whispered soft for me alone—
  "Mi amor! mi corazón!"

Moonlight in the patio,
  Old Señora noddin' near,
Me and Juana talkin' low
  So the Madre couldn't hear—
How those hours would go a-flyin'!
And too soon I'd hear her sighin'
  In her little sorry tone—
  "Adiós, mi corazón."

But one time I had to fly
  For a foolish gamblin' fight,
And we said a swift goodbye
  In that black, unlucky night.
When I'd loosed her arms from clingin'
With her words the hoofs kep' ringin'
  As I galloped north alone—
  "Adiós, mi corazón!"

Never seen her since that night,
  I kain't cross the Line, you know.
She was Mex and I was white;
  Like as not it's better so.
Yet I've always sort of missed her
Since that last wild night I kissed her,
  Left her heart and lost my own—
  "Adiós, mi corazón!"

Text B

I learned Spanish from a girl
  Who lived down Sonora way,
Sparkling eyes as black as jet,
  Hair as fine as softest spray.
I don't claim to be a lover
  Conquering hearts the whole world over,
There's but one whose heart I won,
  Mi amor, mi corazón.

'Neath the mellow yellow moon
  We would meet and part too soon,
We'd converse in tones so low
  So the *madre* wouldn't know.
Oft I kissed her lips so tender,
  Little stars blinked on in wonder,
While the gentle breeze would moan,
  "Mi amor, mi corazón."

While *señora* nodded near
  We would meet where none could hear,
Whispering love as we sat there
  While the moonbeams kissed her hair.
Tender were her words of greeting,
  How my heart would start stampeding,
I still hear her tender tone,
  "Adiós, mi corazón."

'Twas a foolish gambling fight
  That took place that starry night,
Had to say a swift goodbye,
  So we parted, she and I.
On the breeze her words were ringing,
  I still feel her arms a-clinging,
I still hear her pleading tone,
  "Adiós, mi corazón."

Oft I long to go back where
  I can touch her violet hair,
Kiss her lips as soft as down,
  Tell her that my love lives on.
If I dared to cross the border,
  They'd hang me in just short order,
Never more we'll be alone,
  Adiós, mi corazón.

Part Seven

Cowboy Lovers

No. 53
Going West

The unrestrained sentimentality of the folk stands best without commentary. The whole history of our nation: Europe to the eastern shoreline, thence into and over the Appalachians, on to the great mid-continent prairies, the Rockies, and the Pacific Coast, is one of the sadness of separation, and of dreams (mostly unfulfilled) of reuniting. (Melody and text: Library of Congress #69A, recorded by John A., Alan, and Ruby Lomax.)

GOING WEST

I'm go-ing out West be-fore long,____ I'm
go-ing out West be-fore long,____ I'm
go-ing out West where times____ are best, I'm
go-ing out West be-fore long.____

2nd Stanza

My boy, he's gone West, turn back, turn back, My   etc.

I'm going out West before long,
I'm going out West before long,
I'm going out West where times are best;
I'm going out West before long.

My boy, he's gone West, turn back, turn back,
My boy, he's gone West, turn back, turn back,
My boy, he's gone West and he'll never come back;
I'm going out West before long.

Don't cry, little girl, don't cry,
Don't cry, little girlie, don't cry,
Little girlie, don't cry when I tell you good-by;
Oh I'm going out West before long.

Do you know what you promised me?
Do you know what you promised me?
You promised me you'd marry me;
I'm going out West before long.

Oh lay your hand in mine,
Oh lay your hand in mine.
Lay your hand in mine and say you'll be mine;
I'm a-going out West before long.

No. 54
Lily of the West

In the cowboy code true love is disquieting, unique, compulsive, ever-lasting. That the object thereof prove unworthy means nothing: the stricken lover still seeks her out, still loves. (Melody: FAC I 96, sung by Joan O'Bryant. Text A: FAC I 102, recorded by Kathy Dagel. Text B: *Beadle's Dime Song Books,* No. 5 [New York, 1860], p. 48.)

LILY OF THE WEST

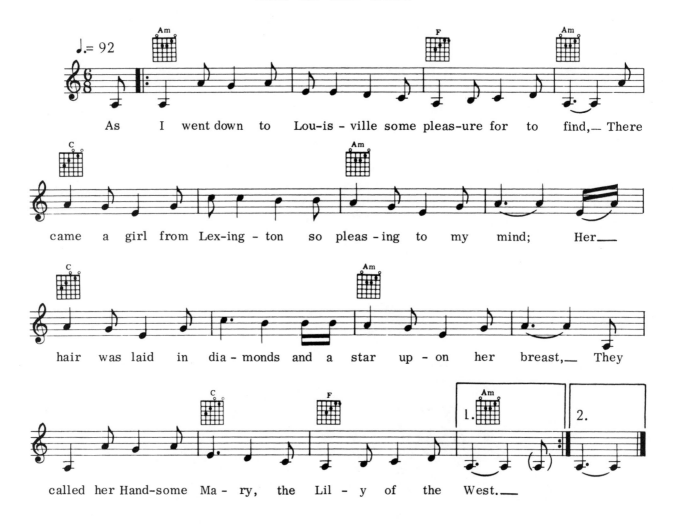

As I went down to Lou-is-ville some pleas-ure for to find,— There came a girl from Lex-ing-ton so pleas-ing to my mind; Her— hair was laid in dia-monds and a star up-on her breast,— They called her Hand-some Ma-ry, the Lil-y of the West.—

TEXT A

As I went down to Louisville some pleasure for to find,
There came a girl from Lexingtown so pleasing to my mind;
Her hair was laid in diamonds and a star upon her breast,
They called her Handsome Mary, the Lily of the West.

She had rings on every finger that come from the distant shores,
Ten thousand hundred dollars laid up for her in store;
'Tis enough to entice the king of Press, how costly she did dress,
And I called her my sweet Mary, the Lily of the West.

I courted her for a long time, her love I expected to gain,
Until she turned her back on to me and I to her the same;
But I never shall forget that day the clod lie on my breast
And I talked to my sweet Mary, the Lily of the West.

One day when I was a-walking down by the shady grove
There come a man from Lexingtown, come dashing with my love;
He sung a song most melodious, it did my soul depress,
And he called her his sweet Mary, the Lily of the West.

My rifle on my shoulder, my dagger in my hand,
I caught him by the collar while bold I bid him stand;
Me being mad and desperated, I quickly pierced his breast,
For talking to my Mary, the Lily of the West.

They took me to the Justice, he only but made my plea,
The jury found me innocent, the judges set me free.
And they did not say more or less
Begone you scornfulish Mary, the Lily of the West.

There was a man among them that was so honorable mean,
He had me bound down in iron chains and brought me back again;
They put me in the guard house, my life to explore,
There are spies at every window, boys, and six at every door.

I went around in the guard house, I surveyed it around and around,
I jumped out at one window and knocked five of them down;
The footmen and the horsemen they quickly followed me,
But I wheeled old Jack four times around and gained my liberty.

I've traveled through the westerns, I've traveled America through,
And a-many pretty cottage girl has come into my view;
But I never shall forget that day the clod lie on my breast
And I talked to my sweet Mary, the Lily of the West.

I just came down from Louisville some pleasure for to find,
A handsome girl from Michigan so pleasing to my mind,
Her rosy cheeks and rolling eyes like arrows pierce my breast,
They call her Handsome Mary, the Lily of the West.

I courted her for many a day, her love I thought to gain;
Too soon, too soon she slighted me which caused me grief and pain.
She robbed me of my liberty, deprived me of my rest,
They call her Handsome Mary, the Lily of the West.

One evening as I rambled down by yon shady grove
I met a lord of high degree conversing with my love;
He sang, he sang so merrily while I was sore oppressed,
He sang for Handsome Mary, the Lily of the West.

I rushed upon my rival, a dagger in my hand,
I tore him from my true love and boldly made him stand;
Being mad to desperation, my dagger pierced his breast,
I was betrayed by Mary, the Lily of the West.

Now my trial has come on and sentenced soon I'll be;
They put me in the criminal box and there convicted me.
She so deceived the jury, so modestly did dress,
She far out-shone bright Venus, the Lily of the West.

Since then I've gained my liberty, I roamed the country through,
I'll travel the city over to find my loved one true;
Although she stole my liberty and deprived me of my rest
I love my Mary, the Lily of the West.

No. 55
Where the Bravest Cowboys Lie

The mysterious resonant tones of this song evoke at one and the same time the anguish and tension of the ancient Scottish border ballads, and the bitterness of life and love on the western fringes of pioneer America: the irrevocable compulsion of romantic love is an all-pervasive theme in cowboy lore. (Melody and text: FAC I 65, from the collection of Alabama folklore made by Ray B. Browne, Bowling Green State University, Ohio.)

WHERE THE BRAVEST COWBOYS LIE

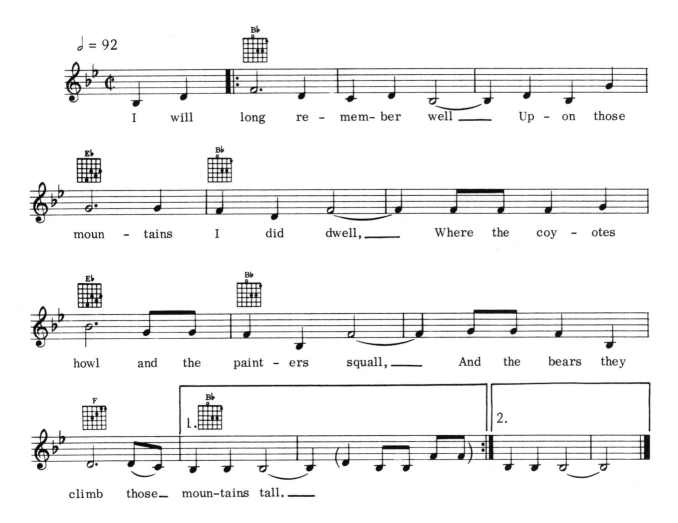

I will long re-mem-ber well ___ Up-on those moun - tains I did dwell, ___ Where the coy - otes howl and the paint - ers squall, ___ And the bears they climb those___ moun-tains tall. ___

I will long remember well
Upon those mountains I did dwell,
Where the coyotes howl and the painters squall,
And the bears they climb those mountains tall.

I had a little girl and I loved her well,
I loved her more than tongue can tell;
I asked her if she'd marry me,
She said she would if a cowboy I'd be.

That night my parents gave me good advice,
To stay at home and live a quiet life;
But to their advice I did not hear,
And for those words I did not care.

That night our beds were snow and sleet,
And not a moment did we sleep;
This morning clouds turned dark and low,
And to our tents we was forced to go.

We rode and rode for nine long hours
Before we could reach those tents of ours;
I'll tell to you an awful tale,
We met those Indians on the trail.

But with our force we cut them down,
You are seen to fall to the frozen ground
All stained in blood; God gave them a name—
The greatest cowboys out on the plain.

If I had the wings and I could fly,
I'd fly to where the bravest cowboys lie,
All stained in blood; God gave them a name——
The bravest cowboys out on the plain.

No. 56
Red River Valley

This is another sentimental classic: cowboy not by origin but by adoption and adaptation. There are scores of texts, including military songs, popular hymns, and dance calls. Anyone who has passed through the limitless expanses of lava, sun, stars, sage, and sky around Spencer, Idaho, will feel the poignancy of our third text. (Melody: traditional. Text A: FAC I 244, as sung by Frank Goodwyn. Text B: FMC II 533, album of Verona Stocks. Text C: PNFQ 271.)

RED RIVER VALLEY

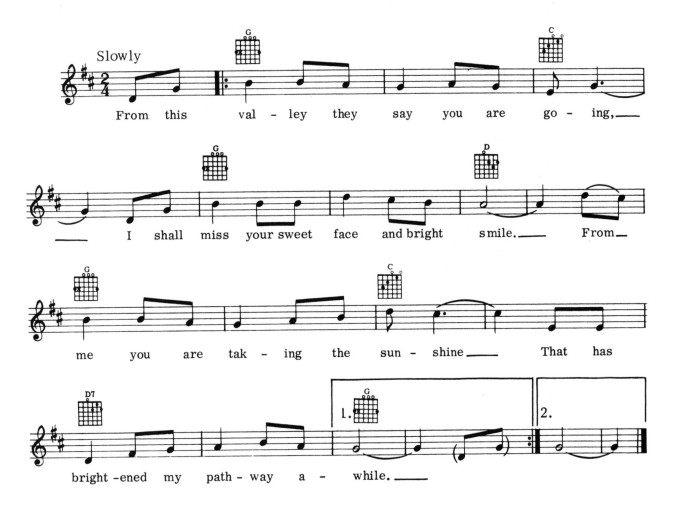

Slowly

From this val - ley they say you are go - ing,____ ____ I shall miss your sweet face and bright smile.____ From____ me you are tak - ing the sun - shine____ That has bright -ened my path - way a - while. ____

TEXT A. RED RIVER VALLEY

From this valley they say you are going,
  I shall miss your sweet face and bright smile.
From me you are taking the sunshine
  That has brightened my pathway awhile.

I've been thinking a long time, my darling,
  Of those sweet words you never would say,
But the last of my fond hopes have vanished
  For they say you are going away.

CHORUS:
    Then come sit here awhile ere you leave us,
      Do not hasten to bid us adieu,
    And remember the Red River Valley
      And the cowboy who loves you so true.

I have promised you, darling, that never
  Would words from my lips cause you pain;
My life will be yours forever
  If you only will love me again.

Must the past with its joys all be blighted
  By a future of sorrow and pain?
Must the vows that were taken be slighted?
  Don't you think you could love me again?

There never could be such a longing
  In the heart of a poor cowboy's breast,
As dwells in this heart you are breaking
  While I wait in my home in the West.

Do you think of this valley you're leaving,
  Oh, how lonely and dreary it will be?
Do you think of the kind hearts you're grieving,
  And the pain you are causing to me?

TEXT B. LITTLE DARLING

Come sit by my side, little darling,
Come lay your cool hand on my brow,
And promise me that you will never
Be nobody's darling but mine—

CHORUS:
    Be nobody's darling but mine, love,
    Be honest, be faithful, be kind,
    And promise me that you will never
    Be nobody's darling but mine.

You are as sweet as the flowers in springtime,
You are as pure as the dew on the rose,
I'd rather be somebody's darling
Than a poor girl that nobody knows.

Mother is dead and in heaven,
Father has gone down below,
Sister has gone to meet mother,
And where I'll go nobody knows.

Mother has often told me,
My sister would do the same,
If anything went wrong around home, love,
I've always taken the blame.

Text C. Lost River Desert

From this desert I know you are leaving,
  I have read the sad news in your eyes,
There's no beauty for you in these prairies,
  And you're blind to the blues of the skies.

I had many fond hopes of your coming,
  I had built my dream castles on air,
But, alas, that fair picture is fading,
  The desert my heart must repair.

Let me point out to you the Great Dipper,
  You may see it wherever you roam,
And some day you may see it and wonder,
  As you picture me here in my home.

From this city you'll write me a letter,
  Remember the lock of your hair,
Just address it to Lost River Desert,
  To the Ranger who welcomes you there.

The coyotes will howl all around me,
  While so sadly I strum my guitar,
While I pour out the love I must vanquish
  Into the mirage of a star.

Some night you may see the Great Dipper,
  And fancy I'm sitting with you,
In the shade of the silent desert,
  The spot where you vowed to be true.

No. 57
Red River Shore

Parental opposition to the course of true love is a typical theme in Old World ballads. Here it is transposed into the western locale, whose code requires that sympathy ever be on the lovers' side, especially if he is a cowboy. (Melody: FAC III 972, commercial recording. Text A: J. Frank Dobie, *Ballads and Songs of the Frontier Folk,* PTFLS [VI, 1927], pp. 158–159 [published by permission of the Texas Folklore Society]. Text B: PNFQ 311.)

RED RIVER SHORE

At the foot of yon moun - tain where the foun - tain doth

flow, The great - est cre - a - tion, where the soft wind doth blow, There

lived a fair maid - en, she's the one I a - dore; She's the

one I would mar - ry on the Red Riv - er shore.

TEXT A. ON RED RIVER SHORE

At the foot of yon mountain where the fountain doth flow,
The greatest creation, where the soft wind doth blow,
There lived a fair maiden; she's the one I adore,
She's the one I would marry on Red River shore.

I spoke to her kindly, saying, "Will you marry me?
My fortune's not great"—"No matter," said she.
"Your beauty's a plenty, you're the one I adore,
You're the one I would marry on Red River shore."

I asked her old father would he give her to me.
"No, sir, she shan't marry no cowboy," said he.
So I jumped on my bronco and away I did ride,
And left my true love on Red River side.

She wrote me a letter, and she wrote it so kind,
And in this letter these words you could find:
"Come back to me, darling, you're the one I adore,
You're the one I would marry on Red River shore."

So I jumped on my bronco and away I did ride
To marry my true love on the Red River side.
But her father the secret had learned,
And gathered an army of twenty and four,
To fight this young cowboy on the Red River shore.

I drew my six-shooter, shooting round after round,
Till six men were wounded and seven were down.
No use of an army of twenty and four.
I'm bound for my true love on Red River shore.

TEXT B. NEW RIVER SHORE

At the foot of yonder mountain where often lay snow,
Amusements containing, while a pleasant wind blow;
I spied a fair damsel and she I adore,
She was a-walking on the New River shore.

Says I, "Pretty fair miss, can you fancy me?
My fortune's not great"—"That's nothing," said she:
"Your beauty is enough and you I adore,
And you I will marry on the New River shore."

As soon as her old father came this for to hear,
He swore he would part her from her dearest dear;
He sent her away where loud cannons did roar,
And left this young man on the New River shore.

She wrote him a letter containing these lines,
"If you'll look in the letter, these words you will find:
'I'll come back again and you I adore,
And you I will marry on the New River shore.'"

As soon as her old father came this news to hear,
He still vowed he'd part her from her dearest dear;
He gathered a company of twenty or more,
To fight this young man on the New River shore.

He drew his broad sword and he waved it around,
Until seven out of twenty lay dead on the ground;
He wounded five more and wounded them full sore,
Thus gained his true love on the New River shore.

No. 58

Down in the Valley

"Down in the Valley," sometimes known as "Birmingham Jail," may well be the sentimental song most widely known among Anglo-Americans. We consider it a classic: it says exactly what is to be said without a superfluous word; it flows straight from the heart without a shade of protective covering, and indulges untold reuse of basic rhythms and images. (Melody: FAC I 413, sung by Paul Kelso. Text: FMC II 507, album of Verona Stocks.)

DOWN IN THE VALLEY

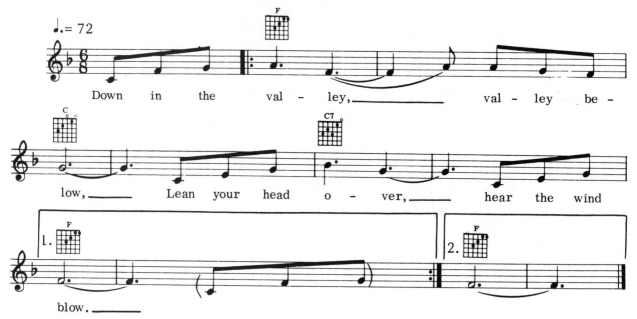

Down in the valley, valley below,
Lean your head over, hear the wind blow.

If you don't love me, love whom you please,
Put your arms 'round me, give my heart ease.

Put your arms 'round me ere it's too late,
Put your arms 'round me, feel my heart break.

Roses love sunshine, violets love dew,
Angels in heaven know I love you.

Know I love you, dear, know I love you,
Angels in heaven know I love you.

Will you be mine, dear? Will you be mine?
Answer my question, "Will you be mine?"

Go build me a castle forty feet high
So I can see him as he goes by.

As he goes by, dear, as he goes by,
So I can see him, as he goes by.

Down on the levy, levy so low,
Late in the evening, hear that train blow.

Hear that train blow, love, hear that train blow,
Late in the evening, hear that train blow.

Write me a letter, send it by mail,
Send it in care of Birmingham jail.

Down in the meadow, down on my knees,
Praying to heaven, give my heart ease.

Pining for you, love, pining for you,
Kiss me once more, love, then I must go.

No. 59
Roving Cowboy

The theme of parental opposition to the course of true love is typical
in the balladry of our British ancestors. It persists in cowboy songs. Here,
only scattered stanzas of a much longer ballad evoke the bitter-sweet
of a love that suffers a double hazard: parental opposition and separation.
There are scores of variants; ours lays out the plot but breaks off before
the typical tragic outcome is reached. (Melody and text: Supertone S2043,
sung by Buell Kazee.)

ROVING COWBOY

Come all you rov-ing cow - boys, bow down your head and
hand, I'll tell to you a sto - ry while you a - round me
stand. I'm goin' to quit this wild west, this
bleak and storm - y plain, Where the In - dians prowl I'll
leave__ you to ne'er re - turn a - gain.__

Come all you roving cowboys, bow down your head and hand,
I'll tell to you a story while you around me stand.
I'm goin' to quit this wild west, this bleak and stormy plain,
Where the Indians prowl I'll leave you to ne'er return again.

I've crossed the Rocky Mountains, I've crossed the rocky hills,
I've crossed the Rocky Mountains where many a brave boy fell.
I've seen the distant country, the Indian and the wild,
I'll never forget that old, old home, and mother's sweetest smile.

There was an old rich merchant who lived a neighbor by,
He had the only daughter, on her I cast my eye.
She was most tall and handsome—blue eyes, and curly hair—
There ain't no one in this wide world to her I can compare.

This lady fair and handsome sat closely by my side;
She promised me so faithfully that she would be my bride.
I kissed away those flowing tears still dimming her blue eyes;
I'll never forget that darling girl, I'll love her till I die.

No. 60
Bucking Broncho

"Bucking Broncho" reveals a young woman's infatuation with the virile cowboy image: his "high-headed" horse, his manner of swinging into the saddle, his unguarded sensuality at their first meeting, his relaxed pleasure in their dancing. To have been loved and abandoned is still not enough to destroy pleasurable memories of his gallantry! The song exists in many forms, from the warm good taste of Jack Thorp's 1908 text which we give, to some "that don't look so good in print." For perspective we include a precowboy relative sung in Ohio in Civil War times. (Melody: FAC I 509, sung by Kathy Dagel. Text A: N. Howard [Jack] Thorp, *Songs of the Cowboys* [Estancia, N.M.: News Print Shop, 1908], pp. 26–27. Text B: Myra E. Hull, "Cowboy Ballads." *The Kansas Historical Quarterly* [Vol. VIII, No. 1, Feb. 1939], p. 57 [published by permission of the Kansas State Historical Society].)

BUCKING BRONCHO

My love is a rid - er, wild bron - chos he breaks, Though he's prom - ised to quit it all, just for my sake. He ties up one foot and the sad - dle puts on, With a swing and a jump he is mount - ed and gone.

TEXT A. BUCKING BRONCHO

My love is a rider, wild bronchos he breaks,
Though he's promised to quit it all, just for my sake.
He ties up one foot and the saddle puts on,
With a swing and a jump he is mounted and gone.

The first time I met him, 'twas early one spring
Riding a broncho a high headed thing
He tipped me a wink as he gaily did go
For he wished me to look at his bucking broncho.

The next time I saw him, 'twas late in the fall
Swinging the girls at Tomlinson's ball
He laughed and he talked, as we danced to and fro
Promised never to ride on another broncho.

He made me some presents, among them a ring
The return that I made him was a far better thing
'Twas a young maiden's heart, I'd have you all know
He'd won it by riding his bucking broncho.

Now all you young maidens, where'er you reside
Beware of the cow-boy who swings the rawhide
He'll court you and pet you and leave you and go
In the spring up the trail on his bucking broncho.

TEXT B. MY LOVER'S A RIDER

My lover's a rider, a rider so fine;
The steed is his sov'reign; the rider is mine.

> La-la-la-la-la-la-la-la-la-la,
> La-la-la-la-la-la-la-la-la-la-la.

Blue eyes and brown hair, and right noble in mien;
Oh, charming and fair is my lover, I ween.

My heart is a castle well-bolted and grim;
My love is the pass-key; it opens to him.

My lover's away, he is over the sea;
I need not be told he is thinking of me.

If you have a lover so noble and true;
I'll finish my song and then listen to you.

No. 61
Powder River

Desperate loneliness has caused this frontiersman to conjure up an image of feminine loveliness out of the muddy waters of the river and the whirlwinds that skitter across the prairies. But the image, no sooner blown to its full loveliness, vanishes like the mirage that it is, leaving emptiness and anguish. (Melody and text: FAC I 79, sung by Joan O'Bryant.)

POWDER RIVER

Last time on that la-zy old riv - er, When last I roamed its qui - et shore, I met a girl who was more like heav-en, And her smile will last for - ev - er - more.

Last time on that lazy old river,
  When last I roamed its quiet shore,
I met a girl who was more like heaven,
  And her smile will last forever more.

Her eyes were of its deep blue water,
  And her skin was as fresh as the dew on the leaf,
And we fell in love right there on the river,
  But from its banks she would not leave.

It seemed like she was born of this water,
  Like her beauty and the river were one of the same,
And my love for her was as strong as the mountain,
  And by force I took her from its domain.

The river struck out like an angry lover;
  He cursed me for my selfish love;
A spirit of the water arose round about me,
  And my love was but for a handful of dust.

Now I'm old and full of grief
And by the river I still roam,
In a valley that was once like heaven
Is now churned with mud and foam.

Part Eight

Treacherous Women

No. 62
The Girl I Left Behind Me

"The Girl I Left Behind Me" has floated in our oral tradition since Revolutionary times. The perennial theme, separation of lovers, got re-worked for every major event in our history: emigration from the Old Country, all our major wars, the Gold Rush, opening of the Oregon territory. It was played and sung in 1867 by "thousands of men led by the firemen and state militia band at the funeral of Julia Bulette, notorious Virginia City prostitute." It is a favorite as a square-dance call. There are so many variants, parodies, etc., that they might best be viewed as an epic cluster pertinent to the whole "western" experience. (Melody: FAC I 160, played by Bill Garlinghouse. Text A: FAC II 712, collected by William L. Alderson from *Oregon Spectator*, July 14, 1854. Text B: PTFLS [Vol. I, 1916], pp. 28–29 [published by permission of the Texas Folklore Society].)

THE GIRL I LEFT BEHIND ME

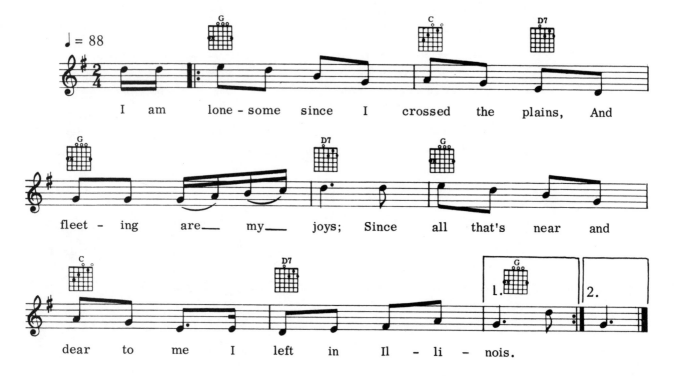

I am lone-some since I crossed the plains, And fleet-ing are my joys; Since all that's near and dear to me I left in Il-li-nois.

TEXT A

I am lonesome since I crossed the plains,
  And fleeting are my joys;
Since all that's near and dear to me
  I left in Illinois.

When I look back to Illinois,
  The tears incline to blind me;
My mind reverts to that sweet home,
  And the friends I left behind me.

I heard of California gold,
  I thought I'd go and try it;
And foolishly I left my home,
  I surely can't deny it.

In California now I am,
  The cradle I am rocking,
And sometimes I am flattered
  That a fortune I am making.

I intend to rock my cradle well
  In places where they mine it;
And if a fortune can be found,
  I'll surely try to find it.

In traveling through this far-famed land,
  I find the people clever;
They treat a stranger with respect,
  I'm sure 'tis their endeavor.

I sometimes meet with ladies kind,
  And girls that do remind me—
Of my kind hearted little girl,
  And the friends I left behind me.

And now may heaven smile on me,
  Let fortune quickly find me;
And speed me back to the dear little girl
  And the friends I left behind me.

TEXT B

The first young gent to the opposite lady,
Swing her by the right hand,
Swing your partner by the left,
And promenade the girl behind you.

    Oh, that girl, that pretty little girl,
      That girl I left behind me,
    Oh, I'll laugh and cry till the day I die
      For the girl I left behind me.

The next young gent to the opposite lady,
Swing her by the right hand,
Swing your partner by the left,
And promenade the girl behind you.

If ever I travel this road again
And the tears don't fall and blind me,
I'm going back to Tennessee
To the girl I left behind me.

    Oh, that girl, that pretty little girl,
      That girl I left behind me,
    With rosy cheeks and curly hair,
      That girl I left behind me.

If ever I travel this road again,
And the angels they don't find me,
I'll reconcile and stay a little while
With the girl I left behind me.

I'll cross the Red River one more time
If the tears don't fall and drown me,
A weeping for that pretty little gal,
The gal I left behind me.

I'll build my nest in a hollow tree
Where the cuckoos they won't find me,
I'll weep and sigh till the day I die
For the gal I left behind me.

If ever I get off this warpath
And the Indians they don't find me,
I'll go right back to see that gal,
The gal I left behind me.

I could buy such girls as you
For fifteen cents a dozen,
But I am going back tomorrow
And marry my country cousin.

No. 63
My Parents Raised Me Tenderly

The cowboy had troubles with his conscience, particularly when it concerned women. No material concern ought mar the course of true love, and once a love-troth has been made, never is it to be severed, most certainly not for a marriage of convenience! (Melody and text: as sung by Mrs. Martha Martin of Granada, Colorado, and published in *Colorado Folksong Bulletin* [Boulder: University of Colorado], Vol. III, 1964, pp. 6–7.)

MY PARENTS RAISED ME TENDERLY

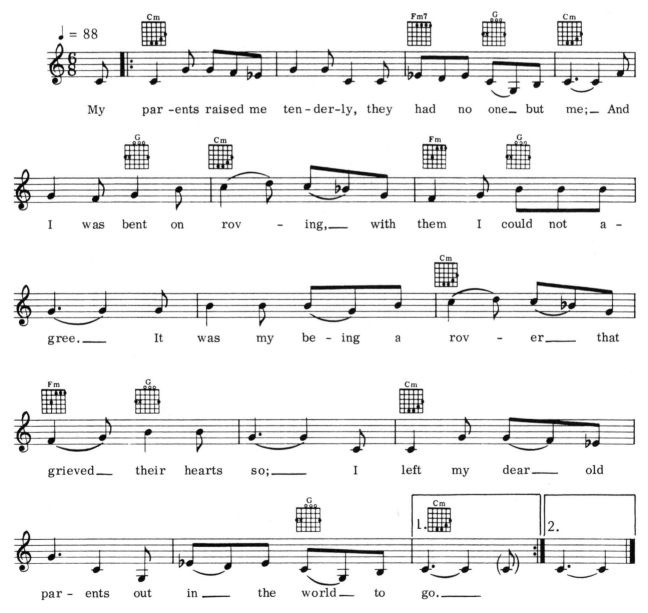

My par-ents raised me ten-der-ly, they had no one__ but me;__ And I was bent on rov - ing,__ with them I could not a - gree.__ It was my be-ing a rov - er__ that grieved__ their hearts so;__ I left my dear__ old par-ents out in __ the world__ to go.__

My parents raised me tenderly, they had no one but me;
And I was bent on roving, with them I could not agree.

It was my being a rover that grieved their hearts so;
I left my dear old parents out in the world to go.

There was a wealthy old farmer who lived on a farm nearby,
He had a lovely daughter on whom I'd cast my eye.

She was a lovely maiden, both beautiful and fair;
There's no other girl in this wide, wide world with her I can compare.

I asked her if she would be willing for me to go away.
She said that she would be willing if I would return some day.

I told her that I would be true to her till death should prove unkind;
I said my last, my last farewell to the girl I left behind.

She said, "I know you love me as dearly as I love you;
But, oh, my heart would be broken if you should prove untrue.

"In God's care do I give you, may He guide your wayward feet,
To overcome temptation and into Glory meet."

I met sweet Willie in Denver, she fell in love with me.
She said, "My pockets being lined with gold, hard labor you may lay o'er,
If you'll consent to marry me and say you'll roam no more."

The gold indeed was tempting, sweet Willie's face was fair;
She was indeed very lovely—blue eyes and light-brown hair.

She was a lovely maiden, but love to me was blind,
For she will never, no never compare with the girl I left behind.

The gold at last has won me, sweet Willie has won the prize,
I've sold my love for a fortune, I've blighted a fair young life.

I've broken a noble, trusting heart—the purest God can give;
A man who'll break a woman's heart on earth ought not to live.

Oh, yes, I have gold and plenty, my wife is very kind,
But, oh, my heart is aching for the girl I left behind.

And when this life is over, and Heaven at last is kind,
I'll see again the fair sweet face of the girl I left behind.

No. 64

The Girl That Wore a Waterfall

Cowboys, especially the younger ones reared on the range, were an easy touch for gamblers and prostitutes when they did get to town— witness the disgrace of the young man in this song. Beauty was, indeed, only skin deep! (Melody: FAC I 525, sung by Jay Bailey. Text: PC–F 77.)

THE GIRL THAT WORE A WATERFALL

Come__ all young men who've been in love and sym - pa - thize with me, For I have loved as fair a maid as ev - er you did see. Her age it was but sev - en - teen, a fig - ure fair and tall, She was a hand-some crea - ture and she wore a wa - ter - fall.

Come all young men who've been in love and sympathize with me,
For I have loved as fair a maid as ever you did see.
Her age it was but seventeen, a figure fair and tall,
She was a handsome creature and she wore a waterfall.

The first time that I met her, I never shall forget,
I'd slipped into a dry goods store some handkerchiefs to get.
She stood behind the counter dressed up just like a doll,
I never saw a face so fair or such a waterfall.

'Twas at a picnic party, I met her after that,
I quickly introduced myself; we had a pleasant chat.
Though many other girls were there, yet none of them at all
Could dance with me except the girl who wore the waterfall.

I saw her home, we marched along, we said we'd never part,
And when she asked me to come in I found I'd lost my heart;
While sitting there I thought I heard some footsteps in the hall,
All sorts of colors turned the girl who wore the waterfall.

A great big fellow six feet high came stalking in the room,
And when he saw me sitting there at once began to fume.
His eyes so hard, his face so harsh, it did my heart appall—
"This is my husband," said the girl who wore the waterfall.

Before I'd time to say a word the fellow at me flew,
And while the maiden held me down he beat me black and blue.
When I got up I found I'd lost watch, money, chain and all—
I never since go near a girl who wears a waterfall.

No. 65
No Use for the Women

We have collected many texts of this song but, unlike most, there is very little variation: it is as if the original song managed to say precisely what was to be said—nothing superfluous, nothing missing. The thesis of the treachery of women is stated, one gripping example thereof is cited, the tragic results are given, and the cowboy's scorn of women is restated with magnified intensity. The whole tragedy rests on an insult to the picture of the girl worshipped by the cowboy, her brash perfidy notwithstanding! (Melody: FAC I 573, sung by Marlin Bingham. Text: Hendren 538.)

NO USE FOR THE WOMEN

Now I've got no use for wom - en, A true one may nev - er be found; They use a man for his mon - ey, When it's gone they'll turn him down. They're all a - like at the bot - tom, Self - ish and grasp - ing for all, They'll stick by a man while he's win - ning, And laugh in his face at his fall.

Now I've got no use for women,
   A true one may never be found;
They use a man for his money,
   When it's gone they'll turn him down.
They're all alike at the bottom,
   Selfish and grasping for all,
They'll stick by a man while he's winning
   And laugh in his face at his fall.

My pal was an honest young puncher,
   Honest, upright and true;
But he turned to a hard shooting gunman
   On account of a girl named Lou.
He fell in with evil companions,
   The kind that are better off dead;
When a gambler insulted her picture
   He filled him full of lead.

All through the long night they trailed him,
   Through mesquite and thick chaparral;
And I couldn't help think of the woman
   As I saw him pitch and fall.
If she'd been the pal that she should have
   He might have been raising a son,
Instead of out there on the prairie,
   To die by the ranger's gun.

Death's sharp sting did not trouble,
   His chances for life were too slim;
But where they were putting his body
   Was all that worried him.
He lifted his head on his elbow,
   The blood from his wounds flowed red,
He gazed at his pals grouped around him
   As he whispered to them and said:

"Oh, bury me out on the prairie
   Where the coyotes may howl o'er my grave;
Bury me out on the prairie,
   But from them my bones please save.
Wrap me up in a blanket
   And bury me deep in the ground,
Cover me over with boulders
   Of granite, gray and round."

So we buried him out on the prairie,
   Where the coyotes can howl o'er his grave,
And his soul is now a-resting
   From the unkind cut she gave.
And many another young puncher
   As he rides past that pile of stones,
Recalls some similar woman
   And envies his mouldering bones.

No. 66

The Trail to Mexico

"Trail to Mexico" is a slow-rhythm (night-herding) song with an engaging melody and theme inherited from the Old World: the heart of woman being fickle, the cowboy's only recourse is high adventure and violent muscular activity. The song has many faces. We give it here in three distinctive cowboy settings (A, B, and E), and two precowboy texts (C and D). (Melody: Brunswick 354, Len Nash. Text A: Library of Congress, WPA #W1033, New Mexico. Text B: Library of Congress, Woody Guthrie Manuscripts, p. 184. Text C: PNFQ 136. Text D: PNFQ 137. Text E: FAC I 247, as sung by Frank Goodwyn.)

THE TRAIL TO MEXICO

I made up my mind to change my way, And to quit my crowd that was so gay, To— leave my na - tive home for a - while, And trav - el west for— man- y a mile.

TEXT A. THE TRAIL TO MEXICO

I made up my mind to change my way
And quit my crowd that was so gay,
To leave my native home for a while
And travel west for many a mile.

'Twas all in the merry month of May
When I started for Texas far away,
I left my darling girl behind—
She said her heart was only mine.

Oh, it was when I embraced her in my arms
I thought she had ten thousand charms;
Her caresses were soft, her kisses were sweet,
Saying, "We will get married next time we meet."

It was in the year of eighty-three
That A. J. Stinson hired me,
He says, "Young fellow, I want you to go
And drive this herd to Mexico."

Oh, it was early in the year
When I went on trail to drive the steer,
I stood my guard through sleet and snow
While on the trail to Mexico.

Oh, it was a long and lonesome go
As our herd rolled on to Mexico;
With laughter light and the cowboy's song
To Mexico we rolled along.

When I arrived in Mexico
I wanted to see my love but could not go;
So I wrote a letter to my dear,
But not a word from her could I hear.

When I arrived at the once loved home
I called for the darling of my own;
They said she had married a richer life,
Therefore, wild cowboy, seek another wife.

Oh, the girl, she is married, I do adore,
And I cannot stay at home any more;
I'll work my way to a foreign land,
Or I'll go back west to my cowboy band.

I'll go back to the western land,
I'll hunt up my cowboy band,
Where the girls are few and the boys are true,
And a false-hearted love I never knew.

"Oh Buddie, oh Buddie, please stay at home,
Don't be forever on the roam,
There is many a girl more true than I,
So pray don't go where the bullets fly."

"It's curse your gold and your silver too,
God pity a girl that won't prove true,
I'll travel west where the bullets fly!
I'll stay on the trail till the day I die."

TEXT B. THE TRAIL TO MEXICO

I made up my mind in the early day
To quit my crowd that was so gay,
To leave my native home for a while,
To travel west for many a mile.

'Twas in the year of '83
That A. J. Simpson hired me;
He said, "Young fellow, I want you to go
And follow my cattle into Mexico."

He gave me a horse and a pack sack too,
With an old tin can and a big bed roll.
We throwed them dogies out on the trail
And we headed them west into Mexico.

We rode the trail where the bullets flew,
Where Indians many and the cowboys few.
We fought our way everywhere we'd go
As we pushed that herd into Mexico.

I wrote a letter to the girl I love,
I said, "I'm true as the stars above."
She said, "I've found me a richer love,
You can follow them cattle into Mexico."

I wrote a letter and this I said,
"You've got you a millionaire instead—
It's curse your gold and your silver too,
God pity a girl that can't prove true!

"I'll shoot my way to the Western trail
Where the Indian bullets fall like hail.
I'll live my life where the dogies go
From old Fort Worth into Mexico."

The days were hot and the nights were cold,
As the dogies cried and the longhorns lowed,
'Twas a long and a lonesome go
From Abilene into Mexico.

I'll get me a girl at the end of the trail,
A cow girl's love will never fail,
You cannot buy her heart for gold
On the sunbaked prairies of Mexico.

TEXT C. EARLY, EARLY IN THE SPRING

It was early, early in one spring,
I was pressed on board to serve my king.
I left my dearest dear behind,
Who ofttimes told me her heart was mine.

It was on a wet and a dreary day,
Our ship had sailed for the merry Kay,
With music sweet and trumpet sound
For old Virginia our ship was bound.

As I was sailing o'er the sea,
I took the opportunity
To write kind letters to my dear,
But nothing from her could I hear.

When I came back to her father's hall,
So loudly for my dear did call;
Her father said, "You must be denied,
For she's just married a richer knight."

If she is married whom I adore,
No longer will I stay on shore.
I'll sail the sea till the day I die,
And split the waves where the bullets fly.

"Oh, Billie, Billie, stay on shore,
Don't sail the seas till the day you die!
Don't split the waves where the bullets fly,
For there's many a prettier girl than I."

"Curse all the gold and the silver, too,
And all fair maids who won't prove true;
Make oaths and vows and then not keep
And marry others for riches' sake."

"If you've wrote letters to this town,
I can but prove I've received none,
If the fault being great, it's none of mine,
So don't reflect on the female kind."

TEXT D. EARLY IN THE SPRING

It was early, early in the spring
I went on board to serve my king,
Leaving my dearest far behind,
She had ofttimes told me her heart was mine.

I wrote letters to my dear,
But nothing from her did I hear,
Until I came to her father's house,
So loud did rap, for her did call.

"Go away, young man, it's don't you know
My daughter's married a long time ago.
My daughter's married for the terms of life,
Go away, young man, and seek another wife."

Curse be the gold and the silver, too,
Curse be the girl that won't prove true;
Curse be the girl that will promise me
And break her vow for treasury.

I will return from whence I came,
I'll plow those seas all over again,
I'll plow those seas till the day I die.
I'll split those waves that roll mountain high.

"O, Johnny, Johnny, don't say so,
Through those dangers you cannot go,
For it was father's fault, it was none of mine,
Don't press too hard on the female kind."

It was early, early in the morn,
She arose, put on her new silk gown.
Straightway to her lover she then did go,
And unto him she did prove true.

"I love my father and mother both,
I love my brothers and sisters all,
I love my friends and relations, too,
But I'll forsake them all and go with you."

TEXT E. GOING TO LEAVE OLD TEXAS

I'm going to leave old Texas now,
They've got no use for the longhorn cow,
They've plowed and fenced my cattle range,
The people there are all so strange.
　　Whoa, dogies, whoa-oh,
　　Whoa-ooh, oooh.
The people there are all so strange.

I'll take my gun, I'll take my rope
And hit the trail upon a lope.
I'll say good-bye to the Alamo
And turn my face toward Mexico.
　　Whoa, dogies, whoa-oh,
　　Whoa-ooh, oooh.
I'll turn my face toward Mexico.

I'll make my home on the wide, wide range,
The people there are not so strange.
The hard, hard ground will be my bed,
A saddle seat will hold my head.
　　Whoa, dogies, whoa-oh,
　　Whoa-ooh, oooh.
A saddle seat will hold my head.

And when I waken from my dreams
I'll eat my bread and my sardines.
And when on earth my life is done
I'll take my turn with the Holy One.
　　Whoa, dogies, whoa-oh,
　　Whoa-ooh, oooh.
I'll take my turn with the Holy One.

Part Nine

Westerners at Work

No. 67
Pattonio

"Pattonio" is the epic of a magnificent western horse that carried a military courier into New Mexico territory, evading and outdistancing a band of hostile Indians: upon arrival it is discovered that an arrow had pinned horseman and mount together. (Melody and text: FAC I 94, recorded by Joan O'Bryant.)

PATTONIO

As you look at the picture that hangs on the wall, As you look at the arrow that hangs by its side, You will say, "Tell a story," You know there is one "Of a horse called Pattonio." The story's begun.

As you look at the picture that hangs on the wall,
As you look at the arrow that hangs by its side,
You will say, "Tell a story"—You know there is one—
"Of a horse called Pattonio." The story's begun.

His hair, like a lady's, was glossy and fine,
He was reckless and proud but gentle and kind;
His arched neck was covered with a dark, flowing mane
And they called him Pattonio, the pride of the plain.

The country was new and the settlers were scarce,
The Indians on the war path were savage and fierce.
Though scouts were sent out every day from the fort,
Yet they never came back so we knew they were lost.

One day the captain said, "Fellows, someone must go
Across the dark borders of New Mexico."
A dozen young fellows straightway answered, "Here."
But the captain spied me, I was standing quite near.

Pattonio was by me, his nose in my hand,
Said the captain, "Your horse is the best in this land.
You're good for the ride, you're the lightest man here,
On the back of that mustang you have nothing to fear."

Then, proud of my pony, I answered, "You know
Pattonio and I are both willing to go.
For speed and endurance I'll trust in my black."
So they all shook my hand and I mounted his back—

Turned down the dark pathway, turned his head to the right;
The black struck a trot and he kept it all night.
When far back behind me I heard a shrill yell
And I knew that the redskins were right on my trail.

I reached down and jingled the bells on Pat's reins,
I spoke to Pattonio, I called him by name;
Pattonio then answered with a nod of his head
And his dark body lengthened and onward we sped.

We were leaving the redskins, the story was plain,
The arrows fell round us like hail and like rain.
Pattonio, he stumbled, I knew he was hurt,
But still he dashed onward and into the fort.

I delivered the message, then tried to dismount
But a pain in my foot was so bad I could not.
By good care and patience Pat and I soon were well,
Of his death many years after I will not try to tell.

As you look at the arrow that hangs on the wall,
It went through my foot, saddle, stirrup, and all;
On many fine horses I've since held the rein
But none like Pattonio, the pride of the plain.

No. 68
The Strawberry Roan

A good song can evolve into an epic cycle in a very short time. "The Strawberry Roan" is a case in point. It was probably written by Curley Fletcher in 1915. Text and tune caught on so well that it was known on every cattle range. Among its parodies we cite "The Bad Brahma Bull," "The Ridge Running Roan," "That Dear Wife of Mine," "What Has Become of the Strawberry Roan," "Goodbye Old Strawberry Roan," and "The Fairchild Abortion." No doubt there are others. (Melody: Melotone 12350, Frank Luther. Text A: FAC I 236, as sung by Frank Goodwyn. Text B: FAC I 204, reproduced with permission of the collector, Dean Emeritus John Donald Robb of the University of New Mexico.)

THE STRAWBERRY ROAN

I was lay-ing round town__ just spend-ing my time, __
Out of a job and not mak-in' a dime, When__ up steps a fel-ler and he
says, "I sup-pose That__ you're a bronc rid-er by the
looks of your clothes?"__

Text A. The Strawberry Roan

I was laying round town just spending my time,
Out of a job and not makin' a dime,
When up steps a feller and he says, "I suppose
That you're a bronc rider by the looks of your clothes?"

He guesses me right. "And a good one I'll claim.
Do you happen to have any bad ones to tame?"
He says he's got one that's a good one to buck,
And at throwing good riders he's had lots of luck.

He says this old pony has never been rode
And the man that gets on him is bound to be throwed.
I gets all excited and I ask what he pays
To ride this old pony a couple of days.

He says, "Ten dollars." I says, "I'm your man;
The bronc never lived that I cannot fan;
The bronc never tried nor never drew breath
That I cannot ride till he starves plumb to death."

He says, "Get your saddle. I'll give you a chance."
We got in the buggy and went to the ranch.
We waited till morning, right after chuck
I went out to see if that outlaw could buck.

Down in the corral, a-standin' alone,
Was this little old *caballo*, a strawberry roan.
He had little pin ears that touched at the tip
And a big forty-four brand was on his left hip.

He was spavined all round and he had pidgeon toes,
Little pig eyes and a big Roman nose.
He was U-necked and old with a long lower jaw—
You could tell at a glance he was a regular outlaw.

I buckled on my spurs, I was feeling plumb fine,
I pulled down my hat and I curls up my twine,
I threw the loop at him, right well I knew then,
Before I had rode him I'd sure earn my ten

I got the blind on him with a terrible fight,
Cinched on the saddle and girded it tight;
Then I steps up on him and pulled down the blind
And sat there in the saddle to see him unwind.

He bowed his old neck and I'll say he unwound,
He seemed to quit living down there on the ground;
He went up to the east and came down to the west
With me in the saddle, a-doing my best.

He sure was frog-walkin', I heaved a big sigh,
He only lacked wings for to be on the fly;
He turned his old belly right up to the sun,
For he was a sun-fishin' son of a gun.

He was the worst bronco I've seen on the range,
He could turn on a nickel and leave you some change.
While he was buckin' he squalled like a shoat,
I tell you that outlaw, he sure got my goat.

I tell all the people that pony could step
And I was still on him a-buildin' a rep;
He came down on all fours and turned up his side,
I don't see how he kept from losing his hide.

I lost my stirrup, I lost my hat,
I was pullin' at leather as blind as a bat;
With a phenomenal jump he made a high dive
And set me a-winding up there through the sky.

I turned forty flips and came down to the earth
And sit there a-cussing the day of his birth.
I know there's some ponies that I cannot ride,
Some of them living, they haven't all died—

But I bet all my money there's no man alive
That can ride Old Strawberry when he makes that high dive.

TEXT B. THE BULL RIDER SONG

As I was snapping out broncs on the old Flying U
At forty a month, a good buckaroo,
When the boss comes around and says, "Say, my lad,
At riding rough ponies, well, you don't look bad:

"At riding the rough strain you're not so slow,
You might do some good at a big rodeo;
You say I ain't got no more ponies to break,
But I'll buy you a ticket and give you a stake.

"Lay off of the liquor and don't you get full
And think you can ride that old big Brahma bull;
He's bad as you make 'em, and don't you forget
He's throwed a lot of riders, he ain't been rode yet."

So I packs up my war bag and starts raising dust,
I'm a-hunting that show and that wild bull to bust.
I enters their contest and pays in my fee,
Then tells 'em to look at a rider, that's me.

Well, they look me all over and said, "Yes, he's full,
Let's give him a shot at that big Brahma bull."
"I've come a long ways and I'm not here to brag,
But I bet you my outfit I'll gentle that stag."

So, while they were gettin' him into the chute
I'm a-buckling the spurs to the heels of my boots,
Then looks that brute over, and to my surprise
He's a foot and a half just between his two eyes.

He's got two high horns that look pretty bad,
He weighs a good ton and that whole ton was mad;
Right over his withers he packs a big hump
So I takes a deep seat right behind that big lump.

Well, I leaned over so to open her wide,
"I'll be back in a minute and bring you his hide."
They opened that chute gate and I'm tellin' you
Right there at the entrance, boys, he come in two.

He hit for the east, but he lit in the west,
I'm a-sittin' up high, I'm sure doing my best;
Those horns are a-tossing right under my chin,
But I'm still sitting straight and trying to grin.

Well, the crowd gets to cheerin' both me and the bull,
But they don't do no good cause I've got my hands full;
He's dipping so low that my boots fill with dirt,
And he's poppin' the buttons right off of my shirt.

He gets the fence rowing and weaving behind,
My head gets to popping, I sorta go blind;
When he takes to hand-springing way up in the air
And leaves me a-sitting on nothing up there.

Up there I turned over, below I can see
He's pawin' the ground, he's sure waiting for me;
I pictures a grave and a slab made of wood
Reading, "Here lies a rider that thought he was good."

I hit on the ground and I've got enough sense
To outrun that bull to a hole in the fence;
I get my old saddle and I'm telling you
I high-tailed her back to that old Flying U.

189

No. 69
Chopo

Jack Thorp's "Chopo" hankers back to Dick Turpin's renowned "Black Bess." Thorp wrote it while reminiscing about the time Chopo helped control a stampede, and then returned his lost rider safely to camp. (Melody: Bluebird B7612A, The Tune Wranglers. Text: N. Howard [Jack] Thorp, *Songs of the Cowboys* [Estancia, N.M.: News Print Shop, 1908], pp. 30–31.)

CHOPO

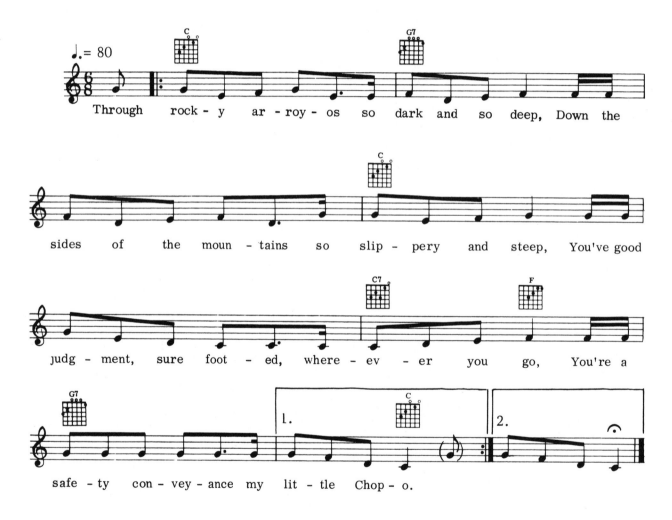

Through rock-y ar-roy-os so dark and so deep, Down the sides of the moun-tains so slip-pery and steep, You've good judg-ment, sure foot-ed, where-ev-er you go, You're a safe-ty con-vey-ance my lit-tle Chop-o.

Through rocky arroyos so dark and so deep
Down the sides of the mountains so slippery and steep
You've good judgment, sure footed, wherever you go
You're a safety conveyance my little Chopo.

Whether single or double or in the lead of a team
Over highways or byways or crossing a stream
You're always in fix and willing to go
Whenever you're called on, my *chico* Chopo.

You're a good roping horse, you were never jerked down
When tied to a steer, you will circle him round
Let him once cross the string, and over he'll go
You *sabe* the business, my cow horse Chopo.

One day on the Llano, a hail storm began
The herds were stampeded, the horses all ran
The lightning it glittered, a cyclone did blow
But you faced the sweet music my little Chopo.

Chopo my pony, Chopo my pride
Chopo my *amigo*, Chopo I will ride
From Mexico's borders 'cross Texas Llanos
To the salt Pecos river I ride you Chopo.

No. 70
Powderhorn

A fine cutting horse in action is a beautiful thing to behold. Out-guessing every move of the stubborn steer that is bent on staying with the bunch, horses of Miss Aledo's instinct can push the critter away from the other steers as the work requires. At its best this maneuver offers beauty of movement and form comparable to that of the classical ballet. (Melody and text: FAC I 200, reproduced with permission of the collector, Dean Emeritus John Donald Robb of the University of New Mexico.)

POWDERHORN

Out in the West you have oft heard it said The

on - ly good paint horse is one that is dead; But to

rules there's ex - cep - tions, and we've one to show, So take a deep

seat, watch this paint fil - ly go. _____

Out in the West you have oft heard it said
The only good paint horse is one that is dead;
But to rules there's exceptions, and we've one to show,
So take a deep seat, watch this paint filly go.

CHORUS:

Miss Aledo, Miss Aledo, swing to and fro,
Watching those dogies wherever they go;
First to the right, and then to the left,
Always out in front of them, doing your best.

It was down at Fort Worth at the big fat stock show
Bob first had the chance to watch this filly go.
He walked right up to 'em, says, "How much would you take?"
They said enough money to make a rent or a stake.

Bob says, "I'll take her, but now let me see,
Will you take a check for the former 'Cross B?'"
The boys says, "No, Bob, it's cash that I want,"
So he gets the two thousand and pays him right off.

CHORUS:

So Miss Aledo, Miss Aledo, swing to and fro,
Watching those dogies wherever they go;
First to the right, then to the left,
Always out in front of them, doing your best.

Watch her go to 'em, she does it so neat,
It looks like the filly's got brains in her feet.
She's always a-watching, she seems to out-guess,
Anything that she's working, she's doing her best.

People will tell you it takes time to show
A good cuttin' pony the right place to go;
But this little paint filly just naturally knows
More than most horses, she's just two years old.

CHORUS:

Miss Aledo, Miss Aledo, swing to and fro,
Watching those dogies wherever they go;
First to the right, then to the left,
Always out in front of 'em, doing your best.

If it's good cutting horses you're wanting to see
Go out north of Stafford upon the Cross B;
Miss Aledo and Powder and Old Yeller Pet,
The best cuttin' hosses the West has seen yet.

No. 71
The Educated Feller (Zebra Dun)

Stories (and ballads) of the trickster tricked are as old as anecdote itself. "The Educated Feller" develops an instance thereof in flamboyant
proportions: the presumptive victim is an outsider; he senses hostility
from the very start and capitalizes it by a bombastic show of naïveté and
arrogance; step by step he leads the tricksters to bait the trap which he
is only too ready to spring. Then in a dramatic demonstration of skill
and showmanship he proves that "he was a thoroughbred and not a gent
from town." (Melody and text: FAC I 217, reproduced with permission
of the collector, Dean Emeritus John Donald Robb of the University of
New Mexico.)

THE EDUCATED FELLER (ZEBRA DUN)

We'd camped out on the plains at the head of the Ci - mar -
ron, —— When a - long had come a stran - ger —— to
stop and ar - gue some.—— He looked so ver - y
fool - ish we be - gan to look a - round,—— We
thought he was a green - horn—— that just es - caped from town.

We'd camped out on the plains at the head of the Cimarron,
When along had come a stranger to stop and argue some.
He looked so very foolish we began to look around,
We thought he was a greenhorn that just escaped from town.

We asked if he'd had his breakfast, he hadn't had a smear,
So we opened up the chuck box and bade him take a share;
He took a cup of coffee, some biscuits, and some beans,
And then began to talk about some foreign kings and queens;

About the Spanish wars and fightings on the seas
With guns as big as steers and ramrods big as trees;
About old Paul Jones, the meanest son-of-a-gun,
'Twas the grittiest cuss that, Lordy, had ever pulled a gun.

When the dude had finished eatin' and had put his plate away
He rolled a cigarette, then asked the time of day;
He talked about the weather, the election, and such things,
But didn't seem to know so much 'bout working on the range.

Such an educated fellow, his talk just came in herds,
He 'stonished all them cowboys with them jaw-breakin' words;
He just kept on a-talking till he made the boys all sick
And they began to look around to play some kind of a trick.

Well, he said he'd lost his job upon the Santa Fe,
A-going across the plains to meet the Seven B.
He didn't say how come it, it was trouble with the boss,
But he would like to borrow a fat, nice saddle hoss.

Well, this tickled all the boys to death, they laughed way down their
    sleeves,
"Well, you can have a saddle horse as fat and nice as you please."
So Shorty grabbed a lariat and he roped the Zebra Dun,
And he turned him to the stranger while we waited for the fun.

Well, old Dun he was an outlaw that'd grown so very wild
He could paw the white right from the moon for every jump a mile.
But he stood right still as if he didn't know
Until he was all saddled and all ready for the go.

When the stranger hit the saddle Old Dunny quit the earth,
A-headed right straight up for all that he was worth,
A-pitchin' and a-squealin' and a-havin' wall-eyed fits,
With his hind feet perpendicular and his front ones in the bits.

Well, you could see the tops of the mountains under Dunny every jump,
But the stranger stayed upon him just like a camel's hump;
The stranger stayed upon him and he curled his black mustache
Just like a summer boarder a-waiting for his hash.

Lord, he thumped him in the shoulders and he spurred him when he
   whirled,
He showed us flunky punchers that he was the wolf of this world;
And when he once more dismounted then again upon the ground
We knew he was a thoroughbred and not a gent from town.

The boss, who'd been a-standing round and watching all the show,
Walked right up to the stranger; he said, "You needn't go;
If you can handle a lariat like you rode old Zebra Dun
Well, you're the man I've looked for ever since the year of one."

Now he could handle a rope, boys, and didn't do it slow,
And when the cows stampeded he was always on the go—
There's one thing and a sure thing I've learned since I've been born:
Every educated feller ain't a plumb greenhorn.

No. 72

The Tenderfoot

The song is a realistic first-person account of an amateur in the employ of a rawhide-rough foreman bent on making or breaking a tenderfoot just as he broke mustangs. The victim is given a stove-up outlaw horse that pitches him fifty ways from Sunday. The boss is satisfied—pleased in fact—with the new hand's start, offers him a new horse for the next day, or the choice of walking back to town. (Melody: FAC I 507, sung by Kathy Dagel. Text: N. Howard [Jack] Thorp, *Songs of the Cowboys* [Boston and New York: Houghton Mifflin Company, 1921], pp. 146–148.)

THE TENDERFOOT

I thought one spring, just for fun, I'd see how cow-punch-ing was done; And when the round-ups had be-gun I tac-kled a cat-tle king.

I thought one spring, just for fun,
I'd see how cow-punching was done;
And when the round-ups had begun
I tackled the cattle-king.
Says he, "My foreman is in town,
He's at the plaza, his name is Brown;
If you'll see him he'll take you down."
Says I, "That's just the thing."

We started for the ranch next day;
Brown augured me most all the way.
He said that cow-punching was child play,
That it was no work at all,—
That all you had to do was ride,
'T was only drifting with the tide;
Oh, how that old cow-puncher lied—
He certainly had his gall.

He put me in charge of a cavyard,
And told me not to work too hard,
That all I had to do was guard
The horses from getting away;
I had one hundred and sixty head,
I sometimes wished that I was dead;
When one got away, Brown's head turned red,
And there was hell to pay.

Straight to the bushes they would take,
As if they were running for a stake,—
I've often wished their neck they'd break,
But they would never fall.
Sometimes I could not head them at all,
Sometimes my horse would catch a fall,
And I'd shoot on like a cannon ball.
Till the earth came in my way.

They saddled me up an old gray hack
With two set-fasts on his back;
They padded him down with a gunny sack
And used my bedding all.
When I got on he quit the ground,
Went up in the air and turned around,
And I came down and hit the ground,—
It was an awful fall.

They picked me up and carried me in
And rubbed me down with an old stake-pin.
"That's the way they all begin;
You're doing well," says Brown.
"And in the morning, if you don't die,
I'll give you another horse to try."
"Oh, say, can't I walk?" says I.
Says he, "Yes—back to town."

I've traveled up and I've traveled down,
I've traveled this country round and round,
I've lived in city and I've lived in town,
But I've got this much to say:
Before you try cow-punching, kiss your wife,
Take a heavy insurance on your life,
Then cut your throat with a barlow knife,—
For it's easier done that way.

No. 73

The Moonshine Steer

Range life was sweetened occasionally by some highly imaginative escapades, especially if there was whiskey to help out. Here is Gail Gardner's account of two punchers who liquored up a range steer. (Melody: FAC I 265, sung by Gail Gardner. Text: Gail I. Gardner, *Orejana Bull for Cowboys Only* [1935, copyright renewed 1963], pp. 11–12 [used with permission].)

THE MOONSHINE STEER

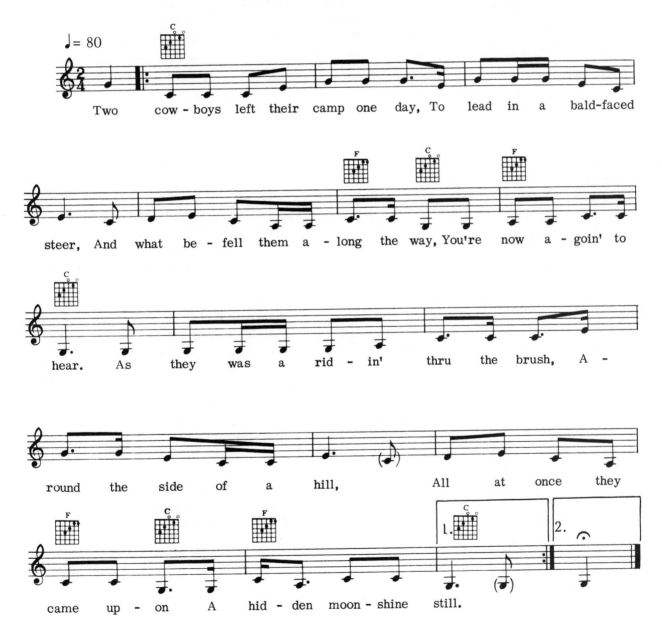

Two cow-boys left their camp one day, To lead in a bald-faced steer, And what be-fell them a-long the way, You're now a-goin' to hear. As they was a rid-in' thru the brush, A-round the side of a hill, All at once they came up-on A hid-den moon-shine still.

Two cowboys left their camp one day,
  To lead in a bald-faced steer,
And what befell them along the way,
  You're now a-goin' to hear.

As they was a-ridin' thru the brush,
  Around the side of a hill,
All at once they come upon,
  A hidden moonshine still.

The moonshiner heard them a-coming,
  A-coming thru the brush,
An' he thought that the sheriff had him shore,
  So he left there all in a rush.

Sez one old boy to the other old boy,
  "Now this here's mighty queer,
I wish that you would tell me the name
  Of this contraption here."

The coil was a gas line stole from a Ford,
  The still was a coal-oil can
But out of the spout and into a jug,
  The old corn liquor ran.

Them boys got down an' hefted the jug,
  And they found her full—pretty nigh,
So they each took a snort right then and there,
  Fer they was tolerable dry.

Sez one old boy, "Let's go from here,
  Fer we've got work to do."
So they got on their horses an' they rode away,
  And the jug it went along too.

When they got to the place where the steer was tied,
  They was a-feelin' mighty gay,
Fer they had stopped to tilt that jug
  Most all along the way.

Sez one old boy, "That's the durndest steer
  That ever I did find,
He's got two heads and a dozen legs,
  And fourteen tails behind."

How they got that oxen loose from the tree,
  It would be hard to tell,
But when they went to lead him away,
  Why, it seems that they just had Hell.

The steer bowed up and sulled again,
  And they seen that he never would lead,
So they figgered that a jolt of moonshine
  Was the very thing he'd need.

So they rolled old steer upon his back,
  And they held him by the horns,
And down his sizzling goozle
  They poured a quart of corn.

Sez one old boy, "Let's turn him loose,
  And git him home real quick;
He's bound to want him a chaser,
  And he'll go right straight to the crick."

But the bald-faced steer he pawed the ground,
  And he bawled and he bellered too;
He walled his eyes and he wrung his tail,
  Then he shook his hocks and flew.

That oxen simply left the world,
  As hard as he could go,
And if he kept on drifting,
  He's down in Mexico.

This story has a moral,
  And you will find it here,
If you ever have any moonshine,
  Don't waste none on no steer.

No. 74
Tying Knots in the Devil's Tail

We like this song for two reasons: first, it is as fine a description of the process of roping and branding on the open range as can be found in print; secondly, it is a classical "western" treatment of the centuries-old Christian tradition concerning devil lore and the dance of death. There is hope for a culture whose folk heroes take Old Nick so deftly in hand! It was written by Gail Gardner in 1917 and has floated in oral tradition. Many variants have developed. (Melody: FAC I 270, sung by Billy Simon. Text: Gail I. Gardner, *Orejana Bull for Cowboys Only* [1935, copyright renewed 1963], pp. 9–10 [used with permission].)

TYING KNOTS IN THE DEVIL'S TAIL

A - way up high in the Sierr - y Petes, Where the yel - ler pines grows tall, Ole Sand - y Bob an' Bus - ter Jig—— Had a ro - deer camp last fall.

Away up high in the Sierry Petes,
   Where the yeller pines grows tall,
Ole Sandy Bob an' Buster Jig
   Had a rodeer camp last fall.

Oh, they taken their hosses and runnin' irons
   And mabbe a dawg or two,
An' they 'lowed they'd brand all the long-yered calves,
   That come within their view.

And any old dogie that flapped long yeres,
   An' didn't bush up by day,
Got his long yeres whittled an' his old hide scortched,
   In a most artistic way.

Now one fine day ole Sandy Bob,
   He throwed his seago down,
"I'm sick of the smell of burnin' hair,
   And I 'lows I'm a-goin' to town."

So they saddles up an' hits 'em a lope,
   Fer it warnt no sight of a ride,
And them was the days when a Buckeroo
   Could ile up his inside.

Oh, they starts her in at the Kaintucky Bar,
   At the head of Whisky Row,
And they winds up down by the Depot House,
   Some forty drinks below.

They then sets up and turns around,
   And goes her the other way,
An' to tell you the Gawd-forsaken truth,
   Them boys got stewed that day.

As they was a-ridin' back to camp,
   A-packin' a pretty good load,
Who should they meet but the Devil himself,
   A-prancin' down the road.

Sez he, "You ornery cowboy skunks,
   You'd better hunt yer holes,
Fer I've come up from Hell's Rim Rock,
   To gather in yer souls."

Sez Sandy Bob, "Old Devil be damned,
  We boys is kinda tight,
But you aint a-goin' to gather no cowboy souls,
  'Thout you has some kind of a fight."

So Sandy Bob punched a hole in his rope,
  And he swang her straight and true,
He lapped it on to the Devil's horns,
  An' he taken his dallies too.

Now Buster Jig was a riata man,
  With his gut-line coiled up neat,
So he shaken her out an' he built him a loop,
  An' he lassoed the Devil's hind feet.

Oh, they stretched him out an' they tailed him down,
  While the irons was a-gettin' hot,
They cropped and swaller-forked his yeres,
  Then they branded him up a lot.

They pruned him up with a de-hornin' saw,
  An' they knotted his tail fer a joke,
They then rid off and left him there,
  Necked to a Black-Jack oak.

If you're ever up high in the Sierry Petes,
  An' you hear one Hell of a wail,
You'll know its that Devil a-bellerin' around,
  About them knots in his tail.

No. 75
Windy Bill

Every culture has its practical jokes: rites of initiation inflicted upon the tenderfoot and the overbearing to cut them down to size. Windy Bill's boasting got its reward in his utter humiliation when he was induced to put a loop on the wrong steer. (Melody and text: FAC I 235, as sung by Frank Goodwyn.)

WINDY BILL

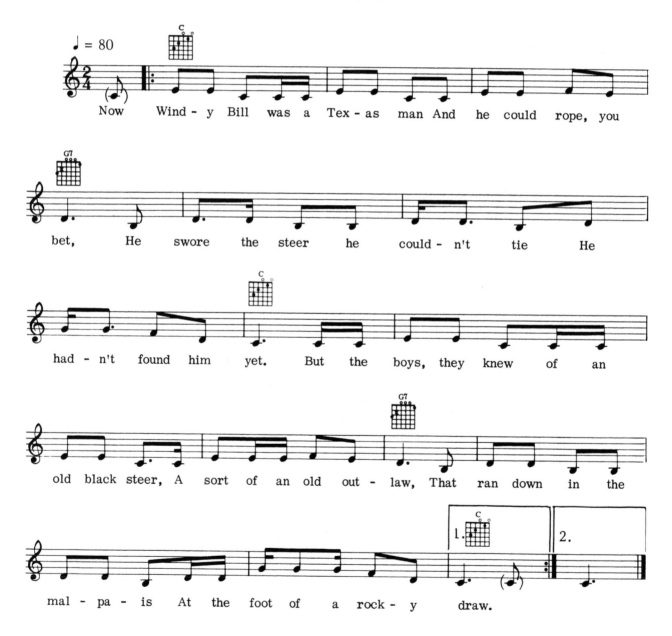

Now Wind-y Bill was a Tex-as man And he could rope, you bet, He swore the steer he could-n't tie He had-n't found him yet. But the boys, they knew of an old black steer, A sort of an old out-law, That ran down in the mal-pa-is At the foot of a rock-y draw.

Now Windy Bill was a Texas man
  And he could rope, you bet,
He swore the steer he couldn't tie
  He hadn't found him yet.
But the boys, they knew of an old black steer,
  A sort of an old outlaw,
That ran down in the malpais
  At the foot of a rocky draw.

This old black steer had stood his ground
  With punchers from everywhere,
And the boys, they bet Bill ten to one
  That he couldn't quite get there.
So Bill brought out his old gray horse,
  His withers and back were raw,
And prepared to tackle that big, black brute
  That ran down in the draw.

With his Brazos bit and his Sam Stack tree
  And his chaps and taps to boot,
And his old maguey tied hard and fast
  Bill swore he'd get that brute.
Now Bill he first came a-ridin' round,
  Old Blackie began to paw,
Then flung his tail right up in the air
  And went a-drifting down the draw.

The old gray horse tore after him,
  For he'd been eatin' corn,
And Bill, he piled his old maguey
  Right around old Blackie's horn.
The old gray horse, he stopped right still,
  The cinches broke like straw,
And the old maguey and the Sam Stack tree
  Went a-drifting down the draw.

Bill, he lit in a flint rock pile,
  His face and hands were scratched.
He said he thought he could rope a snake,
  But he guessed he'd met his match.
He paid his bets like a little man
  Without a bit of jaw,
And allowed old Blackie was the boss
  Of anything in the draw.

Now here's the moral to my story, boys,
  And that you all must see:
Whenever you go to rope a snake
  Don't tie him to your tree.
But take your dally welters
  'Cordin' to California law,
And you'll never see your old rim fire
  Go a-drifting down the draw.

No. 76
Git Along Little Dogies

The slow-jog rhythms of "Git Along Little Dogies" fit trail driving condition and moods. The cattle grazed as they were driven, lest they arrive at the railheads nothing but skin and bone. Trail driving did have its intense and dramatic moments, but for the most part it was downright monotony. This text comes from the journal of Owen Wister, February 21, 1893. (Melody: FAC I 233, as sung by Frank Goodwyn.)

GIT ALONG LITTLE DOGIES

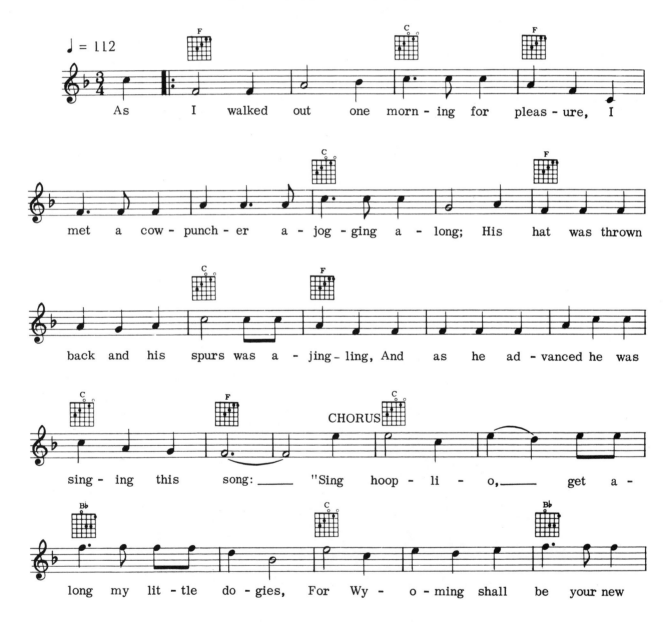

As I walked out one morn-ing for pleas-ure, I met a cow-punch-er a-jog-ging a-long; His hat was thrown back and his spurs was a-jing-ling, And as he ad-vanced he was sing-ing this song: ___ "Sing hoop-li-o, ___ get a-long my lit-tle do-gies, For Wy-o-ming shall be your new

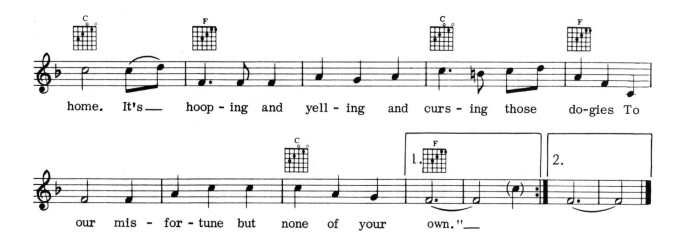

home. It's — hoop - ing and yell - ing and curs - ing those do-gies To

our mis - for - tune but none of your own." —

1. 2.

As I walked out one morning for pleasure,
  I met a cowpuncher a-jogging along;
His hat was thrown back and his spurs was a-jingling,
  And as he advanced he was singing this song—

CHORUS:
  "Sing hooplio, get along my little dogies,
    For Wyoming shall be your new home.
  It's hooping and yelling and cursing those dogies
    To our misfortune but none of your own."

In the Springtime we round up the dogies,
  Slap on the brands and bob off their tails;
Then we cut herd and herd is inspected,
  And then we throw them on the trail.

In the evening we round in the dogies
  As they are grazing from herd all around.
You have no idea the trouble they give us
  As we are holding them on the bedground.

In the morning we throw off the bedground,
  Aiming to graze them an hour or two.
When they are full, you think you can drive them
  On the trail, but be damned if you do.

Some fellows go on the trail for pleasure,
  But they have got this thing down wrong;
If it hadn't been for these troublesome dogies,
  I never would thought of writing this song.

No. 77

Railroad Corral

The metrical perfection of this song confirms its origin from the pen of a poet: it was written by Joseph Mills Hanson, and published first in *Frank Leslie's Popular Monthly* in 1904. It has floated in oral tradition ever since, and with good reason: its images ring true to days of the cowboy era when the drive to the railheads was the culmination of a cowhand's seasonal work. (Melody: Ina Sires, *Songs of the Open Range* [Boston: C. C. Birchard and Co., 1928], p. 22.)

RAILROAD CORRAL

We are up in the morning ere dawning of day
And the grub wagon's busy and flap-jacks in play;
While the herd is astir over hillside and swale
With the night riders rounding them into the trail.

Come, take up your cinches
And shake up your reins;
Come, wake up your broncho
And break for the plains;
Come, roust those red steers from the long chaparral,
For the outfit is off for the railroad corral!

The sun circles upward, the steers as they plod
Are pounding to powder the hot prairie sod;
And, it seems, as the dust turns you dizzy and sick,
That you'll never reach noon and the cool, shady creek.

But tie up your kerchief
And ply up your nag;
Come, dry up your grumbles
And try not to lag;
Come, larrup those steers from the long chaparral,
For we're far on the way to the railroad corral!

The afternoon shadows are starting to lean
When the grub wagon sticks in a marshy ravine;
And the herd scatters further than vision can look,
For you bet all true punchers will help out the cook!

So shake out your rawhide
And snake it up fair;
Come, break your old bronco
To taking his share!
Come, now for the steers in the long chaparral,
For it's all in the drive to the railroad corral!

But the longest of days must reach evening at last,
When the hills are all climbed and the creeks are all passed;
And the tired herd droops in the yellowing light;
Let them loaf if they will, for the railroad's in sight!

So flap up your holster
And snap up your belt;
Come, strap up the saddle
Whose lap you have felt;
Good-by to the steers and the long chaparral!
There's a town that's a trump by the railroad corral!

No. 78
The Old Chisholm Trail

It has been claimed that the stanzas of "The Old Chisholm Trail," written end-on-end, would stretch farther than the trail itself (West Texas to Abilene, Kansas). It is, in fact, a formula-song, like a limerick but much simpler: anyone who can make a simple rhyme and perceive the rhythms of a couplet can turn the trick: hence, "the more whiskey the more verses," as Jack Thorp put it.

Lomax (*Cowboy Songs* [1939], pp. 28–41) offers about a hundred couplets (gathered from multiple sources), and four melodic variations. Here we shall limit ourselves to an early Kansas text, and a unique text which Frank Dobie got from an old-timer in the 1920's. (Melody: Musicraft 299, Dick Thomas. Text A: Myra E. Hull, "Cowboy Ballads." *The Kansas Historical Quarterly* [Vol. VIII, No. 1, Feb. 1939], p. 39 [published by permission of the Kansas State Historical Society]. Text B: J. Frank Dobie, "More Ballads and Songs of the Frontier Folk," PTFLS [No. VII, 1928], pp. 178–180 [published by permission of the Texas Folklore Society].)

THE OLD CHISHOLM TRAIL

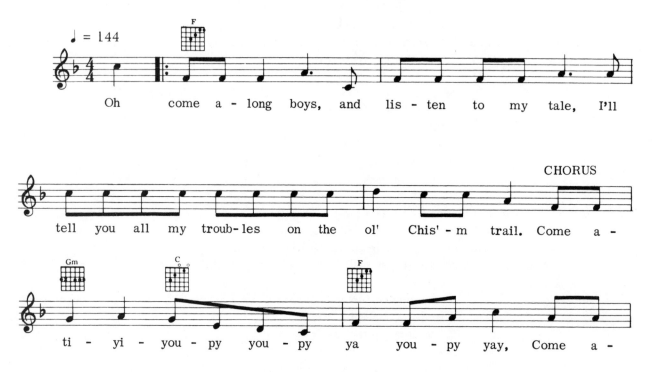

Oh come a-long boys, and lis-ten to my tale, I'll tell you all my troub-les on the ol' Chis'-m trail. Come a-ti-yi-you-py you-py ya you-py yay, Come a-

ti   yi   you - py   you - py   yay.

TEXT A. THE OLD CHISHOLM TRAIL

Oh come along, boys, and listen to my tale,
I'll tell you all my troubles on the ol' Chis'm trail.

CHORUS:
    Come a-ti yi youpy youpy ya youpy yay,
    Come a-ti yi youpy youpy yay.

On a ten-dollar horse and a forty-dollar saddle,
I was ridin', and a-punchin' Texas cattle.

We left ol' Texas October twenty-third,
Drivin' up trail with a 2 U Herd.

I'm up in the mornin' afore daylight,
An' afore I sleep the moon shines bright.

It's bacon and beans most every day,
I'd as soon be eatin' prairie hay.

Old Ben Bolt was a blamed good boss,
But he'd go to see the girls on a sore-backed hoss.

Old Ben Bolt was a mighty good man,
And you'd know there was whisky wherever he'd land.

I woke up one mornin' on the Chisholm trail,
With a rope in my hand and a cow by the tail.

Last night on guard, an' the leader broke the ranks,
I hit my horse down the shoulders an' spurred him in the flanks.

Oh, it's cloudy in the west, and a-lookin' like rain,
And my damned ol' slicker's in the wagon again.

Oh the wind commenced to blow and the rain began to fall,
An' it looked by grab that we was gonna lose 'em all.

I jumped in the saddle an' I grabbed a-holt the horn,
The best damned cowpuncher ever was born.

I was on my best horse, and a-goin' on the run,
The quickest-shootin' cowboy that ever pulled a gun.

No chaps, no slicker, and it's pourin' down rain,
An' I swear, by God, I'll never nightherd again.

I herded and I hollered, and I done pretty well,
Till the boss said, "Boys, just let 'em go to Hell."

I'm goin' to the ranch to draw my money,
Goin' into town to see my Honey.

I went to the boss to draw my roll,
He figgered me out nine dollars in the hole.

So I'll sell my outfit as fast as I can,
And I won't punch cows for no damn man.

So I sold old Baldy and I hung up my saddle,
And I bid farewell to the longhorn cattle.

TEXT B. ELEVEN SLASH SLASH ELEVEN

It's round in your cavy, and it's rope out your hack
And strap your old kack well fast upon his back.

CHORUS:
 Singing hi-yi-yuppy, yuppy, hi-yuppy-yea,
 Singing hi-yi-yuppy, yuppy, hi-yuppy yea.

Your foot in your stirrup and your hand on the horn,
You're the best damned cowboy that ever was born.

You land in the saddle and you give a loud yell,
For the longhorn cattle have got to take the hill.

212

You round up a bunch of dogies and take down the trail,
But the very first thing you land in jail.

But the sheriff's an old puncher and he fixes out your bail,
For it's a damned poor country with a cowboy in jail.

So you round in your foreman and you hit him for your roll,
For you're going to town and act a little bold.

You strap on your chaps, your spurs, and your gun,
For you're going to go to town and have a little fun.

You ride a big bronc that will buck and prance
And you pull out your gun and make the tenderfoot dance.

You go into the gambling house a-looking kinder funny,
For you got every pocket just chock full of money.

You play cards with the gambler who's got a marked pack,
And you walk back to the ranch with the saddle on your back.

Now I've punched cattle from Texas to Maine—
And known some cowboys by their right name;

No matter, though, whatever they claim,
You'll find every dirty cuss exactly the same.

So dig in your spurs and peel your eyes to heaven,
But never overlook a calf with Eleven Slash Slash Eleven.

No. 79

Little Joe, the Wrangler

The popularity of "Little Joe, the Wrangler" has kept expanding since Jack Thorp composed it in 1898. It is a sentimental piece on the perennial theme of the underdog. A boy, abused by a cruel stepmother, has left home, endeared himself to the boss and hands on a cattle drive. In a wild flood of stampeding cattle he makes himself a hero and a martyr. (Melody: FAC I 193, reproduced with permission of the collector, Dean Emeritus John Donald Robb of the University of New Mexico. Text: N. Howard [Jack] Thorp, *Songs of the Cowboy* [Estancia, N.M.: News Print Shop, 1908], pp. 9–11.)

LITTLE JOE, THE WRANGLER

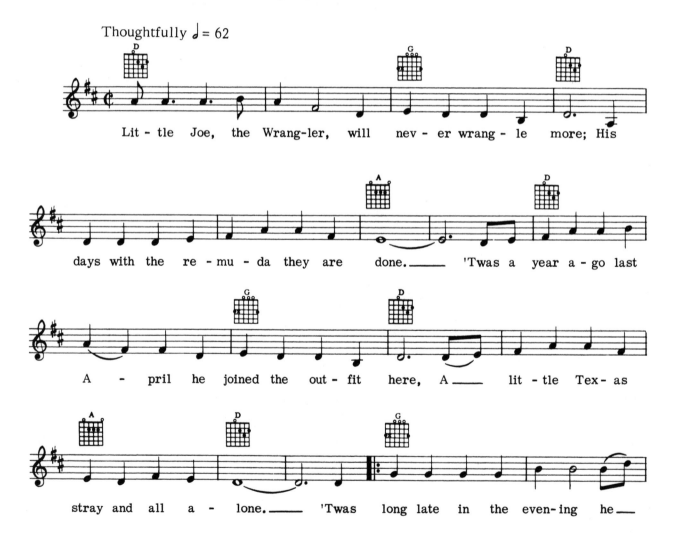

Thoughtfully ♩ = 62

Lit - tle Joe, the Wrang-ler, will nev - er wrang - le more; His days with the re - mu - da they are done.____ 'Twas a year a - go last A - pril he joined the out - fit here, A____ lit - tle Tex - as stray and all a - lone.____ 'Twas long late in the even - ing he____

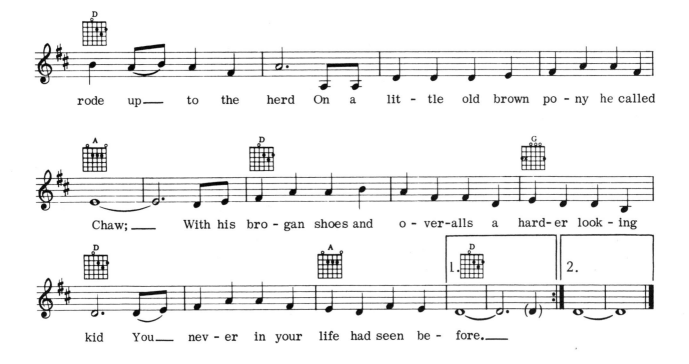

rode up— to the herd On a lit-tle old brown po-ny he called
Chaw; — With his bro-gan shoes and o-ver-alls a hard-er look-ing
kid You— nev-er in your life had seen be-fore.—

1.   2.

Little Joe, the wrangler, will never wrangle more;
   His days with the remuda they are done.
'Twas a year ago last April he joined the outfit here,
   A little Texas stray and all alone.

'Twas long late in the evening he rode up to the herd
   On a little old brown pony he called Chaw;
With his brogan shoes and overalls a harder looking kid
   You never in your life had seen before.

His saddle 'twas a southern kack built many years ago,
   An O.K. spur on one foot idly hung,
While his "hot roll" in a cotton sack was loosely tied behind
   And a canteen from the saddle horn he'd slung.

He said he'd had to leave his home, his daddy'd married twice
   And his new ma beat him every day or two;
So he saddled up old Chaw one night and "Lit a shuck" this way
   Thought he'd try and paddle now his own canoe.

Said he'd try and do the best he could if we'd only give him work
   Though he didn't know "straight" up about a cow,
So the boss he cut him out a mount and kinder put him on
   For he sorter liked the little stray somehow.

Taught him how to herd the horses and to learn to know them all
   To round 'em up by daylight; if he could
To follow the chuck-wagon and to always hitch the team
   And help the "cosinero" rustle wood.

We'd driven to red river and the weather had been fine;
   We were camped down on the south side in a bend
When a norther commenced blowing and we doubled up our guards
   For it took all hands to hold the cattle then.

Little Joe the wrangler was called out with the rest
   And scarcely had the kid got to the herd
When the cattle they stampeded; like a hail storm, long they flew
   And all of us were riding for the lead.

'Tween the streaks of lightning we could see a horse far out ahead
   'Twas little Joe the wrangler in the lead;
He was riding "old Blue Rocket" with his slicker 'bove his head
   Trying to check the leaders in their speed.

At last we got them milling and kinder quieted down
   And the extra guard back to the camp did go
But one of them was missin' and we all knew at a glance
   'Twas our little Texas stray poor wrangler Joe.

Next morning just at sunup we found where Rocket fell
   Down in a washout twenty feet below
Beneath his horse mashed to a pulp his horse had rung the knell
   For our little Texas stray—poor wrangler Joe.

No. 80
Utah Carl

"Utah Carl," a ballad of a cattle stampede, gives many insights into the code of the cowboy: reverence for perfect womanhood even to the point of giving one's life to preserve it; loyal comradeship in work and adventure; the transcendence of life beyond death.

Our text is one of the longest; it moves ploddingly through all the dramatic details like an epic poem. The song is often abbreviated and sung, and with more audience appeal, to one-third the full version. But "Utah Carl" is, at its best, a night-herd song; there is no one to entertain except the singer, and the cattle couldn't care less! (Melody: FAC I 76, recorded by John O'Bryant. Text: Gordon 1005.)

UTAH CARL

And so you ask me, lit – tle friend, why I am si – lent, sad and still, Why my brow is al – ways cloud – ed, like the dark-ness on the hill. Well, pull in your po – ny clos – er while I tell you a sim – ple tale, Of U – tah Carl, my pard – ner, and his last ride on the trail.

And so you ask me, little friend, why I am silent, sad and still,
Why my brow is always clouded, like the darkness on the hill.
Well, pull in your pony closer while I tell you a simple tale,
Of Utah Carl, my pardner, and his last ride on the trail.

'Midst the cactus and the thistles of the Mexicans' far off land,
Where the cattle roam in thousands in many a bunch and band,
There's a grave without a headstone, unmarked with date or name,
There my pardner sleeps in silence—there's the place from where I came.

Long we roamed the range together, for we've ridden side by side;
I loved him like a brother and I wept when Utah died.
Side by side we rode the roundup, roped, cut out, and burned the brand;
Through storm and weary darkness we joined the night herd's weary
    stand.

When the stampede came so sudden and the cowboys form the mill,
There's a ringing voice that is silent—Utah Carl lies cold and still.
Once his voice controlled the stampede as it rang out loud and clear,
And when the cattle heard, it overcame their maddened fear.

Every boy upon the cow range knows how bravely Utah died,
And they pass his grave in silence, and they speak his name with pride.
For he fell as cowboys should, never blanched or quaked with fear,
When he heard the steers upon him and the rush of death was near.

We were rounding up one morning and our work was almost done
When on the right the cattle started in a wild and maddened run.
The boss's little daughter, who was holding on that side,
Started to turn the cattle, and 'twas there my pardner died.

On the saddle of the pony where the boss's daughter sat
Utah Carl that very morning had thrown a red blanket,
Thus the saddle might be easier for Lenore, his little friend,
And the blanket which he placed there brought my pardner to his end.

As Lenore rushed in her pony to the cattle on the right
The red blanket slipped from beneath her, catching on her stirrup tight.
When the cowboys saw the blanket everyone there held his breath;
For should now her pony fail her, none could save Lenore from death.

There is nothing on the range that will cause a steer to fight
Half as quick as some red object, when it's waved within his sight.
When the cattle saw the blanket almost dragging on the ground
They were maddened in an instant and they charged it with a bound.

Lenore saw the threatened danger, quickly turned her pony a pace,
Then leaning from the saddle tried the blanket to displace,
But in leaning lost her balance, fell in front of that wild tide,
When, "Lie still, Lenore, I am coming," were the words my pardner cried.

About fifty yards behind her Utah Carl came riding fast,
Though he little thought that moment that the ride would be his last.
Many times from off his saddle he had caught a trailing rope—
To raise Lenore at full speed was, he saw, his only hope.

As his horse approached the maiden, sure of foot with sturdy bound,
Low he swung from off his saddle to catch Lenore from the ground.
As he hung from off his saddle every cowboy held his breath,
For the feat that he was trying was a feat for life and death.

Low he swung as fast he passed her and he caught her in his arm,
And I thought he was successful and was safe from further harm.
But such weight upon the cinches had never been felt before,
And the hind cinch snapped asunder as he fell beside Lenore.

As Lenore fell from her pony she dragged the blanket down,
It fell there close beside her as she lay upon the ground.
Utah Carl picked up the blanket, and again, "Lie still," he said—
Then, running across the prairie, waved the blanket over his head.

When he started 'cross the prairie every cowboy gave a cry;
He had saved the boss's daughter but they knew he had to die.
He had turned the maddened cattle from Lenore, his little friend,
And he heard the steers upon him, but he stopped to meet his end.

Quickly then from out his holster Utah Carl his pistol drew,
He was bound to die while fighting, like a cowboy bold and true.
The pistol flashed like lightning, the reports rang out loud and clear,
Still on the herd came rushing, though he dropped the leading steer.

Quick the cattle were upon him, and my pardner had to fall—
Never more he'll cinch a bronco, never give a cattle call.
For he died upon the range, and it seemed most awful hard—
I could not make the distance in time to save my pard.

When we broke into the circle on the ground my pardner lay,
From a dozen cuts and bruises his young life flowed away.
I knelt there beside him, and I knew his life was o'er
As I heard him faintly murmur, "I am coming, lie still Lenore."

And these were Utah Carl's last words, he had gone that endless trail,
And she sought his eyes with reverence while his face grew thin and pale.
He had closed life's final roundup at the Master's dread command,
And my tears came down in silence as I clasped my pardner's hand.

There's somewhere a grand, bright future, so I've heard the preachers say,
And I know that my young pardner won't be left on that last day.
And if but an unknown cowboy, he was ready here to die—
I know that my young pardner has a home beyond the sky.

No. 81

When the Work's All Done This Fall

"Momism" has been identified by social psychologists as a distinctive feature of the "western" personality. Here is a sufficient dose to last a long time. After years away from his mother (sufficient time, heaven help! to have come to know a few other honorable women), the puncher resolves to go back. But cruel fate in the guise of a cattle stampede and a not-so-sure-footed horse decrees it shall not be so!

Millions of 78 rpm recordings of "When the Work's All Done This Fall" have been sold, and a score of recording artists have collected royalties on it for more than half a century. Never have folk singers glorified Mom so much, not even the famous Pappy O'Daniels who reputedly sang his way to the governorship of Texas crooning, "The Boy Who Never Grew Too Old to Comb His Mother's Hair." (Melody: Supertone 2017, Bradley Kincaid. Text: PC–F 137.)

WHEN THE WORK'S ALL DONE THIS FALL

A group of jol-ly cow-boys dis-cuss-ing plans at ease, Says one: "I'll tell you some-thing, if you will lis-ten please; I am an old cow-punch-er and here I'm dressed in rags, And I used to be a tough one and take on great big jags."

A group of jolly cowboys discussing plans at ease,
Says one: "I'll tell you something, if you will listen please;
I am an old cowpuncher and here I'm dressed in rags,
And I used to be a tough one and take on great big jags.

"But I've got a home, boys, a good one you all know;
Although I have not seen it since long, long ago.
I'm going back home, boys, once more to see them all;
Yes, I'm going to see my mother when the work is done this fall.

"After the round-up is over and after the shipping is done,
I'm going right straight home, boys, ere all my money is gone.
I have changed my ways, and no more will I fall,
And I am going home, boys, when the work is done this fall.

"When I left home, boys, my mother for me cried,
Begged me not to go, boys, for me she would have died;
My mother's heart is breaking, breaking for me that's all,
And with God's help I'll see her when the work is done this fall."

That very night this cowboy went out to stand his guard;
The night was dark and cloudy, and storming very hard;
The cattle they got frightened, and rushed in wild stampede,
The cowboy tried to head them, riding at full speed.

While riding in the darkness so loudly did he shout,
Trying his best to head them and turn the herd about;
His saddlehorse did stumble, and on him did fall;
The poor boy won't see his mother when the work is done this fall.

They picked him up so gently and laid him on a bed;
His body was so mangled the boys all thought him dead;
He opened wide his blue eyes and looking all around,
He motioned to his comrades to sit near him on the ground.

"Boys, send mother my wages, the wages I have earned,
For I am afraid, boys, my last steer I have turned.
I'm going to a new range, I hear my Master call,
And I'll not see my mother when the work is done this fall.

"Fred, you take my saddle; George, you take my bed;
Bill, you take my pistol after I am dead.
And think upon me kindly when you look upon them all,
For I'll not see my mother when the work is done this fall."

Poor Charlie was buried at sunrise, no tombstone at his head,
Nothing but a little board, and this is what it said:
"Charlie died at daybreak, he died from a fall,
And he'll not see his mother when the work is done this fall."

Part Ten

Night-Herd Moods and Rhythms

No. 82
Night-Herding Song

Night-herding songs have the rhythm and sentiment of lullabies. Their value in calming a herd on the bedground has not been demonstrated scientifically, but their value to a night-herd rider in warding off loneliness is undeniable. (Melody: Bluebird 5189B, Girls of the Golden West. Text: Hendren 338.)

NIGHT-HERDING SONG

Slow down, do-gies, quit your rov-ing a-round; You've wan-dered and tram-pled all o-ver the ground; Oh, haze a-long, do-gies,___ feed kind-a slow, And don't be for-ev-er___ on the go;___ Move slow, lit-tle do-gies, move slow.___ ___ Heigh-ho, heigh-ho, heigh-ho.___ ___ ho.___

Slow down, dogies, quit your roving around,
You've wandered and trampled all over the ground;
Oh, haze along dogies, feed kinda slow,
And don't be forever on the go;
Move slow, little dogies, move slow.
Heigh-ho, heigh-ho, heigh-ho.

I've trail-herded, cross-herded, night-herded too,
But to keep you together is what I can't do;
My horse is leg weary, and I'm awful tired,
But if you get away I'm sure I get fired—
Bunch up, little dogies, bunch up.
Heigh-ho, heigh-ho, heigh-ho.

Oh say, little dogies, when you gonna lay down
And quit this forever shifting around?
My legs they are weary, my seat it is sore,
So lay down, little dogies, like you laid down before—
Lay down, little dogies, lay down,
Heigh-ho, heigh-ho, heigh-ho.

Lay still, little dogies, since you have laid down,
Stretch away out on the big open ground;
Snore loud, little dogies, and still the wild sound
That will go away when the day rolls around—
Lay still, little dogies, lay still.
Heigh-ho, heigh-ho, heigh-ho.

No. 83

Old Paint

Like "Chisholm Trail," "Old Paint" is a formula song: improvisation is easy and hence each singer uses his own selection of couplets. The rhythm is slow and meditative, and the ideas range mostly from bitter-sweet to mournful. This is one of the great among night-herd songs. Echoes of "The Wagoner's Lad" in melody and verses, especially in Text C, suggest colonial origins. (Melody: FAC I 186, reproduced with permission of the collector, Dean Emeritus John Donald Robb of the University of New Mexico. Text A: FAC I 231, as sung by Frank Goodwyn. Text B: Library of Congress #5588, recorded by John A. Lomax. Text C: FAC I 85, recorded by Joan O'Bryant.)

OLD PAINT

I'm rid - ing Old Paint, I'm lead - ing Old Dan, I'm off for Chey - enne ___ to do the hool - i - han. My foot's in the stir - rup, my po - ny won't ___ stand; Good - bye, Old Paint, I'm leav - ing Chey - enne, Good - bye, Old Paint, I'm leav - ing Chey - enne.

TEXT A. GOOD-BYE OLD PAINT

I'm riding Old Paint, I'm leading Old Dan,
I'm off for Cheyenne to do the hoolihan.
My foot's in the stirrup, my pony won't stand:

CHORUS:
    Good-bye, Old Paint, I'm leaving Cheyenne,
    Good-bye, Old Paint, I'm leaving Cheyenne.

Old Paint's a good pony, he paces when he can,
Good-bye, my little Annie, I'm off for Cheyenne.

Go hitch up your horses and feed 'em some hay,
And sit yourself by me as long as you'll stay.

    Good-bye, Old Paint, I'm leaving Cheyenne,
    Good-bye, Old Paint, I'm leaving Cheyenne.

My horses ain't hungry, they won't eat your hay,
My wagon is loaded and rolling away.

They feed in the coulies, they water in the draw,
Their tails are all matted, their backs are all raw.

    Good-bye, Old Paint, I'm leaving Cheyenne,
    Good-bye, Old Paint, I'm leaving Cheyenne.

Bill Jones had two daughters and a song,
One went to Denver, the other went wrong.

His wife she died in a barroom fight,
And still he sings from morning till night.

    Good-bye, Old Paint, I'm leaving Cheyenne,
    Good-bye, Old Paint, I'm leaving Cheyenne.

Oh, when I die, take my saddle from the wall,
Put it on my pony and lead him from the stall;

Tie my bones to his back, turn our faces to the West
And we'll ride the prairie that we have loved best.

    Good-bye, Old Paint, I'm leaving Cheyenne,
    Good-bye, Old Paint, I'm leaving Cheyenne.

TEXT B. OLD PAINT

Farewell, fair ladies, I'm a-leavin' Cheyenne,
Farewell, fair ladies, I'm a-leavin' Cheyenne,
Good-bye my little Doney, my pony won't stand.

CHORUS:
    Old Paint, Old Paint, I'm a-leavin' Cheyenne,
    Good-bye, Old Paint, I'm leavin' Cheyenne,
    Old Paint's a good pony and she paces when she can.

In the middle of the ocean there grows a green tree,
But I'll never prove false to the girl that loves me.

    Old Paint, Old Paint, I'm leavin' Cheyenne,
    Good-bye, Old Paint, I'm leavin' Cheyenne,
    Old Paint's a good pony and she paces when she can.

Oh, we spread down the blankets on the green, grassy ground,
And the horses and cattle were a-grazin' all round.

Old Paint, Old Paint, I'm a-leavin' Cheyenne,
Good-bye, Old Paint, I'm leavin' Cheyenne,
Old Paint's a good pony and she paces when she can.

Oh, the last time I saw her it was late in the fall,
She was riding Old Paint and a-leadin' Old Ball.

Old Paint, Old Paint, I'm a-leavin' Cheyenne,
Good-bye, Old Paint, I'm leavin' Cheyenne,
Old Paint's a good pony and she paces when she can.

Old Paint had a colt down on the Rio Grande,
And the colt couldn't pace and they named it Cheyenne.

Old Paint, Old Paint, I'm a-leavin' Cheyenne,
Good-bye, Old Paint, I'm leavin' Cheyenne,
Old Paint's a good pony and she paces when she can.

Oh, my feet's in my stirrup and my bridle's in my hand,
Good-bye, my little Doney, my pony won't stand.

TEXT C. SWEET LILY

My foot is in my stirrup, the bridle's in my hand,
I'm courting sweet Lily to marry if I can.

CHORUS:
Then Lily, sweet Lily, oh Lily, fare you well,
I'm sorry to leave you, I love you so well.

Your parents don't like me, they say that I'm too poor,
They say that I'm not worthy to enter in your door.

Some say I drink whiskey, my money is my own,
If people don't like me they can let me alone.

No. 84

The Poor Lonesome Cowboy

Self-pity in song is a cathartic for discomfitures of body or soul, of which the cowboy had his share. In this slow-rhythm, dirgelike night-herd song the cowboy's thoughts go back to endearing human relations preceding his isolation on the frontier. It is one of a very few cowboy songs that we have encountered singable to the same melody in both English and Spanish. (Melody and Text A: FAC I 515, sung by Kathy Dagel. Text B: FAC II 133, from "Songs o' th' Cowboys" corralled by "Chuck" Haas. Text C: Gordon 3756. Text D: FAC I 470, sung by Jack Humphrey.)

THE POOR LONESOME COWBOY

Text A. The Poor Lonesome Cowboy

I ain't got no father, I ain't got no father,
I ain't got no father to buy the clothes I wear.

I ain't got no mother, I ain't got no mother,
I ain't got no mother to mend the clothes I wear.

I ain't got no sister, I ain't got no sister,
I ain't got no sister to come and play with me.

I ain't got no brother, I ain't got no brother,
I ain't got no brother to drive the steers with me.

229

I ain't got no sweetheart, I ain't got no sweetheart,
I ain't got no sweetheart to sing and talk with me.

I'm a poor lonesome cowboy, I'm a poor lonesome cowboy,
I'm a poor lonesome cowboy and a long way from home.

TEXT B. POOR LONESOME COWBOY

I'm a poor lonesome cowboy,
Jest a poor lonesome cowboy;
Oh, I'm weary an' loneful,
An' a long ways from home.

CHORUS:
Oh, sunrise is a-coming,
A-coming mighty soon;
Git up and roll little dogies,
Say good morn to the moon.

Oh, I ain't got no father,
I ain't got me no father,
To borrow my tobacco
And buy me boots to wear.

I ain't got me no mother,
Oh, I ain't got no mother,
To feed me milk and honey,
And mend the pants I wear.

Oh, I ain't got no sister,
I nary had a sister,
To make me fancy doo-dads,
And go and dance with me.

I ain't got no brother,
I ain't got me no brother,
To stick burrs 'neath my saddle,
And help me tend the herd.

Oh, I ain't got no sweetheart,
I wish I had a sweetheart,
To take the gold I'm earning
And kiss me when I'm sad.

I'm jest a poor lone cowboy,
A lonesome carefree cowboy,
I ain't no kith nor kinfolk,
The prairie is my home.

TEXT C. SOY POBRE VAQUERO

Soy pobre vaquero,*
No tengo padre,
Ni hermana, ni hermano,
O no, O no, O no.

Soy pobre vaquero,
No tengo madre,
Ni hermana, ni hermano,
O no, O no, O no.

Soy pobre vaquero,
No tengo gato,
Ni perro, ni caballo,
O no, O no, O no.

Soy pobre vaquero,
No tengo dinero,
Ni tequila, ni tabaco,
O no, O no, O no.

TEXT D. SOY POBRE VAQUERO

Yo no tengo dinero†
Yo no tengo papel,
Yo no tengo dinero,
Now ain't that hell!

Yo tengo dinero,
Yo tengo papel,
Yo tengo mujer,
Now ain't that swell!

*I'm a poor cowboy / I have no father, nor sister, nor brother . . . I have no mother, nor sister, nor brother . . . I have no cat, nor dog, nor horse . . . I have no money, nor *tequila,* nor tobacco.

†I have no money . . . cigarette papers. . . . I have money . . . cigarette papers . . . a woman.

230

No. 85
Doney Gal

"Doney Gal" has the maudlin mood and gentle rhythms of the night-herding songs, a kind of lullaby to keep the cattle quiet, and a vehicle for the reflective, bitter-sweet fantasies of the puncher who must move slowly around the herd for a two- to four-hour shift while coyotes shriek their mating calls. In the song we feel the same surges of the un-guarded lyricism that was present in the dawn songs of medieval trouba-dours. Stereotyped western images and rhythms, like old lace or a Bach fugue, are interwoven to produce pulsating effects like the beating of the heart or the alternation of night and day. The song is sung in many variant forms from which we have selected three. (Melody: traditional. Text A: JL 370. Text B: Library of Congress, John A. Lomax manu-scripts. Text C: JL 369.)

DONEY GAL

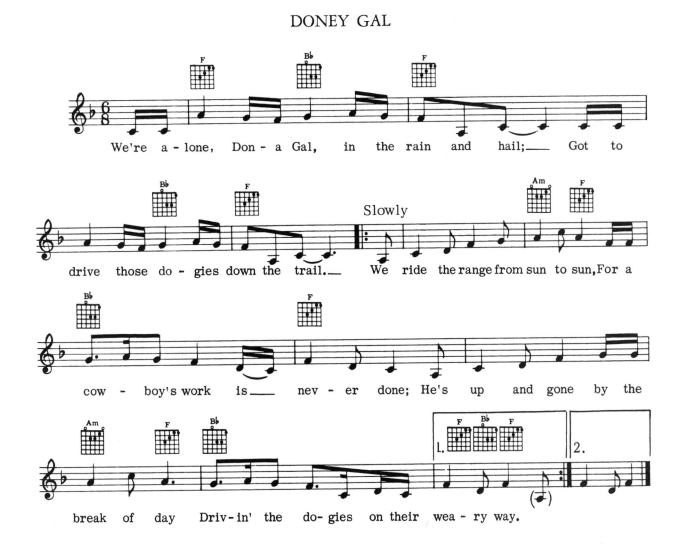

We're a- lone, Don - a Gal, in the rain and hail;___ Got to drive those do - gies down the trail.___ We ride the range from sun to sun, For a cow - boy's work is ___ nev - er done; He's up and gone by the break of day Driv-in' the do - gies on their wea - ry way.

TEXT A. DONA GAL

CHORUS:

We're alone, Dona Gal, in the rain and hail;
Got to drive these dogies down the trail.
[*This part is the old cowboy yodel. Can be sung,
hummed, or can be whistled between verses.*]

We ride the range from sun to sun
For a cowboy's work is never done;
He's up and gone by the break of day
Drivin' the dogies on their weary way.

It's rain or shine, sleet or snow,
Me and my Dona Gal on the go;
Yes, rain or shine, sleet or snow,
Me and my Dona Gal are bound to go.

A cowboy's life is a dreary thing,
For it's rope and brand and ride and sing;
Yes, day or night in the rain or hail,
He'll stay with his dogies out on the trail.

Rain or shine, sleet or snow,
Me and my Dona Gal are on the go;
We travel down that lonesome trail
Where a man and his horse seldom ever fail.

We whoop at the sun and yell through the hail,
But we drive the poor dogies on down the trail;
And we'll laugh at the storms, the sleet and snow,
When we reach the little town of San Antonio.

TEXT B. DONEY GAL

Way out West on the lonesome trail,
Where man and his rope seldom ever fail,
We ride the range from sun to sun,
For a cowboy's work is never done.

Rain or shine, sleet or snow,
I'm just a wild cowboy and bound to go.

A cowboy's life is a dreary thing,
For it's rope and brand and ride and sing;
Yes, day or night in the rain or hail,
He'll stay with his dogies out on the trail.

Rain or shine, sleet or snow,
A poor lonesome cowboy and bound to go.

We whoop at the sun and yell through the hail,
But we drive the poor dogies on up the trail;
And we'll laugh at the storms, the sleet and snow,
When we camp near the town of San Antonio.

Rain or shine, sleet or snow,
Me and my Doney Gal are on the go.

Tired and hungry, far from home,
Just a poor cowboy and bound to roam;
Starless nights, lightning's glare,
Danger and darkness everywhere.

Rain or shine, sleet or snow,
Me and my Doney Gal are on the go.

Drifting my Doney Gal round and round
The sleeping steers on the bedding ground;
Riding on night-herd all night long,
Singing them softly a cowboy song.

Rain or shine, sleet or snow,
A poor lonesome cowboy and bound to go.

Swimming the rivers across our way,
We push for the North Star day by day.
The storm cloud breaks; at furious speed
We follow the steers in their wild stampede.

Rain or shine, sleet or snow,
Me and my Doney Gal are bound to go.

Over the prairies lean and brown,
On through the wastes where there ain't no town;
Bucking the dust storms, wind and hail,
Pushing the longhorns up the trail.

    Rain or shine, sleet or snow,
    Me and my Doney Gal are bound to go.

Trailing the herd through mountains green,
We pen the dogies at Abilene.
'Round the campfires' flickering glow
We sing the songs of long ago.

    Rain or shine, sleet or snow,
    Me and my Doney Gal are bound to go.

Text C. The Lonesome Trail

Traveling up the Lonesome Trail
Where man and his horse seldom ever fail;
Rain and hail, sleet and snow,
Me and my Doney Gal a-bound to go.

Tagging along through fog and dew
Wishing for sunny days and you;
Rain and hail, sleet and snow,
Me and my Doney Gal a-bound to go.

Over the prairies lean and brown,
On through the wastes where stands no town;
Rain and hail, sleet and snow,
Me and my Doney Gal a-bound to go.

Swimming the rivers across our way
We fight on forward day end on day;
Rain and hail, sleet and snow,
Me and my Doney Gal a-bound to go.

Bedding the cattle, singing a song,
We ride the night herd all night long;
Rain and hail, sleet and snow,
Me and my Doney Gal a-bound to go.

When the storm breaks on the quiet mead
We follow the cattle on their wild stampede;
Rain and hail, sleet and snow,
Me and my Doney Gal a-bound to go.

Trailing the herd through mountains green,
We pen the cattle in Abilene;
Rain and shine, sleet and snow,
Me and my Doney Gal a-bound to go.

Round the campfire's flickering glow
We sing the songs of long ago;
Rain and shine, sleet and snow,
Me and my Doney Gal a-bound to go.

No. 86
The Cowboy's Life

Here again we have the rhythms and moods of a night-herding song. The bitterness of cowboy labor is expressed with a noble resignation and the suggestion that man's soul is fulfilled through struggle. The humorous twist about "tying on to a cross-eyed wife" may be deeper than humor: the female kind is just one more adversity that the frontiersmen must endure. The rich internal rhyme, the smooth rhythmic flow of language, suggest that singers with a mite of sophistication have had their hand and heart in the making of this song. Our melody is not of the same source as any of the three texts: still, with a little bending of the rhythms to the words, or vice versa, they can be sung thereto. (Melody: J. Frank Dobie, "More Ballads and Songs of the Frontier Folk," PTFLS [No. VII, 1928], pp. 173–174 [published by permission of the Texas Folklore Society]. Text A: PNFQ 116. Text B: FAC II 389, from the Indiana University Folklore Archives, Richard M. Dorson, director. Text C: *The Cattleman* [Fort Worth, Texas], July 1915.)

THE COWBOY'S LIFE

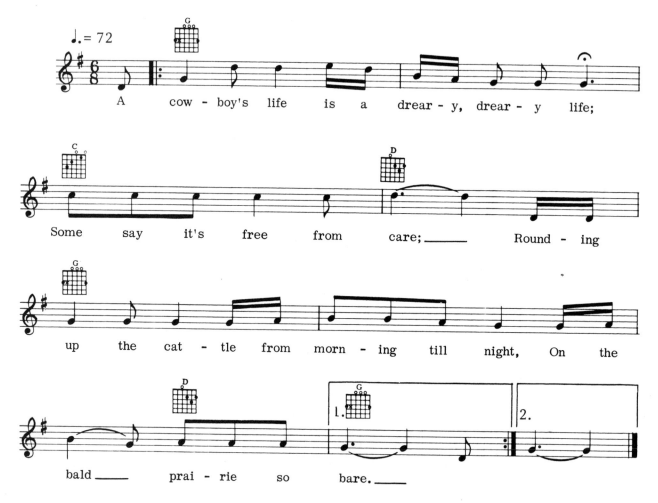

A cow-boy's life is a drear-y, drear-y life;
Some say it's free from care; ____ Round-ing
up the cat-tle from morn-ing till night, On the
bald ____ prai-rie so bare. ____

TEXT A. THE DREARY, DREARY LIFE

A cowboy's life is a dreary, dreary life;
   Some say it's free of care;
Rounding up the cattle from morning till night,
   On the bald prairie so bare.

Just about four o'clock old cook will holler out:
   "Roll out, boys; it's almost day."
Through his broken slumbers the puncher he will ask:
   "Has the short summer night passed away?"

The cowboy's life is a dreary, dreary life;
   He's driven through the heat and cold,
While the rich man's a-sleeping on his velvet couch,
   Dreaming of his silver and his gold.

When the spring work sets in, then our troubles will begin,
   The weather being fierce and cold;
We're almost froze, with the water on our clothes,
   And the cattle we can scarcely hold.

The cowboy's life is a dreary, weary one;
   He works all day to the setting of the sun,
And then his day's work is not done,
   For there's his night guard to go on.

"Saddle up! Saddle up!" the boss will holler out,
   When camped down by the Pecos stream,
Where the wolves and owls with their terrifying howls
   Will disturb us in our midnight dream.

You are speaking of your farms; you are speaking of your charms;
   You are speaking of your silver and gold;
But a cowboy's life is a dreary, weary life;
   He's driven through the heat and cold.

Once I loved to roam, but now I stay at home.
   All you punchers take my advice:
Sell your bridle and your saddle, quit your roaming and your travel,
   And tie on to a cross-eyed wife.

TEXT B. THE COWBOY'S LIFE

The bawl of a steer to a cowboy's ear
  Is music of sweetest strain;
And the whelping notes of the gray coyotes
  To him are a glad refrain.
And his jolly songs speed him along
  As he thinks of the little gal,
With golden hair who is waiting there
  At the bars of the home corral.

For a kingly crown in the noisy town
  His saddle he wouldn't change;
No life so free as the life we see
  Way out on the Yaso Range.
His eyes are bright and his heart as light
  As the smoke of his cigarette;
There's never a care for his soul to bear,
  To trouble, to make him fret.

The rapid beat of his bronco's feet
  On the sod as he speeds along,
Keeps living time to the ringing rhyme
  Of his rollicking cowboy song.
Hike it, cowboys, for the range away
  On the back of a bronc of steel,
With a careless flirt of the rawhide quirt
  And the dig of a rolled heel.

The winds may blow and the thunder growl,
  Or the breeze may safely moan;
A cowboy's life is a royal life,
  His saddle his kingly throne.
Saddle up, boys, for the work is play
  When love's in the cowboy's eyes;
When his heart is light and the clouds of white
  That swim in the summer skies.

TEXT C. BORDER BALLAD

Oh, the cowboy's life is the life of the wind
  As he clatters across the plains,
With a laugh and a yell and a hearty word,
  And a smile at the driving rains.

Oh, the cowboy's life is a life of flame
  As he clatters across the plain,
While the coyotes howl in the gathering night,
  But the dreams he sees are vain.

Oh, the cowboy's life is a life of dust,
  Though the cowboy laughs at fear,
But when he travels the last, long trail
  Is there no one to drop him a tear?

No. 87
Wee Little Piute

Images of cowboys, Indians, and the West have contributed to the formation of many American lullabies: witness this delicate song. (Melody by Casse Lyman Monson and text by Albert R. Lyman, FAC I 112.)

WEE LITTLE PIUTE

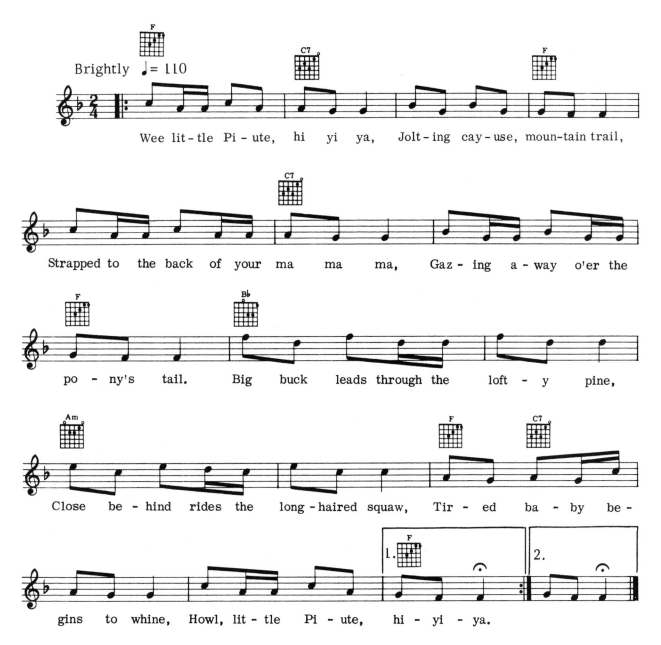

Brightly ♩ = 110

Wee lit-tle Pi-ute, hi yi ya, Jolt-ing cay-use, moun-tain trail,

Strapped to the back of your ma ma ma, Gaz-ing a-way o'er the

po-ny's tail. Big buck leads through the loft-y pine,

Close be-hind rides the long-haired squaw, Tir-ed ba-by be-

1. 2.

gins to whine, Howl, lit-tle Pi-ute, hi-yi-ya.

Wee little Piute, hi yi ya,
  Jolting cayuse, mountain trail,
Strapped to the back of your ma ma ma,
  Gazing away o'er the pony's tail.
Big buck leads through the lofty pine,
  Close behind rides the long-haired squaw,
Tired baby begins to whine,
  Howl, little Piute, hi yi ya.

Wee little Piute, hi yi ya,
  Buckskin cover, soft, dry bark,
Snug in the wickiup, hi yi ya,
  Night on the mountain, voices hark.
Big owl hoots from the limb above,
  Coyotes howl in the rocky draw,
Kind hands reaching, a mother's love,
  Sleep, little Piute, hi yi ya.

No. 88
Blue Mountain

Many cowboys drifted from ranch to ranch through a dozen western states. Owning nothing except a cow pony, saddle, and "hot roll," they rode the "chuck line"—begged, that is—from ranch to ranch, staying out their welcome at each before moving on. This song expresses a subtle balance between moods of violence and sentimentality that fits the cowboy image, and rhythms that fit the movements of a horse paced for a long day's trek. Judge F. W. Keller wrote it in Monticello, Utah. (Melody and text: FAC I 608, sung by Loyal Bailey [reproduced by permission of Judge F. W. Keller].)

BLUE MOUNTAIN

My home it was in Texas,
My past you must not know;
I seek a refuge from the law
Where the sage and piñon grow.

Blue Mountain, you're azure deep,
Blue Mountain with sides so steep,
Blue Mountain with horse head on your side,
You have won my love to keep.

For the brand "LC" I ride,
And the sleeper calves on the side,
I'll own the "Hip-Side-and-Shoulder" when I grow older,
Zapitaro, don't tan my hide!

I chum with Latigo Gordon,
I drink at the Blue Goose saloon,
I dance at night with the Mormon girls,
And ride home beneath the moon.

I trade at Mons' store
With bullet holes in the door;
His calico treasure my horse can measure
When I'm drunk and feeling sore.

Yarn Gallus with shortened lope
Doc Few-Clothes without any soap,
In the little green valley have made their sally,
And for Slicks there's still some hope.

In the summer time it's fine,
In the winter the wind doth whine,
But say, dear brother, if you want a mother,
There's Ev on the old chuck line.

No. 89
Cowboy's Home Sweet Home

Often the cowboy is presented as an eternal wanderer whose past will not bear inquiry: an impetuous crime has driven him West and remorse haunts him unto death. The fact that one cannot "go back" is, of course, of the nature of life itself and a source of anguish to all, even one whose conscience is not overburdened. "Cowboy's Home Sweet Home" dramatizes this kernel of existential truth like a Sartre play. We offer two texts: one that is fresh from the ranges, the other polished by artists of the '30's. (Melody and Text A: Victor 40156, Arthur Miles. Text B: Gordon 1189.)

COWBOY'S HOME SWEET HOME

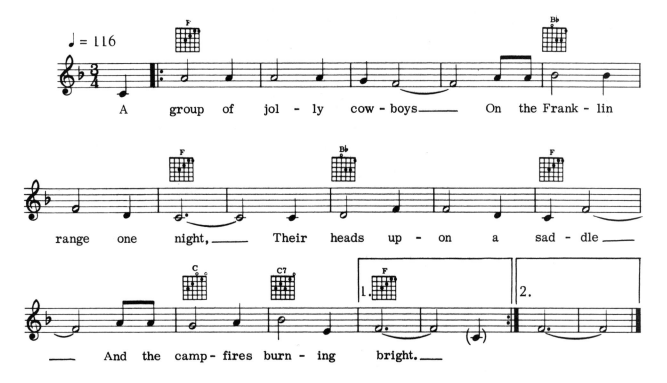

♩ = 116

A group of jol - ly cow - boys____ On the Frank - lin range one night,____ Their heads up - on a sad - dle____ ____ And the camp - fires burn - ing bright.____

TEXT A. THE LONELY COWBOY

A group of jolly cowboys
  On the Franklin range one night,
Their heads upon a saddle
  And the campfires burning bright.

Some were telling stories,
  And some were singing songs,
And some were smoking cigarettes
  While the hours rolled along.

At once they began their talking
  Of distant friends so dear.
A boy raised his head from his saddle
  And brushed away a tear.

This boy was tall and handsome
  And his face showed a lack of good cheer,
His eyes were of a heavenly blue
  And he had light wavy hair.

We asked him why he left his home,
  It being so dear to him.
He raised his head from his saddle,
  With tears his eyes grew dim.

As he raised his head from his saddle,
  And he gives a rub right o'er,
Said, "Boys, I'll tell you the reason why
  I stay at home no more.

"I fell in love with the neighbor's girl,
  Her cheeks was fair and white.
Another fellow loved this girl
  And it ended in a fight.

"This fellow's name was Tommy Smith
  And we had been great chums,
We'd shared each other's troubles, boys,
  We'd shared each other's fun.

"It almost makes me shudder
  To think of that sad night!
When Tom and I was quarrelling
  I stuck him with my knife.

"I fell on my knees beside him
  And tried to stop the blood
That flowed down so gently
  It was like a crimson flood.

"I can almost hear Tommy's voice
  As the boys all gathered around,
Saying, 'Bob, old boy, you'll remember
  When I am under the ground.'

"Now boys, you know the reason why
  That I'm compelled to roam,
And why I am so far away
  From dear old home sweet home."

Text B. Cowboy's Home Sweet Home

We were lying on the prairie
  At Frank Slaughter's ranch one night,
With our heads on our saddles
  And fires were burning bright.

While some were telling stories
  And some were singing songs,
And others were idly smoking
  As the hours rolled along.

At last we fell to talking
  Of our distant friends so dear;
A boy raised his head from his saddle
  And brushed away a tear.

We asked him why he left his home
  If it was so dear to him;
He gazed to the ground for a moment
  And his eyes with tears grew dim.

He raised his head from his saddle
  And looked that rough crowd o'er,
He says, "Boys, I'll tell you the reason why
  I left old Kansas' shore.

"I fell in love with a beautiful girl
  Whose cheeks were soft and bright,
Another fellow loved her too
  And it ended in a fight.

"The other fellow's name was Tom Smith,
  We'd been friends since boys,
We always shared each other alike
  In all our trials and joys.

"It always makes me shudder
  To think of that sad night
When Tom and I first quarreled,
  And I stuck him with my knife.

"I fell to the ground beside him
  And tried to stop the blood
That was so swiftly spouting
  From his side in a crimson flood.

"I can hear Tom's voice as in a dream
  As he fell to the ground and said,
'Oh, Bob, old boy, you'll be sorry
  When you see me lying dead!'

"Now, boys, you know the reason why
  I am compelled to roam;
I am a sinner in the deepest of sin,
  Far away from home sweet home.

"Home, home sweet home, boys,
  There's no place like home.
I'd give my saddle and pony
  For a glimpse of home sweet home."

No. 90
Curtains of Night

"Curtains of Night" is one of the great love songs of a century ago. Its majestic first stanza survives in oral tradition as a favorite among night-herd songs. (Melody: Victor 21289, Teneva Ramblers. Text: *The Family Guide Songster* [c. 1875], Vol. II, p. 8.)

CURTAINS OF NIGHT

When the cur-tains of night are pinned back by the stars And the beau-ti-ful

moon sweeps the skies,___ And the dew-drops of heav-en are kiss- ing the

rose, It is then that my mem- o - ry flies,___ As___ if on the

wings of some beau- ti -ful dove, In ___ haste with the mes-sage it

bears, ___ To___ bring you a kiss of af - fec-tion and say, "I re-

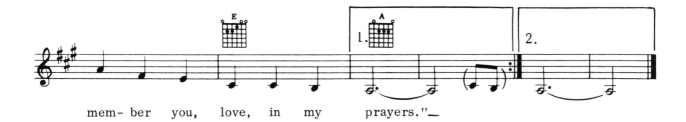

mem- ber   you,   love,   in   my   prayers."—

When the curtains of night are pinned back by the stars
    And the beautiful moon sweeps the skies,
And the dewdrops of heaven are kissing the rose,
    It is then that my memory flies,
As if on the wings of some beautiful dove,
    In haste with the message it bears,
To bring you a kiss of affection and say—
    "I remember you, love, in my prayers."

CHORUS:
    Go where you will, on land or at sea,
        I'll share all your sorrows and cares;
    And at night when I kneel by my bedside to pray,
        I'll remember you, love, in my prayers.

I have loved you too fondly to ever forget
    The love you have spoken for me;
The kiss of affection still worn on my lips
    When you told me how true you would be.
I know not if fortune be fickle or friend
    Or if time or your memory wear,
I know that I love you wherever you roam,
    And remember you, love, in my prayers.

When heavenly angels are guarding the good,
    As God has ordained them to do,
In answer to prayers I have offered to Him,
    I know there is one watching you.
And may its bright spirit be with you through life
    To guide you up heaven's bright stairs,
And meet with one who has loved you so true
    And remembers you, love, in her prayers.

Part Eleven

Outlaws

No. 91
Bring Him Back Dead or Alive

The bitter irony of involuntary fratricide is an appropriate topic for the balladry of violence on the frontier. The bandit's quick offense when he knows himself cornered culminates with the all-too-late discovery that he has killed his own brother. As with the biblical Cain, a brother's curse will haunt him as long as they allow him to live. Melodic structure is not well stabilized, as if the song were still in the process of creation. We have encountered it only once, sung by Paul Kelso at Denton, Texas, in 1959 (FAC I 66).

BRING HIM BACK DEAD OR ALIVE

Gan-non killed a man in Den-ton in the year of for-ty-five, Bring him back dead or a-live!___ And the sher-iff swore an oath on-ly one would sur-vive, He'd bring him back dead or a-live. Gan-non he was run-ning, he head-ed for Gaines-ville, Bring him back dead or a-live! Sher-iff swore to get him, "By God I will! I'll bring him back dead or a-live!"___ Gan-non on the cor-ner with a

dead or a - live!__ "If you will hang me quick I'll es - cape my broth-er's

voice!" Bring him back dead or a - live,__ Bring him back

rit. - - - - - -

dead or a - live,__ Bring him back dead or a - live! __

Gannon killed a man in Denton in the year of forty-five,
  Bring him back dead or alive!
And the sheriff swore an oath only one would survive,
  He'd bring him back dead or alive.

Gannon he was running, he headed for Gainesville,
  Bring him back dead or alive!
Sheriff swore to get him, "By God I will!
  I'll bring him back dead or alive!"

Gannon on the corner with a wild and feverish mind,
  Bring him back dead or alive!
He knew that the sheriff was not far behind,
  And he'd bring him back dead or alive,
  Bring him back dead or alive!

The sheriff cornered and he called him,
  And Gannon shot him down in the streets,
  Bring him back dead or alive!
And there he saw his brother, he was lying at his feet,
  Bring him back dead or alive,
  Bring him back dead or alive, great God!
  Bring him back dead or alive!

"You can have my guns and horse and I will surrender, boys."
  Bring him back dead or alive!
"If you will hang me quick I'll escape my brother's voice!"
  Bring him back dead or alive,
  Bring him back dead or alive,
  Bring him back dead or alive!

No. 92

I've Been All Around This World

One man against the whole of society is always a bitter pill. Too many of this breed haunted the frontier. If we are to judge by the evocation in this ballad of mother, father, and little sister, the badman was a softie at heart. It is not love and hate that are opposites, but rather love and indifference. (Melody and text: FAC I 368, collected by Bob Duncan.)

I'VE BEEN ALL AROUND THIS WORLD

Way up on the O - sage moun - tain where the wind blows chill - y and cold, Way up on the O - sage moun - tain where the wind blows chill- y and cold, Where I hid out last win - ter, starved and ver - y near - ly froze; Lord knows I've been all_____ a - round this world.

Way up on the Osage mountain where the wind blows chilly and cold,
Way up on the Osage mountain where the wind blows chilly and cold,
Where I hid out last winter, starved and very nearly froze;
   Lord knows, I've been all around this world.

Way up on the Osage mountains, it's there I made my stand,
Way up on the Osage mountains, it's there I made my stand,
With a Winchester on my saddle and a six-shooter in each hand.
   Lord knows, I've been all around this world.

They arrested me on Broadway Street and there they made me stand,
They arrested me on Broadway Street and there they made me stand,
With a six-shooter in my face and shackles on my hands.
   Lord knows, I've been all around this world.

Well, I took off my overcoat and I hung it on my wall,
Well, I took off my overcoat and I hung it on my wall,
Whipped out two six-shooters, God knows I made 'em bawl.
   Lord knows, I've been all around this world.

Oh hang me, oh hang me, oh hang me good and high,
Oh hang me, oh hang me, oh hang me good and high,
And telegraph to mother to come and see me die.
   Lord knows, I've been all around this world.

There's mother and father, little sister she counts three,
There's mother and father, little sister she counts three,
To follow down to the gallows and see the last of me.
   Lord knows, I've been all around this world.

The railroad is finished, the cars is on the track,
The railroad is finished and the cars is on the track,
Just telegraph to mother, her money will bring me back.
   Lord knows, I've been all around this world.

No. 93

Jesse James

Jesse James is the most sung of all the outlaws. A dozen different ballads exalt him as an American Robin Hood—bold, charitable, defiant of the law as a symbol of man's oppression, victim of a sneaking turncoat. There are hundreds of texts and innumerable parodies. A research project is needed to assemble the popular songs and poems about Jesse James, to collate texts, to unravel their complex interrelationships, to compare their content with Jesse's biography, and finally to make an assessment of the impact that the James epic has had on "western" folk. Here we are giving five of the best known Jesse James ballads. Text D is unique in that, instead of praising the bandit, it extracts a moral precept from his deviant career. (Melody A: King 847, Grandpa Jones. Text A: Gordon 433. Text B: Library of Congress, Woody Guthrie Manuscripts, p. 200. Melody C: FAC I 479, collected by Edith Fowke from Tom Powell, Napanee, Ontario, Canada. Text C: Gordon 3217. Melody D: Montgomery-Ward 4443, The Vagabonds. Text D: Hendren 308. Melody and Text E: commercial recording, Frank Luther.)

JESSE JAMES

♩ = 100

Jes - se James was a lad that killed man - y a man, He robbed the Dan - ville train. But that dirt - y lit - tle cow - ard that shot Mr. How - ard Has laid poor Jes - se in his grave. Poor

CHORUS

Jes - se had a wife to mourn for his life, Three child - ren, they were brave, But the dirt - y lit - tle cow - ard that shot Mr. How - ard Has

1. laid poor___ Jes - se in his grave. 2.

TEXT A. JESSE JAMES

Jesse James was a lad that killed many a man,
   He robbed the Danville train.
But that dirty little coward that shot Mr. Howard
   Has laid poor Jesse in his grave.

Poor Jesse had a wife to mourn for his life,
   Three children, they were brave,
But the dirty little coward that shot Mr. Howard
   Has laid poor Jesse in his grave.

It was Robert Ford, that dirty little coward,
   I wonder how he did feel,
For he ate of Jesse's bread, and he slept in Jesse's bed,
   Then he laid poor Jesse in his grave.

Jesse was a man, a friend to the poor,
   He never would see a man suffer pain;
And with his brother Frank, he robbed the Chicago bank,
   And stopped the Glendale train.

It was his brother Frank that robbed the Gallatin bank,
   And carried the money from the town;
It was in this very place that they had a little race,
   For they shot Captain Sheets to the ground.

They went to the crossing, not very far from there,
   And there they did the same;
With the agent on his knees, he delivered up the keys
   To the outlaws, Frank and Jesse James.

It was Wednesday night, the moon was shining bright,
   They robbed the Glendale train.
The people they did say, for many miles away
   It was robbed by Frank and Jesse James.

It was Saturday night, Jesse was at home,
   Talking with his family brave.
Robert Ford came along like a thief in the night
   And laid poor Jesse in his grave.

The people held their breath when they heard of Jesse's death,
   And wondered how he came to die;
It was one of the gang called little Robert Ford,
   He shot poor Jesse on the sly.

Jesse went to his rest with hand on his breast;
   The devil will be upon his knee.
He was born one day in the County of Clay
   And came from a solitary race.

This song was made by Billy Gashade
   As soon as the news did arrive.
He said there was no man, with the law in his hand,
   Who could take Jesse James while alive.

TEXT B. JESSE JAMES AND HIS BOYS

Jesse James and his boys rode the Dodge City trail,
   They held up the midnight southern mail.
Every sheriff knew them well on that Dodge City trail,
   But they could not keep Jesse in a jail.

Jesse James and his boys stopped the Coffeyville Express
   They caught the agent at the station door,
With the agent on his knees he delivered up the keys
   To the muzzle of Jesse's forty-four.

The outlaw Jesse James would never rob the poor
   Or frighten a mother with a child,
But he took from the rich and delivered to the poor
   And they shot poor Jesse on the sly.

It was Mr. Robert Ford, a man that was a coward,
   He paid Jesse James a friendly call,
Robert Ford, it's a fact, shot Jesse in the back
   While Jesse hung a picture on the wall.

He posed as Jesse's friend and brought him to his end,
   And the people true and brave,
They say Robert Ford was a dirty little coward
   For he laid Jesse James in his grave.

Now Jesse had a wife who was proud of her life,
   Three children, they were brave,
But that dirty little coward you call Robert Ford
   Has laid poor Jesse in his grave.

Lyrics under the music staff:

Liv-ing in Mis-sour-i was a bad bold man, He was known— from Se-at-tle down to Birm-ing-ham, From Bos-ton, Mas-sa-chu-setts, right a-cross the states,— Ne- vad-a, Col-o-rad-o, and the Gold-en Gates.

Text and Melody C. Jesse James

Living in Missouri was a bad bold man,
He was known from Seattle down to Birmingham,
From Boston, Massachusetts, right across the states,
Nevada, Colorado, and the Golden Gates.

chorus:
       Some people will forget a lot of famous names,
       But every nook and corner knows of Jesse James.
       We used to read about him in our homes at night,
       When the wind blew down the chimney we would shake with fright.

Jesse said, "Boys, some coin we need,"
Polished up his rifle, got his trusty steed,
Then he galloped over to his brother Frank,
And said, "We're going to make a raid on the Pittsfield bank."

Next morning they arrived in town at ten o'clock;
The cashier at the bank got an awful shock,
While Jesse had him covered with his "forty-four"
His pals took out a half million "bones" or more.

257

Jesse in his cabin one day all alone,
His wife had left him there to straighten up the home—
Scrubbing out the kitchen when the door bell rang,
In walked Ford, a member of the outlaw gang.

A picture of Jesse's wife was hanging on the wall.
Jesse says to Ford, "Tonight we make a haul,
The western mail will run through town,"
Went to get his rifle, knocked the picture down.

Jesse says to Ford, "I'll hang it up again."
So he stepped and stood upon a chair,
Then Ford aimed his forty-four at Jesse's head,
And the news went round the country that Jesse James was dead.

Now we know that Jesse never would have lost his life
If it hadn't been for the picture of his absent wife.
Next week on his tombstone the legend ran,
"If you want to be a bandit, stay a single man."

'Twas way down in Mis-sour-i, there lived a shoot-in'
man, Tall and dark and slen-der, he'd ride out with his
band, Their guns all bright-ly pol-ished, and their
hors-es all well groomed, They had in mind a
bank, and they would rob it soon.

Text and Melody D. The Death of Jesse James

'Twas way down in Missouri, there lived a shootin' man,
Tall and dark and slender, he'd ride out with his band,
Their guns all brightly polished, and their horses all well groomed,
They had in mind a bank, and they would rob it soon.

The folks they all were sleeping when the robbers they did ride
Into that silent village, where the robbers they did hide.
The sheriff unsuspecting was guarding money there,
When Jesse James, the bandit, came to that village fair.

Next morning when they found him, the sheriff he was dead,
The doctor looked him over, found a bullet in his head.
They said it was a bullet from the gun of Jesse James,
He killed our poor Mike Murphy, the sheriff that was slain.

Though Jesse James, the bandit, was well known in this town,
He married a girl who loved him, and then he drug her down.
The people they were sorry to see her in this plight,
They knew that Jesse the robber would come back some night.

One day when Jesse was hanging a picture on the wall,
Then Ford, the dirty coward, caused poor Jesse to fall,
With a bullet from his pistol, though he was Jesse's friend.
Now folks you've heard the story of a bandit's dreadful end.

Though Jesse was just a roamer o'er valley, hill and plain,
He found that with his pistol there was nothing to be gained.
So now, good folks, take warning, wherever your life you spend,
Be honest, true, and faithful and miss this tragic end.

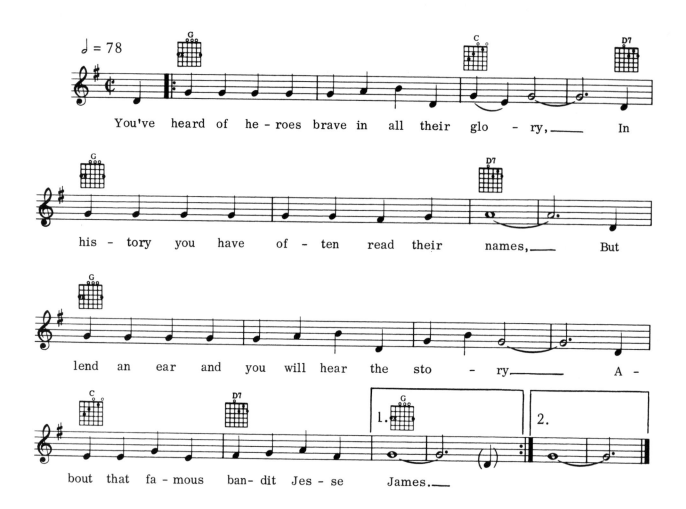

You've heard of he-roes brave in all their glo-ry,___ In his-tory you have of-ten read their names,___ But lend an ear and you will hear the sto-ry___ A-bout that fa-mous ban-dit Jes-se James.___

Text and Melody E. Jesse James

You've heard of heroes brave in all their glory,
  In history you have often read their names,
But lend an ear and you will hear the story
  About that famous bandit Jesse James.

When just a lad he joined the bad guerrillas
  And there he learned to play their wicked games,
With brother Frank and other famous killers
  Began the bold career of Jesse James.

He roamed all over Kansas and Missouri,
  At robbing banks he was a clever hand,
He never had to face a trial by jury
  And soon became the leader of his band.

He even roamed way down in old Kentucky,
  They claim he first invented robbing trains;
His life was short, he sure was mighty lucky
  They never got the goods on Jesse James.

The Pinkertons were always out to catch him,
  But could they do it? No! Not on your life!
It took a simple little gal to catch him,
  And later on he took her for his wife.

Now after years of hanging around with outlaws
  He met up with a gent named Robert Ford.
This traitor, though he didn't care about the laws,
  He knew on Jesse's head was a reward.

He walked into the house one early morning
  While Jesse was dustin' pictures in their frames,
He shot him in the back without a warning,
  And that's the end of Mr. Jesse James.

So good folks, what's the use of us pretending,
  It doesn't pay to play those crooked games.
Beware of any such unhappy ending,
  Just profit by the death of Jesse James.

No. 94

Cole Younger

This is a first-person account of a life of lawlessness on the frontier: train, bank, and other robberies committed by the Younger and the James brothers. The thread of remorse that runs through the song throws some light upon frontier character: trains and banks, being symbols of law and order, do not count unless you are caught. But to take the ready cash from a lone California miner is to stoop about as low as is possible. (Melody and text: FAC I 429, reproduced with permission of the collector, Dean Emeritus John Donald Robb of the University of New Mexico.)

COLE YOUNGER

I am a high-way ban-dit man, Cole Young-er is my name, Though many a dep-re-da-tion has brought my life to shame. A-rob-bing of the North-field bank was a shame I'll nev-er de-ny, I'm doomed a poor pris-on-er, in the Still-wa-ter Jail I lie.

I am a highway bandit man, Cole Younger is my name,
Though many a depredation has brought my life to shame.
A-robbing of the Northfield bank was a shame I'll never deny;
I'm doomed a poor prisoner, in the Stillwater Jail I lie.

'Tis one of the high, bold robberies the truth to you I'll tell,
A Californee miner whose fate to us befell,
Saying, "Hand your money over and make no long delay,"
A trick that I'll be sorry of until my dying day.

Then we left good old Texas, that good old Lone Star State,
Out on Nebraskee prairies the James boys we did meet.
With knives, guns, and revolvers we all sat down to play
A good old game of poker to pass the time away.

Out on Nebraskee prairies the Denver came along,
Says I to Bob, "Let's rob her as she goes rolling on."
Killed the engineer and fireman, conductor 'scaped alive;
Their bodies now lie moulding beneath Nebraska's skies.

We saddled up our horses and northward we did go
To the God forsaken country called Minnesot-ee-oh.
I had my eye on the Northfield bank when brother Bob did say,
"Cole, if you undertake that job, you'll always curse the day."

We stationed out our pickets and up to the bank did go,
It was there upon the counter I struck my fatal blow,
Saying, "Hand your money over and make no long delay
For we're the noted Younger boys, and 'low no time to stay."

The cashier, being a true Westfield, refused our noble band;
It was Jesse James that pulled the trigger that killed that faithful man.
In vain we searched for the money drawers while the battle raged outside,
Until we saw our safety was a quick and desperate ride.

It was Charlie pitched off by his post, Doc Wheeler drew his gun;
He shot poor Charlie through the heart, who cried, "My God, I'm done."
Again Doc Wheeler drew his gun, results of which you'll see,
Well, Miller he fell from his horse in mortal agony.

"Come boys, and ride for life and death; there's hundreds on our trail!"
The Younger boys were doomed to fate and landed right in jail,
They've taken us to the Stillwater Jail to worry our lives away,
The James boys they can tell the tale of that eventful day.

No. 95
Sam Bass

The style of this song, which has relatively little variation from text to text, is that of an author close to the historical facts. The essentials of Sam's biography are told with journalistic verve, sympathy for the bandits, and open censure for the turncoat whose betrayal led to Sam's demise. (Melody and text: FAC I 197, reproduced with permission of the collector, Dean Emeritus John Donald Robb of the University of New Mexico.)

SAM BASS

Sam Bass was born in In-di-a-na,— it was his na-tive home,— And at the age of sev-en-teen young Sam be-gan to roam.— Sam first came to Tex-as— a cow-boy to be;— A kind-er heart-ed fel-low you sel-dom ev-er see.—

Sam Bass was born in Indiana, it was his native home,
And at the age of seventeen young Sam began to roam.
Sam first came to Texas a cowboy to be,
A kinder-hearted fellow you seldom ever see.

Sam used to deal in race stock, one called the Denton mare,
He matched her in scrub races and took her to the fair.
Sam used to coin the money and spent it rather free,
He always drank good whiskey wherever he might be.

Sam left the Collins' ranch in the early month of May
With a herd of Texas cattle the Black Hills to see,
Sold out at Custer City and then got on a spree,
And a tougher set of cowboys you seldom ever see.

On their way back to Texas they robbed the U. P. train,
They then split up in couples and started out again.
Joe Collins and his partner was over-taken soon,
With all their hard-earned money they had to meet their doom.

Sam made it back to Texas all right side up with care,
Rode into the town of Denton with all his friends to share.
Sam's life was short in Texas, three robberies he did do,
He robbed all the passengers, the mail and express too.

Sam had four bold companions, four bold and daring lads,
Frank Jackson, Henry Underwood, Joe Collins, and Old Dad;
Four bold and daring cowboys the rangers never knew,
They whipped the Texas Rangers and ran the boys in blue.

Sam had another companion called Arkansas for short,
Was shot by a Texas Ranger by the name of Thompson Floyd.
Old Tom was a big six-footer and thinks he's mighty fly,
But I can tell you like his racket, he's a dead beat on the sly.

Jim Murphy was arrested and then released on bail,
He jumped his bond at Tyler and took the trail for Terrell.
But Major Barnes had posted him and that was all a stall,
It was a plan to capture Sam before the coming fall.

Sam met his fate at Round Rock July the twenty-first,
They pierced poor Sam with rifle balls and emptied out his purse.
Sam is now a corpse and six feet under clay
And Jackson's on the border still trying to get away.

Jim had borrowed Sam's good gold and didn't want to pay,
The only way he saw to win was to give poor Sam away.
He sold out Sam and Barnes and left their friends to mourn,
And what a scorchin' Jim will get when Gabriel toots the horn.

And so he sold out Sam and Barnes and left their friends to mourn,
And what a scorchin' Jim will get when Gabriel blows his horn.
Perhaps he's got to heaven, there's none of us can say,
But if I'm right in my surmise he's gone the other way.

No. 96

Billy the Kid

Billy was one of the most notorious of the western outlaws, and the balladry about him may yet make an epic poem. We have abandoned the classic six-stanza text in favor of a longer and more realistic variant which comes to us as learned in 1927 by a noted silent-movie stunt man, Chuck Haas, from the lips of Dodge City's notorious sheriff, Wyatt Earp.

An even longer Billy the Kid ballad, authored by Henry Herbert Knibbs, is singable to the same tune. We also give a realistic four-stanza piece about the Kid for which we have no music. Texts of a dozen or so other "Kid" ballads are also available, though space will not permit their inclusion here. (Melody: commercial recording, Pat Patterson. Text A: FAC II 133, from "Songs o' th' Cowboys" corraled by "Chuck" Haas. Text B: Henry Herbert Knibbs, *Songs of the Lost Frontier* [Boston and New York: Houghton Mifflin Company, 1930], pp. 34–37. Text C: Hendren 695.)

BILLY THE KID

I'll sing you a true song of Bil - ly the Kid, And tell of the des - per - ate deeds that he did, Out here in the West, boys, in New Mex - i - co, When a man's_ best friend was his old for - ty four.

TEXT A. BILLY THE KID

I'll sing you a true song of Billy the Kid,
And tell of the desperate deeds that he did,
Out here in the West, boys, in New Mexico,
When a man's best friend was his old Forty-four.

When Billy the Kid was a very young lad,
In Old Silver City, he went to the bad;
At twelve years of age the Kid killed his first man,
Then blazed a wide trail with a gun in each hand.

Fair Mexican maidens played soft on guitars
And sang of *Billito* their king 'neath the stars;
He was a brave lover, and proud of his fame,
And no man could stand 'gainst the Kid's deadly aim.

Now Billy ranged wide, and his killings were vile;
He shot fast, and first, when his blood got a-rile,
And, 'fore his young manhood did reach its sad end,
His six-guns held notches for twenty-one men.

Then Gov'ner Lew Wallace sent word to the Kid
To ride in and talk, for a pardon to bid:
But Billy said: "I ain't a-feered of the law;
Thar's no man a-living can beat me to the draw!"

The Gov'ner then sent for another fast man:
Pat Garrett, the Sheriff, and told of a plan
To catch Billy napping at his gal's; so he said:
"We'll bring him to Justice: alive or plumb dead!"

'Twas on that same night, into town Billy rid,
And said: "*Mis amigos*, all hark to the Kid!
There's twenty-one men I have put bullets through
And Sheriff Pat Garrett must make twenty-two!"

Now this is how Billy the Kid met his fate:
The bright moon was shining, the hour was late;
To Pete Maxwell's place Billy went in all pride,
Not knowing the dark hid the Sheriff inside.

As Billy show'd plain in the moon-lighted door,
He fell in his tracks, and lay dead on the floor;
Shot down by Pat Garrett, who once was his friend,
Young Billy, the Outlaw, and his life did end!

There's many a boy with a fine face and air
That starts in his life with the chances all fair;
But, like young *Billito*, he wanders astray
And departs his life in the same hardful way!

TEXT B. THE BALLAD OF BILLY THE KID

No man in the West ever won such renown
As young Billy Bonney of Santa Fe town,
And of all the wild outlaws that met a bad end,
None so quick with a pistol or true to a friend.

It was in Silver City his first trouble came,
A man called Billy's mother a very foul name;
Billy swore to get even, his chance it came soon,
When he stabbed that young man in Joe Dyer's saloon.

He kissed his poor mother and fled from the scene,
A bold desperado and not yet fifteen;
He hid in a sheep-camp but short was his stay,
For he stole an old pony and rode far away.

At monte and faro he next took a hand,
And lived in Tucson on the fat of the land;
But the game was too easy, the life was too slow,
So he drifted alone into Old Mexico.

It was not very long before Billy came back,
With a notch in his gun and some gold in a sack;
He struck for the Pecos his comrades to see,
And they all rode to Lincoln and went on a spree.

There he met his friend Tunstall and hired as a hand
To fight with the braves of the Jingle-bob brand;
Then Tunstall was murdered and left in his gore;
To avenge that foul murder Young Billy he swore.

First Morton and Baker he swiftly did kill,
Then he slaughtered Bill Roberts at Blazer's sawmill;
Sheriff Brady and Hindman in Lincoln he slew,
Then he rode to John Chisum's along with his crew.

There he stood off a posse and drove them away.
In McSween's house in Lincoln he made his next play;
Surrounded he fought till the house was burned down,
But he dashed through the flames and escaped from the town.

Young Billy rode north and Young Billy rode south,
He plundered and killed with a smile on his mouth,
But he always came back to Fort Sumner again
For his Mexican sweetheart was living there then.

His trackers were many, they followed him fast,
In Arroyo Tiván he was captured at last;
He was taken to Lincoln and put under guard,
And sentenced to hang in the old court-house yard.

J. Bell and Bob Ollinger watched day and night,
Young Billy gave Ollinger scarcely a glance,
But sat very still and awaited his chance.

One day he played cards with J. Bell in the room,
Who had no idea how close was his doom;
Billy slipped off a handcuff, hit Bell on the head,
Then he snatched for the pistol and shot him down dead.

Bob Ollinger heard and he ran to the spot
To see what had happened and who had been shot;
Young Billy looked down from a window and fired,
Bob Ollinger sank to the ground and expired.

Then Young Billy escaped on a horse that was near,
As he rode forth from Lincoln he let out a cheer;
Though his foes they were many he feared not a one,
So long as a cartridge remained in his gun.

But his comrades were dead or had fled from the land,
It was up to Young Billy to play a lone hand;
And Sheriff Pat Garrett he searched far and wide,
Never thinking the Kid in Fort Sumner would hide.

But when Garrett heard Billy was hiding in town,
He went to Pete Maxwell's when the sun had gone down;
The door was wide open, the night it was hot,
So Pat Garrett walked in and sat down by Pete's cot.

Young Billy had gone for to cut him some meat,
No hat on his head and no boots on his feet;
When he saw two strange men on the porch in the gloom,
He pulled his gun quick and backed into the room.

Billy said, "Who is that?" and he spoke Maxwell's name,
Then from Pat Garrett's pistol the answer it came—
The swift, cruel bullet went true to its mark,
And Young Billy fell dead on the floor in the dark.

So Young Billy Bonney he came to his end,
Shot down by Pat Garrett who once was his friend;
Though for coolness and courage both gunmen ranked high,
It was Fate that decided Young Billy should die.

Each year of his life was a notch in his gun,
For in twenty-one years he had slain twenty-one.
His grave is unmarked and by desert sands hid,
And so ends the true story of Billy the Kid.

TEXT C. BILLY THE KID

Billy was a bad man
  And carried a big gun.
He was always after greasers
  And kept 'em on the run.

He shot one every morning
  For to make his morning meal.
And let a white man sass him
  He was sure to feel his steel.

He kept folks in hot water,
  And he stole from many a stage,
And when he was full of liquor
  He was always in a rage.

But one day he met a man
  Who was a whole lot badder.
And now he's dead and we
  Ain't none the sadder.

No. 97
Queen of the Desperadoes

This rough-hewn ballad has a central theme that hearkens back to the thirteenth century when woman was indeed queen, and the highest ideal of an errant knight was but to do her bidding. Belle Starr was certainly no Lady Gwendolyn! But frontiersmen behaved as though she were. What a pity that no melody has been found! Perhaps a reader can help us? (Text A: FAC II 133, from "Songs o' th' Cowboys" corralled by "Chuck" Haas. Text B: PNFQ 376.)

QUEEN OF THE DESPERADOES

Text A

She was a two-gun woman, Belle Shirley was her name,
'Twas in the State of Texas Belle won undying fame.

Jim Reed was her first lover, Belle eloped one night with him,
Her pap chased them crost Texas to stage a fight with Jim.

The lovers lived all happy till Jim got in a tight,
And drilled plum through by Morris and cashed-in the same night!

When Jim from her was taken, Belle took the wildsome trail,
And starts a life of rambling that sure was bound to fail.

I was a poor young cowboy, but money was too slow,
So I joined Belle's wild riders in north New Mexico.

We raided the Panhandle, then holed-up in the Strip.
When we ran out of money we'd make another trip!

We knew no Law nor order, 'cept pretty Belle's command,
As we rode free and reckless acrost that wildsome land.

Then Belle fell sorely wounded, 'twas traitor Watson's cause!
Though, like us, he was guilty of breaking Texas' laws.

But Belle was soon recovered, and I rode by her side . . .
The last of all her riders! By my hand Watson died!

Then Henry Starr Belle married and moved to Younger's Bend
On the Canadian River . . . She lived there till the end!

TEXT B

She was a two-gun woman:
  Miss Belle Shirley was her name.
The Lone Star State of Texas
  Was where she won her fame.

CHORUS:

  Oh, I was a puncher in an old slouch hat,
  But I couldn't make any money at that;
  So I said: "Belle, let me join your show,
  An' if it gets too hot, I'll ride to Old Mexico,
  I'll ride to Old Mexico-o-o."

Jim Reed was her first lover,
  And she eloped with him one night,
Whilst her dad chases her clear across Texas,
  Trying to stage a fight.

When Jim Reed was drilled by Morris
  Belle, she took to the trail,
And started a life of wandering
  That everyone knew would fail.

When Belle, she married Mr. Starr,
  She moved to Younger's Bend
And lived on Canadian River
  Until the very end.

Belle fell from under her steed one day;
  The traitor Watson was the cause;
But both of them was guilty, like the rest of us,
  Of breaking the territory's laws.

Oh, come, cowhand and herder,
  Every gambler, prospector, and bum;
Don't tinker with gun-totin' ladies
  Or drink too much niggerhead rum.

For Belle was a beautiful tough one,
  And she led all her gang to the grave;
But while they were up and kickin'
  Each one of them was her slave.

Part Twelve

Swing Your Partner

No. 98

Shoot the Buffalo

"Shoot the Buffalo" is much older than the cowboy era. It was a favorite among people moving West from the early 1800's. Its form is so simple that any rhymed couplet with the right rhythms may be added. It served for the play-parties that were popular wherever and whenever arm-in-arm dancing was taboo. It was popular also for square dancing. (Melody: collected, adapted and arranged by John A. Lomax and Alan Lomax, *Best Loved American Folk Songs* [New York: Grosset & Dunlap, 1947], p. 103 [© Copyright 1934 and renewed 1962 Ludlow Music, Inc., New York, N.Y. Used by permission]. Text A: Library of Congress #895A1, recorded by John A. Lomax. Text B: Library of Congress, WPA, Arkansas, W305–306. Text C: Library of Congress, miscellaneous texts.)

SHOOT THE BUFFALO

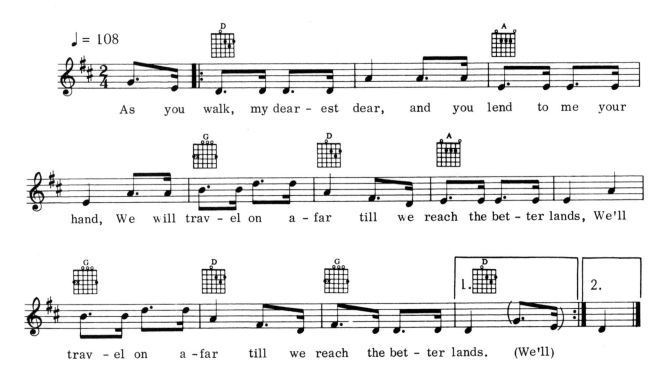

As you walk, my dear-est dear, and you lend to me your hand, We will trav-el on a-far till we reach the bet-ter lands, We'll trav-el on a-far till we reach the bet-ter lands. (We'll)

Text A

As you walk, my dearest dear, and you lend to me your hand,
We will travel on afar till we reach the better lands,
Till we reach the better lands, till we reach the better lands,
We'll travel on afar till we reach the better lands.

CHORUS:
> We'll shoot the buffalo, oh we'll shoot the buffalo,
> We'll rally round the cane brake and shoot the buffalo.
> We'll shoot the buffalo, oh we'll shoot the buffalo,
> We'll rally round the cane brake and shoot the buffalo.

The boys will plow and hoe and the girls will knit and sew,
And we'll all work together wherever we may go,
Wherever we may go, wherever we may go,
We'll all work together wherever we may go.

And when the preacher's done we will pass around the rum,
And while they say the blessing I'll be loading up my gun,
I'll be loading up my gun, I'll be loading up my gun,
And while they say the blessing I'll be loading up my gun.

And the girls could go to school, and the boys will like to fool,
And go to town together and play a game of pool,
We'll play a game of pool, we will play a game of pool,
We will go to town together and play a game of pool.

And the girls will sew and spin, and the boys will laugh and grin,
And will hug and kiss each other, and run away again,
And will run away again, and will run away again,
Will hug and kiss each other and run away again.

Text B

Right hand across and you don't get lost,
Rally round the cane-brake, shoot the buffalo,
Left hand back and you don't get sacked,
Rally round the cane-brake, shoot the buffalo.
Oh, shoot the buffalo, oh, shoot the buffalo,
Rally round the cane-brake, shoot the buffalo.

Briar in my finger, splinter in my toe,
Run around the cane-brake, shoot the buffalo.
If you want to get to Heaven, go right straight through,
Run around the cane-brake, shoot the buffalo.

The buffalo is dead, because I shot him in the head,
Run around the cane-brake, shoot the buffalo.
If she don't like biscuit, feed her cornbread,
Run around the cane-brake, shoot the buffalo.
Oh, shoot the buffalo, shoot the buffalo,
Rally around the cane-brake, shoot the buffalo.

TEXT C

Rise ye up, my dearest dear, and present to me your hand,
And we'll wander off together to a far and distant land,

Where the girls they cuss and swear, and the boys can curl their hair,
And we'll rally round the cane brake and shoot the buffalo.

CHORUS:
    Yes, we'll shoot the buffalo,
    Yes, we'll shoot the buffalo,
    Yes, we'll shoot the buffalo,
    We'll rally round the cane brake
    And shoot the buffalo.

Swing your right hand partner, then your own true love,
Swing your opposite partner and then your turtle dove.

I went down to the neighbor's well to get a bucket of water,
I put one arm around his wife and the other round his daughter.

And if I had a needle and thread as fine as I could sew,
I'd sew it through my true love's dress and down the river we'd go.

Great big house in New Orleans, fourteen stories high,
And every room that I pass through was lined with chicken or punkin
   pie.

It's a rainin' and a hailin', it ain't gonna rain any more,
The lakes and ponds will all go dry and we won't have any more tadpole
   pie.

No. 99
Skip to My Lou

The play-party song is not made for listening but to establish a rhythm for group dancing or games. Circles or opposing lines were formed and the dance figures were conceived for group execution, not for couples, as is typical in the square dance. (Melody and text: FAC I 534, sung by Bill Koch, formerly of Hecla, South Dakota, now of Manhattan, Kansas.)

SKIP TO MY LOU

Lou, Lou, skip to my Lou; Lou, Lou, skip to my Lou;
Lou, Lou, skip to my Lou; Skip to my Lou, my dar - ling.

Lou, Lou, skip to my Lou;
Lou, Lou, skip to my Lou;
Lou, Lou, skip to my Lou;
   Skip to my Lou, my darling.

Little red wagon, paint it blue;
Little red wagon, paint it blue;
Little red wagon, paint it blue;
   Skip to my Lou, my darling.

CHORUS:
   She's gone again, skip to my Lou;
   Gone again, skip to my Lou;
   Gone again, skip to my Lou;
      Skip to my Lou, my darling.

Fly's in the buttermilk, shoo, fly, shoo;
Fly's in the buttermilk, shoo, fly, shoo;
Fly's in the buttermilk, shoo, fly, shoo;
   Skip to my Lou, my darling.

Cows in the cornfield, two by two;
Cows in the cornfield, two by two;
Cows in the cornfield, two by two;
   Skip to my Lou, my darling.

I'll get another one better'n you;
I'll get another one better'n you;
I'll get another one better'n you;
   Skip to my Lou, my darling.

No. 100

Up and Down the Railroad Track

Everything indicates that pioneer Western square dance figures were on the simple side. Once the figures and their sequence were learned, the same ones in the same sequence got used over and over, and the caller no longer called these figures by their names. Rather, he chanted sundry stanzas from a traditional repertoire so long as their rhythms fit. In "Up and Down the Railroad Track" we suspect that one stanza and the chorus gave all the rhythms necessary for one full sequence. Music is not available. (Text: *Journal of American Folklore,* Vol. 27 [1914], pp. 302–303.)

UP AND DOWN THE RAILROAD TRACK

Up and down the railroad track
    And half-way swing around,
Back to the center and two couples swing
    With four hands cast around.

CHORUS:
        Docey doe my darling,
            Miss fair-you-well, I'm gone,
        Docey doe my darling,
            Miss with the white slippers on.

The higher up a cherry tree
    The riper grows the cherries,
The sooner a young man courts the girls
    The younger he will marry.

I used to ride an old gray horse
    And now I ride a roan,
You can hug and kiss your own sweetheart
    But you'd better leave mine alone.

I wish I had a needle and thread
    As fine as I could sew,
I would sew my girl to my coat-tail
    And down that river I would go.

I used to drive a four-horse team
    And hooked Old Nag behind,
Since I got a new sweetheart
    You are no girl of mine.

No. 101
Buffalo Gals

"Buffalo Gals" was a favorite play-party or square dance call during the cowboy era and before. Stanzas vary ad infinitum. Our first text is accompanied by explicit instructions for its use at a play-party. The second and third were used in the Midwest in the 1880's as square dance calls. (Melody: FAC I 201, reproduced with permission of the collector, Dean Emeritus John Donald Robb of the University of New Mexico. Text A: Library of Congress, WPA, Arkansas W304. Text B: PC–F 21. Text C: PC–F 23.)

BUFFALO GALS

Buf - fa - lo gals won't you come out to - night, Won't you come out to - night, won't you come out to - night; Buf- fa - lo gals won't you come out to - night, And dance by the light of the moon?

DIRECTIONS FOR PLAYING "BUFFALO GALS":

Players do the swinging. Boys choose partners. Players form circle and walk around as chorus is sung. Then break and "Two couples all around." They catch hands and swing. A designated couple catches hands with the couple on their right. The four swing around. Each boy swings the opposite girl (in the ring of four), then his partner. Then they swing again. The designated couple goes on to the next couple to the right and the routine is repeated. This keeps up until the couple reaches its original position. The game may be repeated until each couple has been completely around the circle.

TEXT A

Buffalo gals won't you come out tonight,
Won't you come out tonight, won't you come out tonight;
Buffalo gals won't you come out tonight,
   And dance by the light of the moon?

Break and bounce with the couple on the right,
The couple on the right, the couple on the right;
Break and bounce with the couple on the right,
   And swing four hands around.

Everybody wait 'til we get all around,
'Til we get all around, 'til we get all around;
Everybody wait 'til we get all around,
   And swing four hands around.

TEXT B

First lady swing with the right hand gent,
With the right hand round, with the right hand round,
Partner with the left, and the left hand round,—
Lady in the center and seven hands round.

Buffalo gals ain't you comin' out to-night,
Ain't you comin' out to-night, ain't you comin' out to-night?

Lady swing out and the gent swing in,
Join your hands and go round again.

All of the gals are a comin' out to-night,
Are a comin' out to-night, are a comin' out to-night,
All of the gals are a comin' out to-night
To dance by the light of the moon.

Second lady, etc.

TEXT C

First lady swing with the right hand gent,
With the right hand round, the right hand round,
Pardner with the left, and the left hand round,
Birdie in a cage and seven hands round.

Lady in the center and seven hands round;
Seven hands round, seven hands round,
Buffalo gals, ain't you comin' out tonight,
Birdie in a cage and seven hands round.

Ain't you coming out tonight, ain't you comin' out tonight
And birdie hop out and a crow hop in,
Lady swing out and the gent swing in,
And join your paddies and go round again.

No. 102
Red River Gal

This square dance call was a favorite in the cowboy era; it is, still, among thousands of square dance groups throughout the nation. (Melody: traditional. Text: FAC II 127, collected by Bill Koch, formerly of Hecla, South Dakota, now of Manhattan, Kansas.)

RED RIVER GAL

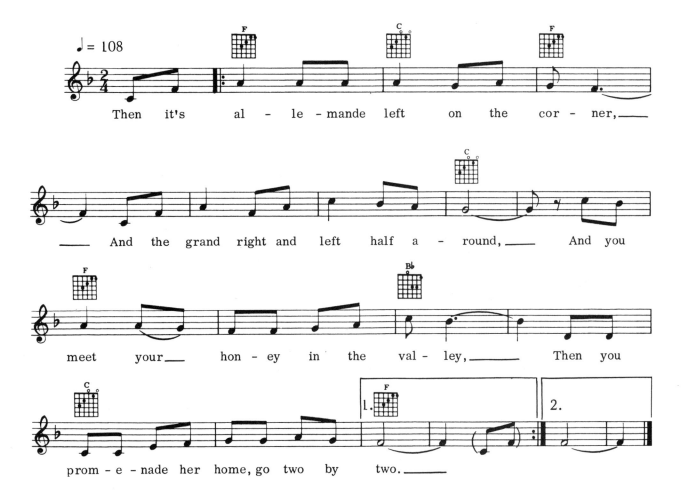

Then it's al - le - mande left on the cor - ner,____ ____ And the grand right and left half a - round, ____ And you meet your__ hon - ey in the val - ley, _____ Then you prom - e - nade her home, go two by two. ____

Then it's allemande * left on the corner,
And the grand right and left go half around,
And you met your honey in the valley,
Then you promenade her home—go two by two.

The first couple right and you circle,
Circle to the left and go all the way,
Then you swing with the other fellow's lady,
Then you swing with your Red River gal.

Then it's on to the next and you circle,
Circle to the left and go all the way,
Then you swing with the other fellow's lady,
Then you swing with your Red River gal.

* Lloyd Shaw, *Cowboy Dances* (Caldwell, Idaho: Caxton Printers, 1941), p. 47:
". . . it is necessary for the caller to explain . . . that a *Grand right and left* is
almost universally preceded by a little introductory turn called *Allemande left.*"

No. 103
Bunkhouse Orchestra

Folks were sparsely scattered on the frontier. It is little wonder that loneliness plagued them so much—little wonder, also, that when they did get together they really whooped it up. (Melody: "Turkey in the Straw." Text: Charles Badger Clark, *Sun and Saddle Leather* [Boston: Richard G. Badger, 1920], pp. 45-48.)

BUNKHOUSE ORCHESTRA

Shin-in' a - do - be fire - place, shad-ows on the wall, See old Short - y's friv'- lous toes a - twitch - in' at the call; It's the best grand high that there is with - in the law, When sev - en jol - ly punch-ers tac - kle "Tur - key in the Straw."

[Note: We have collected folk versions of this song twice; in both cases only the in-set stanzas were used. However, we offer it in its complete text.]

Wrangle up your mouth-harps, drag your banjo out,
Tune your old guitarra till she twangs right stout,
For the snow is on the mountains and the wind is on the plain,
But we'll cut the chimney's moanin' with a livelier refrain.

    Shinin' 'dobe fireplace, shadows on the wall—
    (See old Shorty's friv'lous toes a-twitchin' at the call:)
    It's the best grand high that there is within the law
    When seven jolly punchers tackle "Turkey in the Straw."

Freezy was the day's ride, lengthy was the trail,
Ev'ry steer was haughty with a high arched tail,
But we held 'em and we shoved 'em, for our longin' hearts were tried
By a yearnin' for tobacker and our dear fireside.

    Swing 'er into stop-time, don't you let 'er droop!
    (You're about as tuneful as a coyote with the croup!)
    Ay, the cold wind bit when we drifted down the draw,
    But we drifted on to comfort and to "Turkey in the Straw."

Snarlin' when the rain whipped, cussin' at the ford—
Ev'ry mile of twenty was a long discord,
But the night is brimmin' music and its glory is complete
When the eye is razzle-dazzled by the flip o' Shorty's feet!

Snappy for the dance, now till she up and shoots!
(Don't he beat the devil's wife for jiggin' in 'is boots?)
Shorty got throwed high and we laughed till he was raw,
But tonight he's done forgot it prancin' "Turkey in the Straw."

Rainy dark or firelight, bacon rind or pie,
Livin' is a luxury that don't come high;
Oh, be happy and onruly while our years and luck allow,
For we all must die or marry less than forty years from now!

Lively on the last turn! lope 'er to the death!
(Reddy's soul is willin' but he's gettin' short o' breath.)
Ay, the storm wind sings and old trouble sucks his paw
When we have an hour of firelight set to "Turkey in the Straw."

No. 104
The High-Toned Dance

Much of the uniqueness of the cowboy image derives from a willful primitivistic pose: an actual overplaying of the role that myth thrusts upon him. Such is the case of the puncher in this song who really cut a swath when forced to attend a swanky affair in Denver. (Melody and text: FAC I 68, as sung by Frank Goodwyn.)

THE HIGH-TONED DANCE

♩ = 112

Now you can't ex-pect a cow-boy to ag - i - tate his shanks In the

et - i - quet - tish fash - ion of ar - is - to - crat - ic ranks, When he's

al - ways been ac - cus - tomed to shake the heel and toe, In the

rat - tling ranch - er's dan - ces where much et - i - quette don't go. You can

bet I set there laugh- ing in quite an ex-cit - ed way, A

giv - ing of the squint- ers an as - ton-ished sort of play, When I

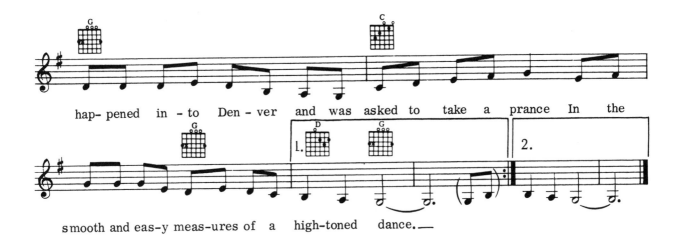

hap- pened in - to Den - ver and was asked to take a prance In the

smooth and eas-y meas-ures of a high-toned dance. —

Now you can't expect a cowboy to agitate his shanks
In the etiquettish fashion of aristocratic ranks,
When he's always been accustomed to shake the heel and toe,
In the rattling ranchers' dances where much etiquette don't go.
You can bet I set there laughing in quite an excited way,
A giving of the squinters an astonished sort of play,
When I happened into Denver and was asked to take a prance
In the smooth and easy measures of a high-toned dance.

When I got among the ladies in their frocks of fleecy white,
And the dudes togged out in wrappings that was simply out of sight,
Tell you what, I was embarrassed and somehow I couldn't keep
From feeling like a burro in a purty flock of sheep.
Every step I took was awkward and I blushed a flaming red,
Like the upper decorations of a turkey gobbler's head.
And the ladies said 'twas seldom they had ever had a chance
To see an old-time puncher at a high-toned dance.

I cut me out a heifer from that bunch of purty girls,
And I yanked her to the center to dance those dreamy whirls.
She laid her head upon my breast in a loving sort of way,
And we drifted into heaven while the band began to play.
I could feel my neck a burning from her nose's breathing heat
As she docey-doed around me, half the time upon my feet.
She looked up into my blinkers with a soul-dissolving glance
Quite conducive to the pleasures of a high-toned dance.

Every nerve just got to dancing to the music of delight,
And I hugged that little sagehen uncomfortably tight;
But she never made a beller and the glances of her eyes
Seemed to thank me for the pleasures of a genuine surprise.
She cuddled up against me in a loving sort of way,
And I hugged her all the tighter for her trustifying play,
Tell you what, the joys of heaven ain't a cussed circumstance
To the huggamania pleasures of a high-toned dance.

When they struck the old cotillon on that music bill of fare,
Every bit of devil in me seemed to bust out on a tear;
I fetched a cowboy war whoop and I started in to rag
Till the rafters started sinking and the floor began to sag.
My partner she got sea sick, and then she staggered for a seat,
And I balanced to the next one but she dodged me slick and neat.
Tell you what, I took the creases from my go-to-meeting pants
When I put the cowboy trimmings on that high-toned dance.

No. 105
At a Cowboy Dance

The images of range life are adequate to the figures of a square dance, just as they are to the life of the soul. When you've danced a gal to "At a Cowboy Dance" she knows she's been danced! Music is not available. (Text: James Barton Adams, *Breezy Western Verse* [Denver: The Post Printing Co., 1889], pp. 103–104.)

AT A COWBOY DANCE

Git yo' little sage hens ready,
  Trot 'em out upon the floor—
Line 'em up there, you cusses! Steady!
  Lively now! One couple more.
Shorty, shed that ol' sombrero;
  Bronco, douse that cigarette!
Stop yer cussin', Cassimero,
  'Fore the ladies. Now, all set!

Salute yer ladies all together!
  Ladies opposite the same;
Hit the lumber with yer leather!
  Balance all and swing yer dame!
Bunch the heifers in the middle!
  Circle stags, and doe-se-doe—
Pay attention to the fiddle;
  Swing her round an' off you go!

First four forward! Back to places!
  Second foller! Shuffle back!
Now you've got it down to cases!
  Swing 'em till their trotters crack!
Gents all right a heel an' toein'!
  Swing 'em: Kiss 'em if you kin!
On to next an' keep a-goin'
  Till yo' hit yer pards agin!

Gents to center; ladies round 'em!
  Form a basket; balance all!
Whirl yo' gals to where yo' found 'em;
  Promenade around the hall!
Balance to yo' pards and trot 'em
  Round the circle double quick!
Grab and kiss 'em while you've got 'em!
  Hold 'em to it if they kick!

Ladies, left hand to yer sonnies!
  Aleman! Grand right and left!
Balance all an' swing yo' honies—
  Pick 'em up an' feel their heft!
Promenade like skeery cattle!
  Balance all, an' swing yer sweets!
Shake yer spurs and make 'em rattle!
  Keno! Promenade to seats.

No. 106

Snagtooth Sal

Women are so idealized in the code of the cowboy that a comic effect is achieved whenever the image of an ugly woman is evoked: "Clementine" and "Snagtooth Sal" are typical. The latter was standard in the play-party repertoire. (Melody: Capitol P–8332, Roger Wagner Chorale. Text: Gordon 675.)

SNAGTOOTH SAL

♩. = 108 Lively

I was young and hap - py, my heart was light and gay,

Sing - ing, al - ways sing - ing through the sun - ny sum - mer day,

Hap - py as a liz - ard in the wav - ing cha - par - ral,

Walk - ing down through Lar - a - mie with Snag - tooth Sal.

CHORUS

Sal, Sal, — my heart it broke to - day; Broke in two for - ev - er when they

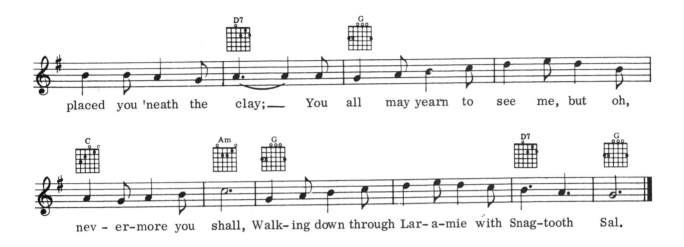

placed you 'neath the clay; — You all may yearn to see me, but oh,

nev - er-more you shall, Walk-ing down through Lar-a-mie with Snag-tooth Sal.

I was young and happy, my heart was light and gay,
Singing, always singing through the sunny summer day,
Happy as a lizard in the waving chaparral,
Walking down through Laramie with Snagtooth Sal.

CHORUS:
    Sal, Sal, Sal, my heart it broke today;
    Broke in two forever when they placed you 'neath the clay;
    You all may yearn to see me, but oh, nevermore you shall,
    Walking down through Laramie with Snagtooth Sal.

Bury me tomorrow where the lily blossoms spring,
Underneath the willows where the little birdies sing.
She told me that she loved me, she swore she'd be my pal,
But she turned me down completely, did my Snagtooth Sal.

I met her in the evening when the stars were shining bright,
We walked and talked and billed and cooed till twelve o'clock at night.
I thought I had her safely in my aching heart's corral,
But she died and left me longing for my Snagtooth Sal.

Plant a little stone above the little mound of sod,
Write, "Here lies a loving and a busted heart, begod."
Never more you'll see him walking proudly with his gal,
Walking down through Laramie with Snagtooth Sal.

No. 107
Ragtime Cowboy Joe

"Ragtime Cowboy Joe" is presented to remind readers that the commercial exploitation of the cowboy image did not lag far behind the era of the open range itself. Far from being a cowboy's image of himself, this beloved song merely uses the western theme in the sophisticated ragtime musical style of the turn of the century. (Melody from sheet music, 1912, by Lewis F. Muir and Maurice Abrahams. Text: PNFQ 377.)

RAGTIME COWBOY JOE

Out in Ar - i - zo - na where the bad men are, And the on - ly friend to guide you is an even - ing star;___ The rough-est tough-est man by far,___ Is Rag - time Cow-boy Joe.___ Got his name from sing - ing to the cows and sheep,___ Ev - ery night they say he sings the herd to sleep, In a bas - so

rich and deep,___ Croon - ing soft and low.___ He al - ways

sings___ rag - gy mu - sic to the cat - tle, As he swings___ back and

for - ward in the sad - dle On a horse ___ that is

syn - co - pat - ed, gait - ed. And there's such a fun - ny me - ter to the

roar of his re - peat - er, How they run ___ when they

hear that fel - low's gun, Be - cause the west - ern folks all

know, He's a high fa - lu - ting, scoot-ing, shoot-ing son-of-a-gun from Ar - i - zo - na,

Rag - time Cow - boy Joe. He al - ways Joe.

291

Out in Arizona where the bad men are,
And the only friend to guide you is an evening star;
The roughest, toughest man by far
    Is Ragtime Cowboy Joe.
Got his name from singing to the cows and sheep,
Every night they say he sings the herd to sleep,
In a basso rich and deep,
    Crooning soft and low.

CHORUS:

    He always sings raggy music to the cattle,
    As he swings back and forward in the saddle
    On a horse that is syncopated gaited.
    And there's such a funny meter to the roar of his repeater,
    How they run when they hear that fellow's gun,
        Because the western folks all know,
        He's a high-faluting, scooting, shooting son-of-a-gun from Arizona,
        Ragtime Cowboy Joe.

Dressed up every Sunday in his Sunday clothes,
He beats it for the village where he always goes.
And every girl in town is Joe's
    'Cause he's a ragtime bear.
When he starts a spieling on the dance hall floor,
No one but a lunatic would start a war.
Wise men know his forty-four
    Makes men dance for fair.

292

Part Thirteen

Passing of the Frontier

No. 108
Home on the Range

"Home on the Range" became the best-known cowboy song in the 1930's when, thanks to Franklin Delano Roosevelt's enthusiasm for it, it came near being another national anthem. The story of claims and counterclaims to authorship, in court and out, would itself make a "who-dun-it" to top them all. It is a cowboy song by adoption only, the ranges in question being land surveyed by the federal government for homestead purposes, and not the cattle range. It was written by Dr. Brewster Higley, and first published in the *Kirwin* (Kansas) *Chief* on Saturday, February 26, 1876. The tune was set to it shortly after by Daniel E. Kelley, also of Kansas.

Here we give, in addition to Dr. Higley's original text, the text of a western miner's adaptation of the song, written by William and Mary Goodwin in 1904 and copyrighted by Balmer and Webber Music Co.; we also give John A. Lomax's 1910 text on which the texts popularized in the 1930's were based. (Melody: Library of Congress #3215A3, recorded by Sidney Robertson. Text A: *Kirwin Chief*, February 26, 1876. Text B: JL 124. Text C: John A. Lomax, *Cowboy Songs* [1910], pp. 39-40.)

HOME ON THE RANGE

Oh, give me a home where the Buf - fa - lo roam Where the Deer and the An - te - lope play;__ Where nev - er is heard a dis- cour - ag - ing word, And the sky is not cloud - ed all day.__ A

TEXT A. WESTERN HOME

Oh! give me a home where the Buffalo roam,
  Where the Deer and the Antelope play;
Where never is heard a discouraging word,
  And the sky is not clouded all day.

CHORUS:
  A home! A home!
    Where the Deer and the Antelope play,
  Where seldom is heard a discouraging word,
    And the sky is not clouded all day.

Oh! give me a land where the bright diamond sand,
  Throws its light from the glittering streams,
Where glideth along the graceful white swan,
  Like the maid in her heavenly dreams.

Oh! give me a gale of the Solomon vale,
  Where the life streams with buoyancy flow;
On the banks of the Beaver, where seldom if ever,
  Any poisonous herbage doth grow.

How often at night, when the heavens were bright,
  With the light of the twinkling stars
Have I stood here amazed, and asked as I gazed,
  If their glory exceed that of ours.

I love the wild flowers in this bright land of ours,
  I love the wild curlew's shrill scream;
The bluffs and white rocks, and antelope flocks
  That graze on the mountains so green.

The air is so pure and the breezes so fine,
  The zephyrs so balmy and light,
That I would not exchange my home here to range,
  Forever in azures so bright.

TEXT B. ARIZONA HOME

Oh, give me a home where the buffalo roam,
    Where the deer and the antelope play;
There seldom is heard a discouraging word
    And the sky is not cloudy all day.

Yes, give me the gleam of the swift mountain stream
    And the place where no hurricane blows;
Oh, give me the park where the prairie dogs bark
    And the mountain all covered with snow.

CHORUS:
    A home, a home
        Where the deer and the antelope play,
    There seldom is heard a discouraging word
        And the sky is not cloudy all day.

Oh, give me the hills and the ring of the drills
    And the rich silver ore in the ground;
Yes, give me the gulch where the miner can sluice
    And the bright, yellow gold can be found.

Oh, give me the mine where the prospectors find
    The gold in its own native land;
And the hot springs below where the sick people go
    And camp on the banks of the Grande.

Oh, give me the steed and the gun that I need
    To shoot game for my own cabin home;
Then give me the camp where the fire is the lamp
    And the wild Rocky Mountains to roam.

Yes, give me the home where the prospectors roam
    Their business is always alive
In these wild western hills, midst the ring of the drills,
    Oh, there let me live till I die.

TEXT C. HOME ON THE RANGE

Oh, give me a home where the buffalo roam,
    Where the deer and the antelope play,
Where seldom is heard a discouraging word
    And the skies are not cloudy all day.

CHORUS:
    Home, home on the range,
        Where the deer and the antelope play;
    Where seldom is heard a discouraging word
        And the skies are not cloudy all day.

Where the air is so pure, the zephyrs so free,
    The breezes so balmy and light,
That I would not exchange my home on the range
    For all of the cities so bright.

The red man was pressed from this part of the West,
    He's likely no more to return,
To the banks of Red River where seldom if ever
    Their flickering camp-fires burn.

How often at night when the heavens are bright
    With the light from the glittering stars,
Have I stood here amazed and asked as I gazed
    If their glory exceeds that of ours.

Oh, I love these wild flowers in this dear land of ours,
    The curlew I love to hear scream,
And I love the white rocks and the antelope flocks
    That graze on the mountain-tops green.

Oh, give me a land where the bright diamond sand
    Flows leisurely down the stream;
Where the graceful white swan goes gliding along
    Like a maid in a heavenly dream.

Then I would not exchange my home on the range,
    Where the deer and the antelope play;
Where seldom is heard a discouraging word
    And the skies are not cloudy all day.

    Home, home on the range,
        Where the deer and the antelope play,
    Where seldom is heard a discouraging word
        And the skies are not cloudy all day.

No. 109
The Cowboy's Ride

For sheer lyricism this song is hard to beat! It is metrically so perfect and its images so subtly drawn that we sense behind it a poet inspired both by the prairies of the West and the Anglo-American literary heritage. It is encountered in less perfect form in oral tradition. (Melody and text: Library of Congress #1338A1, recorded by John A. Lomax.)

THE COWBOY'S RIDE

Oh, for a ride o'er the prai - ries free, On a
fi - ery un - tamed steed, Where the cur - lews fly____
____ and the coy - otes cry And the west - ern wind____
____ goes sweep - ing by, For my heart en - joys the speed.

Oh, for a ride o'er the prairies free,
  On a fiery untamed steed,
Where the curlews fly and the coyotes cry
And the western wind goes sweeping by,
  For my heart enjoys the speed.

With my left hand light on the bridle rein,
  And saddle girth pinched behind,
With a lariat tied at the pony's side
By my stout right arm that's true and tried,
  We race with the whistling wind.

We're up and away in the morning light
  As swift as a shooting star,
That suddenly flies across the sky,
And the wild birds whirl in quick surprise
  At the cowboy's gay "Hurrah!"

As free as a bird o'er the rolling sea
  We skim the pasture wide,
Like a seagull strong we hurry along,
And the earth resounds with a galloping song
  As we sail through the fragrant tide.

You can have your ride in the crowded town!
  Give me the prairies free.
Where the curlews fly and the coyotes cry,
And the heart expands 'neath the open sky:
  Oh, that's the ride for me!

No. 110
The Old Cowboy

An aged puncher reminisces about the classical era of cowpunching in mellowed and nostalgic tones. Homeric images such as the one about turning the stampeding cattle by the light of the lightning flashing on their horns more than compensates for the heap of doggerel you have to plow through if you are to feel the cowboy and western mood. (Melody and text: FAC I 408, sung by Paul Kelso.)

THE OLD COWBOY

I rode a line on the open range
    When cow-punching was not slow;
I turned the longhorn one way, boys,
    And the other the buffalo.

I went up the trail in the eighties
    And the hardships that I have stood,
I've drunk water from the cow tracks, boys,
    When you bet it tasted good.

I've starved and ate of the prickly pear,
  And I've slickered it out in the rain;
Been tortured by the Apaches
  Till I could not bear the pain.

I've been in many a stampede, too,
  I've heard the roaring noise,
And the light we had to turn them by
  Was the lightning on their horns.

But many a man I worked with then
  Is sleeping on Boot Hill;
And the last cow drive was made to Dodge
  Over the Jones and Plummer Trail.

I used to be a tough one, boys,
  Hell-bending I did go;
Killed a man in old Cheyenne,
  But now I'm getting slow.

They're building towns and railroads now
  Where we used to bed our cows;
And the man with the mule and the plow and the hoe
  Is digging up our old bed ground.

The old cowboy has watched the change,
  Has seen the good times go;
And the old cowboy will soon leave the plain
  Just like the buffalo.

No. 111
Cattle Call

By the 1930's the cowboy mentality had about played itself out; blue yodels, sentimentality, and histrionics began to supplant realism and simplicity. One might properly call this the decadent phase in the evolution of cowboy songs. At their best, however, as here, the yodels did evoke the cattle calls that were used on the drives in earlier days. (Melody and text: FAC I 202, reproduced with permission of the collector, Dean Emeritus John Donald Robb of the University of New Mexico.)

CATTLE CALL

Hm   Hm   Hm _____   Hoo   Hoo   Hoo _____

Hoo - pl - ee   Hm   Hm   Hm _____   Hoo _____

Hoo _____   Hoo _____   When   the   dew   day   is

dawn - ing   I   wake   up   a - yawn - ing,   Drink - ing   my

cof - fee   strong; ___   Make   my   bed   in   a   roll,   down   the

trail   I   will   stroll ___   Sing - ing   this   old   cat - tle   call. ___

(Yodel)

When the dew day is dawning I wake up a-yawning,
   Drinking my coffee strong;
Make my bed in a roll, down the trail I will stroll
   Singing this old cattle call—

With my saddle all shedded and the cattle all bedded
   Nothing wild seems to be wrong;
Make my bed 'neath the skies, I look up at the stars,
   And then I can sing you this call—

Well, each day I do ride o'er a range far and wide.
   I'm goin' home this fall;
Well, I don't mind the weather, my heart's like a feather,
   'Cause always I'll sing you this call—

No. 112
The Pecos Punchers

The song gives a sweeping and realistic view of the cowboy's commitments to life and the image he made of himself: his wearing apparel and gear; sleeping out; night-herding; roping, branding; bronc-riding; whiskey and the dance hall; even the inevitable "Last Ride." Music is lacking. (Text: JL 22.)

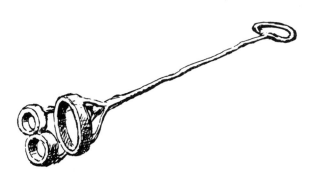

THE PECOS PUNCHERS

I'm a gay puncher, fresh from the Pecos Flat,
I wear the high heels, also the white hat,
I ride the Meyers saddle, my chaps are the best,
My bits, boots, and spurs can't be beat in the West.

I'm noted in Texas out on the Staked Plains,
Also from the Pecos to the Rio Grande range;
I ride up the trail and take down the rawhide,
And there never was a bronco but what I could ride.

I ride in the wagon, I ride in pursuit,
To hear the cook holler, "Chuck away! grab a root!"
We roll out our bedding on the ground cold and hard,
For shortly we have to stand three hours guard.

Next morning at daybreak in a circle we ride,
We round up the dogies, take down the rawhide;
We rope them and brand them like in days of old,
Upon the left shoulder we stamp the Eight-O.

I've worked for the Mallets, also the Long-S,
But as for the Eight-O's, I think them the best;
The nights are so dark, can hardly see at all,
As I ride to the sound of some maverick's bawl.

Now as for maverick stealing, I confess true enough,
But to the young cowman it seems mighty tough;
But what cares the puncher as he rides the range o'er?
The cowman will get there or else make a roar.

Now as for bronc riding, I've got quite enough,
I'll go East like Wild Bill and there play the tough,
Let my beard grow long and dance on the stage,
I'll tell they eat cactus out West and chew sage.

As for saddle and bridle I have no more use,
I'll ride to the home ranch and turn my bronc loose;
I'll hang up my saddle where it will keep dry,
For I may need it in the sweet by-and-by.

No. 113

Way Out in Idaho

Dreams of El Dorado pervade the oral and literary tradition of mankind almost everywhere. In Civil War times Idaho became for Midwesterners that ethereal land where easy fortunes awaited all who might venture so far to the west. (Melody: FAC I 32, recorded by Rosalie Sorrels. Text: Gordon 2716.)

WAY OUT IN IDAHO

They say there is a land,___ Where crys - tal wa - ters flow ___ O'er beds of quartz and pur - est gold, Way out in I - da - ho. ___ Oh, wait, I - da - ho; ___ We're com - ing, I - da - ho, ___ Our four horse team will soon be seen, Way out in I - da - ho. ___

They say there is a land,
  Where crystal waters flow
O'er beds of quartz and purest gold,
  Way out in Idaho.

CHORUS:

    Oh, wait, Idaho;
      We're coming, Idaho,
    Our four horse team will soon be seen,
      Way out in Idaho.

We're bound to cross the plains,
  And up the mountains go,
We're bound to see our fortunes there,
  Way out in Idaho.

We'll need no pick or spade,
  No shovel, pan, or hoe,
The largest chunks are top of ground,
  Way out in Idaho.

We'll see hard times no more,
  And want we'll never know,
When once we've filled our sacks with gold,
  Way out in Idaho.

No. 114
Lone Star Trail

"Lone Star Trail" encompasses a cluster of song subjects that range from the painful separation of lovers to the grim realism of life on the trail. Typically in these songs, trailing and cowpunching loom as compulsions that drive men onward and away from the amenities of a highly organized society. What drives them thus? Riding and twisting the lasso, dust, stampeding longhorns and the fire that plays on their horns! Were Ulysses and his crew driven by more compelling forces? (Melody and Text A: Columbia 2310D, Ken Maynard. Text B: Library of Congress #658A2, recorded by John A. Lomax.)

LONE STAR TRAIL

Oh, I am a lone-ly cow-boy and I'm off of the Tex-as trail, My trade is cinch-in' sad-dles and pull-in' bri-dle reins; For I can twist a las-so with the great-est skill and ease, Or rope and ride a bron-co most an-y-where I please. Oh, I love the roll-ing prai-rie that's far from trial and

strife, Be - hind a bunch of long-horns I'll jour-ney all my

life. But if I had a stake, boys, soon mar-ried I would

be To the sweet- est girl in this wide world, just fell in love with

me._____ Tee wee____ hee - wee_____ ee - wee

wee - wee - ee - wee. _____

TEXT A

Oh, I am a lonely cowboy, and I'm off of the Texas trail,
My trade is cinchin' saddles and pullin' bridle reins;
For I can twist a lasso with the greatest skill and ease,
Or rope and ride a bronco most anywhere I please.

Oh, I love the rolling prairie that's far from trial and strife,
Behind a bunch of longhorns I'll journey all my life.
But if I had a stake, boys, soon married I would be
To the sweetest girl in this wide world, just fell in love with me.

(Yodel)

Oh, when we get on the trail, boys, the dusty billows ride,
It's fifty miles from water and the grass is scorching dry;
Oh, the boss is mad and ringy, you all can plainly see,
I'll have to pull out the longhorns, I'm a cowboy here to be.

But when it comes a rain, boys, one of the gentle kind,
When the lakes are full of water and the grass is waving fine,
Oh, the boss'll shed his frown, boys, and a pleasant smile you'll see,
I'll have to pull out the longhorns, I'm a cowboy here to be.

Oh, when we get 'em bedded we sink down for the night,
Some horse'll shake his saddle, it'll give the herd a fright,
They'll bound to their feet, boys, and madly stampede away,
In one moment's time, boys, you can hear a cowboy say:

Oh, when we get 'em bedded we feel most inclined,
When a cloud'll rise in the west, boys, and the fire play on their horns.
Oh, the old boss rides around them, your pay you'll get in gold,
So I'll have to pull out the longhorns until I am too old.

Text B

'Twas down on the Lone Star Trail in eighteen seventy-three,
'Twas there I met a comrade and he was dear to me.
I love him like a brother, and that is hard to say,
But we rode the ranges together for many and many a day.

I am a Texas cowboy and I do ride the range,
My trade is cinches and saddles and ropes and bridle reins.
With Stetson hat and jingling spurs and leather up to my knees,
Gray-backs as big as chili beans, and fighting like hell with fleas.

And if I had a little stake I soon would married be,
But another week and I must go, the boss said so today.
My girl must cheer up courage, and choose some other one,
For I am bound to follow the Lone Star Trail until my race is run.

No. 115

The Last Longhorn

This song, written in the 1890's, already anticipates the end of the cowboy era. Nesters (i.e., dirt farmers and cattlemen operating small herds on fenced lands) severed the trails over which herds had been driven to market. Domestic breeds of cattle came to supplant the rugged longhorns, and domesticated breeds of men to supplant the cowboys. (Melody: Victor 40197, Carl T. Sprague. Text: *The Cattleman* [Fort Worth, Texas], March 1917.)

THE LAST LONGHORN

An aged long-horn bo-vine lay dy-ing on the riv-er, There was lack of veg-e-ta-tion and the cold winds made him shiv-er. But a cow-boy stood be-side him with sad-ness on his face To watch the fi-nal pass-ing, the last of all the race.

An aged longhorn bovine lay dying on the river,
There was lack of vegetation and the cold winds made him shiver.
But a cowboy stood beside him with sadness on his face
To watch the final passing, the last of all the race.

The aged bovine struggled and raised his shaking head,
But he said, "I care not to remain when all my friends are dead;
These Jerseys and these Holsteins, they are no friends of mine,
For they have come from Bingen on the Rhine.

"Tell the Herefords and the Durhams when they come a-grazing round
And find me lying cold and still upon the frozen ground,
That I don't want them to bellow when they find that I am dead,
For I was Groesbeck, fair Groesbeck on the Red.

"Tell the coyotes when they come around a-seeking for their prey
They might as well go further for they'll find it will not pay;
When they attempt to eat me, they very soon will see
My bones and hide are petrified, they'll find no beef on me.

"I remember back in '80's, some nineteen summers past,
With grass and water plenty, but 'twas too good to last;
I little dreamed what would transpire, just a few seasons hence,
When the Nesters came a-moving in and brought the wire fence.

"Before the fine-haired cattle came I oft would go and see
My friends upon the Pease River, they were branded S T V.
And then go down to Wichita, 'twould only take a day,
And have a general round-up along the U L A.

"It was only one short year ago that some of them remained,
But they were embalmed to feed the boys who were a-fighting Spain.
The heel-fly will soon be around and they torment me so,
I would not die in springtime so now is the time to go."

His voice sank to a murmur, his breath came short and quick,
The cowboy tried to skin him when he saw he could not kick.
He rubbed his knife upon his boot until he made it shine,
But he failed to skin old longhorn, he could not cut the rind.

And the cowboy rose up sadly and mounted his cayuse,
Saying, "The time has come when Longhorns and Cowboys are no use."
And gazing sadly backward upon the dead bovine
His horse stepped in a dog hole and fell and broke his spine.

The cowboys and the longhorns that were here in '84
Have gone to their last round-up over on the other shore.
They answered well their purpose when they used to ride the line,
But their glory has departed in 1889.

No. 116
Cowboy Again for a Day

This song is a nostalgic benediction upon the cowboy era. The frontier
has passed and the old-timer, through his mind's eye, reviews the images
of the grand moments: the birth, that is, of his own milieu, his very own
since he is the one who made it. Our second text goes one step further
by panning Hollywood's phony stereotypes of cowboy life. There is a
quaint coincidence in the fact that two manuscript texts of a fragment
of this song, one in the Robert W. Gordon Collection and another in the
John A. Lomax papers, ascribe the song to ROSODORE THEOVELT. (Melody:
Jules Verne Allen, *Cowboy Lore* [San Antonio: The Naylor Co., 1933,
1950], pp. 143–144. Text A: *Hoofs and Horns*, Vol. 4, January 1935,
p. 6. Text B: JL 147.)

COWBOY AGAIN FOR A DAY

Back - ward, turn back - ward, oh time with your wheels,

Air-planes, and wag-ons, and au - to - mo - biles; Give me once more my som-

rope and to brand, Out where the sage - brush is

dust - y and gray Make me a cow - boy a - gain for a day.

bre - ro and flaps, Spurs, flan - nel shirt, — slick - er, and chaps.

Put a six shoot - er or two in my hand, Show me a year - ling to

Text A. Cowboy Again for a Day

Backward, turn backward, oh time with your wheels,
Airplanes, and wagons, and automobiles;
Give me once more my sombrero and flaps,
Spurs, flannel shirt, slicker, and chaps.
Put a six-shooter or two in my hand,
Show me a yearling to rope and to brand,
Out where the sagebrush is dusty and gray
Make me a cowboy again for a day.

Give me a bronc that knows how to dance,
Buckskin in color and wicked of glance;
New to the feelin' of bridle and bit—
Give me a quirt that will sting when it hits.
Strap on the blanket behind in a roll,
Pass me the rope that is dear to my soul;
Over the trail let me gallop away—
Make me a cowboy again for a day.

Thunder of hoofs on the range as you ride,
Hissing of iron and sizzling of hide;
Bellows of cattle and snort of cayuse,
Longhorns from Texas as wild as the deuce.
Midnight stampedes and milling of herds,
Yells of the cowboys too angry for words;
Right in the thick of it all would I stay—
Make me a cowboy again for a day.

Under the star-studded heavens so vast,
Campfire and coffee and comfort at last;
Bacon that sizzles and crisps in the pan
After the roundup smells good to a man.
Stories of cowmen and rustlers retold
Over the pipe as the embers grow cold;
Those are the times that old memories play—
Make me a cowboy again for a day.

Text B. Moving Picture Cowboy

Backward, turn backward, film guy in your flight,
And turn out a cowboy that does the game right.
Put on a picture that won't look so strange
To us old punchers who've rode on the range.

Don't have the daughter the old man loves best
Skip with some hard-ridin' son of the West.
Backward, turn backward, 'til folks get a clue
To some of the things that a cowboy don't do.

Show us a cowboy that has more work to do
Than merely to ride a wild bronco or two.
Picture him riding away in the rain
Roundin' up steers on the mud-splattered plain.

Make him the way that he really is seen
And not as they make him appear on the screen.
Backward, turn backward, 'til people will know
Exactly how things on a cattle ranch go.

Picture a cowboy whose job is above
Close-herdin' damsels and fallin' in love.
Make him appear in a far different light
Than hangin' around the saloons half the night.

Picture him cuttin' out steers from the bunch
And not with some girl at a picnic or lunch.
Backward, turn backward, you actors who try
To mimic a callin' that's nearly gone by.
Pull off those chaps, those guns and those spurs
And get a real puncher to tell what occurs.

After you hear the long years of the West,
Of storm, stampede, poor crop and all the rest,
Then all you film guys trot out your machine
And picture a cowboy just as he is seen.

No. 117

The Dying Cowboy

Perhaps the greatest of cowboy songs, "The Dying Cowboy," was created as a parody of "The Ocean Burial" copyrighted as the work of George N. Allen in 1850. It concentrates the classical images of the West —coyote, prairie grasses, buffalo, buzzard, rattlesnake—and places them in sharp contrast with the gentler images of the abandoned home. Notions of perfect womanhood—mother, sister, sweetheart—are rallied to sustain the bitter pill of death. But tragedy haunts the cowboy for he is buried on the lone prairie despite his wish.

In oral tradition it appears in a brief form, such as in the Woody Guthrie text, rather than in the extended form given by J. Frank Dobie. Our third text suggests the many ways in which "The Dying Cowboy" has been reused in other cowboy songs. (Melody A: Library of Congress #2621B, recorded by John A. Lomax. Text A: Library of Congress, Woody Guthrie Manuscripts, p. 131. Melody B: FAC I 178, reproduced with permission of the collector, Dean Emeritus John Donald Robb of the University of New Mexico. Text B: J. Frank Dobie, "Ballads and Songs of the Frontier Folk." PTFLS [VI, 1927], pp. 181–183 [published by permission of the Texas Folklore Society]. Text C: Columbia 15141, Obed Pickard.)

THE DYING COWBOY

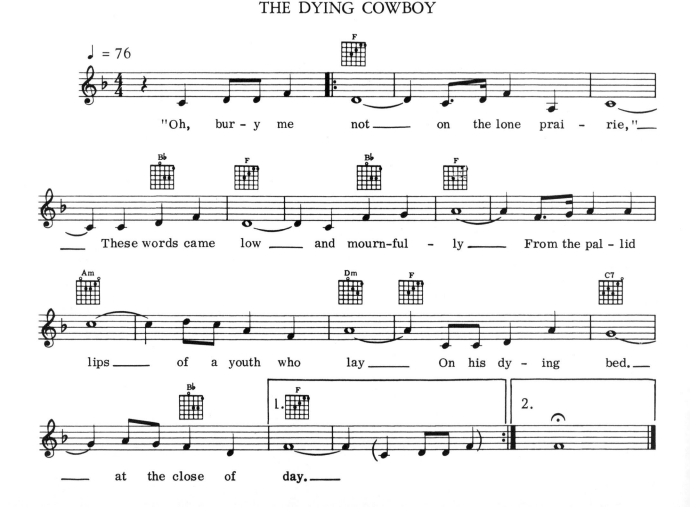

"Oh, bury me not on the lone prairie,"—
These words came low and mournfully
From the pallid lips of a youth who lay
On his dying bed at the close of day.

He had wailed in pain till o'er his brow
The Shadow of Death was a gathering now.
He thought of his home and his loved ones nig
As the cowboys gathered to see him die.

"Oh, bury me not on the lone prairie
Where the wild coyotes will howl o'er me,
In a narrow grave just six by three
Oh, bury me not on the lone prairie.

"It matters not, I've oft been told,
Where the body lies when the heart grows cold,
Yet grant, oh grant this wish to me,
And bury me not on the lone prairie.

"Oh, bury me not,"—and his voice failed there—
But we took no heed of his dying prayer;
In a narrow grave just six by three
We buried him there on the lone prairie.

Oh, we buried him there on the lone prairie
Where the rattlesnakes rattle and the wind sports free,
Where the buffalo roams and the tumbleweeds
Will cover his grave on the lone prairie.

And the cowboys now as they roam the plains—
They have marked the spot where his bones are lain—
Fling a handful of roses o'er his grave
And pray to Him that his soul be saved.

The moon comes up when the sun goes down
And it lights the grave where we laid him down.
His pale young face never more we'll see,
We buried him there on the lone prairie.

"Oh, bury me not on the lone prairie"—
These words came slow and mournfully
From the pallid lips of a youth who lay
On his cold damp bed at the close of day.

He had wasted and pined till on his brow
Death's shades were slowly gathering now;
He thought of his home and his loved ones nigh,
As the cowboys gathered to see him die.

    Oh, bury me not on the lone prairie,
    Where the wild coyotes will howl o'er me,
    Where the west wind sweeps and the grasses wave,
    And sunbeams rest on the prairie grave.

Again he listened to the well-known words,
To the wind's soft sigh and the song of birds;
And he thought of his home and his native bowers,
Where he loved to roam in his childhood hours.

"It matters not, I've oft been told,
Where the body lies when the heart grows cold.
Yet grant, oh, grant, this wish to me,
Oh, bury me not on the lone prairie.

"Then bury me not on the lone prairie
In a narrow grave six foot by three,
Where the buffalo paws on the prairie sea,
Oh, bury me not on the lone prairie.

"I've always wished that when I died
My grave might be on the old hillside.
There let the place of my last rest be,
Oh, bury me not on the lone prairie.

"O'er me then a mother's prayer
And a sister's tears might mingle there,
Where my friends can come and weep o'er me,
Oh, bury me not on the lone prairie.

"Oh, bury me not on the lone prairie
In a narrow grave just six by three,
Where the buzzard waits and the wind blows free,
Oh, bury me not on the lone prairie.

"There is another whose tears may shed
For one who lies on a prairie bed—
It pained me then and it pains me now—
She has curled these locks, she has kissed this brow.

"Oh, why did I roam o'er the wild prairie?
She's waiting there at home for me,
But her lovely face ne'er more I'll see.
Oh, bury me not on the lone prairie.

"These locks she has curled, shall the rattlesnake kiss?
This brow she has kissed, shall the cold grave press?
For the sake of her who will weep for me,
Oh, bury me not on the lone prairie.

"Oh, bury me not on the lone prairie,
Where the wild coyotes will howl o'er me,
Where the buzzard beats and the wind goes free.
Oh, bury me not on the lone prairie.

"Oh, bury me not"—and his voice failed there,
But we took no heed of the dying prayer;
In a narrow grave six foot by three,
We buried him there on the lone prairie.

Where the dewdrops glow and the butterflies rest,
And the flowers bloom o'er the prairie's crest;
Where the wild coyote and winds sport free
On a wet saddle blanket lay a cowboy-ee.

"Oh, bury me not on the lone prairie,
Where the wild coyotes will howl o'er me,
Where the rattlesnakes hiss and the crow flies free,
Oh, bury me not on the lone prairie."

Oh, we buried him there on the lone prairie,
Where the wild rose blooms and the wind blows free;
Oh, his young face ne'er more to see,
For we buried him there on the wild prairie.

Yes, we buried him there on the lone prairie,
Where the owl all night hoots mournfully,
And the buzzard beats and the wind blows free
O'er his lonely grave on the lone prairie.

May the light-winged butterfly pause to rest
O'er him who sleeps on the prairie's crest;
May the Texas rose in the breezes wave
O'er him who sleeps in the prairie grave.

And the cowboys now as they roam the plain—
For they marked the spot where his bones are lain—
Fling a handful of roses o'er his grave,
With a prayer to God his soul to save.

    "Oh, bury me not on the lone prairie,
    Where the wolves can howl and growl o'er me.
    Fling a handful of roses o'er my grave
    With a prayer to Him Who my soul will save.

TEXT C (SUNG TO "NO USE FOR THE WOMEN," NO. 65)

Oh, listen, kind friends, I'll tell you
  A story you all know well,
The dying words of a cowboy
  On a western plain where he fell.

'Twas the same old sweetheart story,
  With another she had fled,
And as he lay there dying
  These farewell words he said:

"Oh, bury me not on the prairie,"
These words came mournfully
From the pallid lips of a boy who lay
On his dying bed that day.

"Oh, bury me not on the prairie
  Where the coyotes howl o'er my grave,
Place a bunch of roses o'er me
  And a prayer for my soul to be saved,
  Yes, a prayer for my soul to be saved."

We all kneeled down on the prairie
  And begged for this boy's request,
To save his soul in heaven
  As we gently laid him to rest.

Oh, listen, kind friends, I'll tell you
  A story you all know well:
The dying words of a cowboy
  When he said his last farewell.

Then we buried him there on the prairie
  Where the winds howl mournfully,
And the blizzards beat and the wind blows free
  O'er the grave in that lonely prairie.

Yes, we buried him there on the prairie
  Where the coyotes howl o'er his grave,
Where the blizzards beat and the wind blows free
  O'er the grave in that lonely prairie.

No. 118

The Dying Outlaw

Death laments are as old as poetry, and as universal. Here it is the story of a Canadian outlaw brought to bay by a Mounty. Note the outlaw's basic concerns: the prairie, the beat of horses' hooves, the "last great roundup." (Melody and text: FAC I 484, collected by Edith Fowke from Stanley Botting, Naramata, B.C.)

THE DYING OUTLAW

Come gath - er a - round me, my com - rades and friends, For sun___ it is set - ting on life's short day; For I'm wound - ed to die and there's noth-ing to do But wait 'til my life ebbs a - way.___ Oh, bur - y me on the lone prai - rie, Where the hoofs of the hors - es shall fall,___ Where the ech - o - ing

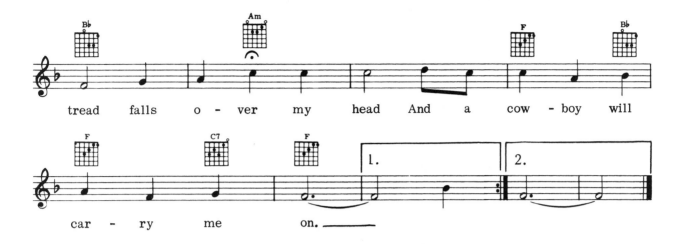

tread   falls   o - ver   my   head   And   a   cow - boy   will

car - ry   me   on. _____

1.   2.

Come gather around me, my comrades and friends,
    For sun it is setting on life's short day;
For I'm wounded to die and there's nothing to do
    But wait 'til my life ebbs away.

    Oh, bury me on the lone prairie,
        Where the hoofs of the horses shall fall,
    Where the echoing tread falls over my head
        And a cowboy will carry me on.

I've rode on the prairie by night and by day,
    No danger I feared as I rode along;
But a red-coated foreman has written my doom,
    And a cowboy will carry me on.

Be kind to my pony while with you he stays,
    Then bury him beside me when he must go,
How often I've tried him and I know he won't fail
    When we ride in that great rodeo.

319

No. 119

The Streets of Laredo

The song deals with the death of a sinner: sin, remorse, death—note these words carefully for they are all of deep concern to the kind of men who pioneered America. The cowboy, dying in a street or on a barroom floor, captures the ear of a fellow cowboy to purge his soul for the Last Ride. At this crucial moment he is concerned with human beings most near and dear—wife or sweetheart, mother, sister, father, brother—not with their physical well-being, but rather with remorse for the anguish brought upon them by the cowboy's dishonorable life. At the threshold of death, the cowboy also wants a ritual that ties man not so much to eternity and God as to mankind as he knows it. In various versions not cited here there are sixteen gamblers, six pretty maidens, the thrown lasso, brandy sprinkled on his coffin, whiskey to assuage the pallbearers' thirst, the dashing horse, even the fife and drum, which are like mementos of the precowboy origins of our American culture. The cowboy also harbors an underlying human dignity that forces him to admonish his own kind into paths of righteousness. Still more important is his deep surge toward oneness with men of his own breed. In this desire the cowboy is rewarded for, quite oblivious to his "sinful" life, his friends rally to his funeral procession with love and affection despite (or should we say "because of") his self-assigned wrongdoings. Within this broad frame, each of the scores of texts of "The Cowboy's Lament" makes its own specific choices and embroiders its own details like the interwoven motifs of a patchwork quilt. Its variants, parodies, and antecedents give it the proportions of an epic poem. (Melody: Myra E. Hull, "Cowboy Ballads," *The Kansas Historical Quarterly* [Feb. 1939], VIII, No. 1, p. 50 [published by permission of the Kansas State Historical Society]. Text A: N. Howard [Jack] Thorp, *Songs of the Cowboys* [Estancia, N.M.: News Print Shop, 1908], pp. 29-30. Text B: JL 320.)

THE STREETS OF LAREDO

TEXT A

'Twas once in my saddle I used to be happy,
    'Twas once in my saddle I used to be gay;
But I first took to drinking, then to gambling,
    A shot from a six-shooter took my life away.

My curse let it rest, let it rest on the fair one
    Who drove me from friends that I loved and from home,
Who told me she loved me, just to deceive me,
    My curse rest upon her, wherever she roam.

Oh she was fair, Oh she was lovely,
    The belle of the Viliage [*sic*], the fairest of all;
But her heart was as cold as the snow on the mountains,
    She gave me up for the glitter of gold.

I arrived in Galveston in old Texas,
    Drinking and gambling I went to give o'er,
But, I met with a Greaser and my life he has finished,
    Home and relations I ne'er shall see more.

Send for my father, Oh send for mother,
  Send for the surgeon to look at my wounds,
But I fear it is useless, I feel I am dying,
  I'm a young cow-boy cut down in my bloom.

Farewell my friends, farewell my relations,
  My earthly career has cost me sore.
The cow-boy ceased talking, they knew he was dying,
  His trials on earth, forever were o'er.

Beat your drums lightly, play your fifes merrily,
  Sing your death march as you bear me along;
Take me to the grave yard, lay the sod o'er me,
  I'm a young cow-boy and know I've done wrong.

TEXT B

As I was passing by Tom Sherwin's bar room—
  Tom Sherwin's bar room so early one day—
Who should I see but a handsome young cowboy
  Stretched out on a blanket and all pale and gray.

Oh, his eyes were fast glazing, and death was approaching,
  His white lips were curled and tortured with pain;
As he spoke in a whisper of a scene far behind him,
  Of his home in the East which he'd ne'er see again.

"Oh, tell my old father I've tried to live honest—
  Tried to shoot square and give all men their due—
But I first took to drinking and then to gambling
  Which brought me to trouble, and now I am through.

"Oh, tell him I wish I had heeded his warning,
  But now it's too late, and I bid him adieu;
Got shot in the breast by a Dodge City gambler
  Who dealt from the bottom, and I'm dying today.

"Please gather up my last hand of poker—
  The one that I dropped when I got my death wound—
Send it and my six gun home to my brother
  After you've buried me deep in the tomb.

"Tell him these things are what ruined his brother
  And never to part with the last fatal hand,
But carry it always just as a reminder
  If e'er he should drift to this wild cattle land.

"Oh, write me a letter to my gray-haired mother
  And break the news gently to my sister so dear;
But not one word of this shall you mention
  When a crowd gathers round you my story to hear.

"Tell them I loved them all through my wild wanderings
  And that nobody here knows my name;
I got in a battle while playing stud poker
  And I don't want my people to share in my shame.

"Oh, there is another as dear as my sister,
  Lovely and pure as the dew on a rose;
Tell her to wait for her lover no longer
  For he sleeps where the prairie wind smoothly blows.

"Tell her that her image has always been with me,
  Carrying me up through the long, lonely days,
And that I'm taking it down through the valley
  Locked in my heart to be with me always."

Part Fourteen

The Last Roundup

No. 120
The Dying Cowboy of Rim Rock Ranch

This "Dying Cowboy" is a folkish bending of cowboy imagery to transcendental notions basic in the Christian faith. Life and salvation are for man what the roundup and trail drive are for the dogies. Note how the realistic range images of the first text get molded, in the second one, into the transcendental images of life and death. (Melody and Text A: Library of Congress #856B2, recorded by John A. Lomax. Text B: Library of Congress, collected by John A. Lomax.)

THE DYING COWBOY OF RIM ROCK RANCH

Good - bye to my pals of the prai - rie,____ Good -
bye to the sad - dle__ and the trail;__ Good - bye to the morn-ing's first
gleam - ing,__ Good - bye to the prai - ries and vale. For I'm

CHORUS

rid - ing a-way on life's round - up___ Where the sun is a - sink - ing

low; ___ Yes, I'm rid´- ing a - way on life's round - up ___ Where the

sun ___ is sink - ing low. ___

Text A

Good-bye to my pals of the prairie,
   Good-bye to the saddle and the trail;
Good-bye to the morning's first gleaming,
   Good-bye to the prairies and vale.

CHORUS:
   For I'm riding away on life's roundup
     Where the sun is a-sinking low;
   Yes, I'm riding away on life's roundup
     Where the sun is sinking low.

Good-bye to the cracking of the pistol,
   Good-bye to the clinking of the spurs;
Good-bye to the morning's first gleaming,
   Good-bye to the wild life's whirl.

Good-bye to the lurking of coyotes,
   Good-bye to the calls of the dove;
Good-bye to the rimrock races,
   Good-bye to the girl that I love.

Oh boys, when you're far from the rimrock
   You lean over the canyon below,
You can think of the spot where I'm resting
   For the Roundup of the Eternal Soul.

Text B

Goodbye to the cracking of the pistol,
   Goodbye to the clinking of the spur,
Goodbye to the morning for sleeping,
   Goodbye to the wild Irish girl.

CHORUS:
   For I'm riding away on my brown girl,
     Where the sun is sinking low;
   For I'm riding away on my brown girl,
     Where the sun is sinking low.

Goodbye to the yapping of the coyote,
   Goodbye to the calls of the dove,
Goodbye to the Rim Rock ranches,
   Goodbye to the girl that I love.

Oh, boys, when you're far from the Rim Rock
   You know there's a cabin on that shore,
You can think of the spot where I left you,
   For the roundup where we all must go.

Goodbye to my pals of the prairie,
   Goodbye to the cattle and trail,
Goodbye to the morning for sleeping,
   Goodbye to the prairie and vale.

No. 121
Cowboy's Meditation

This meditation is a classic of cowboy verse. Life after death and its corollary with life on the cattle ranges are expressed as a speculation, not as a dogma. The song has an engaging structural unity: the range hand settles for a night's sleep; his meditation lulls him to sleep and dreams; dawn breaks, and from his Neoplatonic meditation (Neoplatonic because the afterlife is seen as a perfected form of life in the here and now) the cowboy is roused once more to a life of action. (Melody: FAC I 504, sung by Kathy Dagel. Text: FAC I 167, sung by Robert E. Voris.)

COWBOY'S MEDITATION

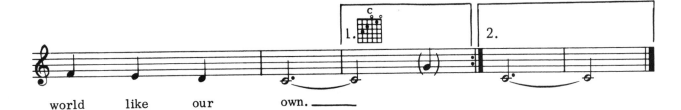

world like our own. _____

At midnight when cattle are sleeping
 On my saddle I pillow my head,
And up at the heavens lie peeping
 From out of my cold, grassy bed.
And it's often and often I've wondered
 At night while lying alone,
If each tiny star way up yonder
 Is a great peopled world like our own.

Are they worlds with their ranges and ranches,
 Do they ring with rough rider's refrain,
Do the cowboys scrap with the Comanches
 And other redmen of the plains?
Are the hills covered over with cattle
 In those mystic worlds so far, far away,
Do the ranch houses ring with the prattle
 Of sweet little children at play?

In evening in the bright stars up yonder
 Do the cowboys lie down to their rest,
Do they gaze at this wide world and wonder
 If rough riders dash over its crest?
Do they list' to the wolves in the canyon,
 Do they watch the night owl in its flight?
Are their horses their only companions
 While guiding their herds through the night?

Sometimes when a star is twinkling
 Like a diamond set in the sky
I've oft found myself lying and thinking
 If maybe God's heaven is nigh.
And I wondered if there I shall meet her—
 My mother whom God took away—
It's up in stars heavens I'll greet her
 At the round-up on that last day.

In the east the great daylight is breaking
 And into my saddle I'll spring,
The cattle from sleep are awaking,
 My heavenward thoughts now take wing.
The eyes of my bronco are flashing,
 He impatiently pulls at the reins,
While out 'round the herd I'll go dashing,
 Just a reckless cowboy of the plains.

No. 122
The Grand Roundup

"The Grand Roundup" is a full-blown hymn in which the essential Christian notions about life, morality, and salvation are viewed through cowboy images. We have it in scores of texts, many of which present their own distinctive images, stanzas, and even melodic lines. (Melody: FAC I 169, sung by Robert E. Voris. Text A: FAC II 125, collected by J. Frank Dobie. Text B: W. S. James, *Cow-Boy Life in Texas* [Chicago: Donohue, Henneberry and Co., 1893], pp. 212–213.)

THE GRAND ROUNDUP

Last night as I lay on the prai - rie,—— Look-ing up to the stars in the sky,—— I won-dered if ev - er a cow - boy—— Would get to that sweet bye and bye.—— Oh, yes, there will be a great round - up —— Where— cow - boys like cat - tle will stand,—— To be "cut" by the Rid - er of Judg - ment,—— Who is

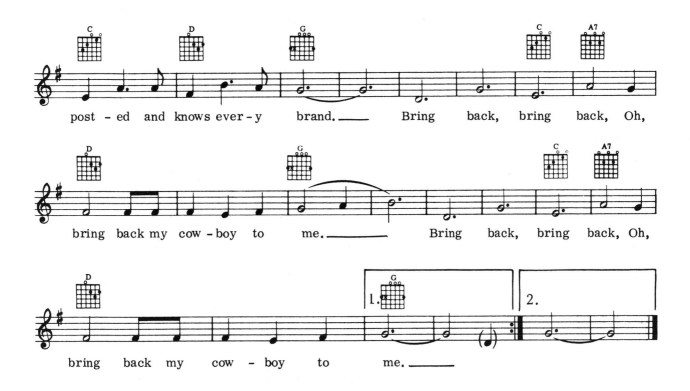

post-ed and knows ever-y brand.___ Bring back, bring back, Oh,

bring back my cow-boy to me.___ Bring back, bring back, Oh,

bring back my cow-boy to me.___

TEXT A. THE COWBOY'S VISION

Last night as I lay on the prairie,
  Looking up to the stars in the sky,
I wondered if ever a cowboy
  Would get to that sweet bye and bye.
Oh, yes, there will be a great roundup
  Where cowboys like cattle will stand,
To be "cut" by the Rider of Judgment,
  Who is posted and knows every brand.

CHORUS:
    Bring back, bring back,
      Oh, bring back my cowboy to me.
    Bring back, bring back,
      Oh, bring back my cowboy to me.

The canyons and gorges are many
  And "dogies" go often astray,
But the pale-horsed rider will gather
  Everyone to that great judgment day.
In that day of the great final judgment,
  When we all come around the white throne,
How happy will be every cowboy,
  To whom the Lord sayeth, "Well done!"

How sad, as we come to that roundup,
  If our hearts do not have the right brand,
For no "maverick" or "stray" in the judgment
  Will ever be able to stand.
Then my brother, let's come to the branding,
  Our owner is calling today;
If he touches and blesses and owns you
  You'll be glad in that great judgment day.

TEXT B. LAST ROUNDUP

When I think of the last great roundup
    On the eve of Eternity's dawn,
I think of the host of cow-boys
    Who have been with us here and have gone,
And I wonder if any will greet me
    On the sands of the evergreen shore;
With a hearty "God bless you, old fellow,"
    That I've met with so often before.

I think of the big-hearted fellows
    Who will divide with you blanket and bread,
With a piece of stray beef well roasted,
    And charge for it never a "red."
I often look upward and wonder,
    If the green fields will seem half so fair;
If any the wrong trail have taken
    And fail to "be in" over there.

For the trail that leads down to perdition
    Is paved all the way with good deeds;
But in the great roundup of ages,
    Dear boys, this won't answer your needs.
But the way to green pastures, though narrow,
    Leads straight to the home in the sky;
And Jesus will give you the passports
    To the land of the sweet by-and-by.

For the Saviour has taken the contract
    To deliver all those who believe,
At the headquarters ranch of His Father,
    In the great range where none can deceive.
The Inspector will stand at the gate-way,
    And the herd, one and all must go by;
The roundup by the angels of judgment
    Must pass 'neath His all-searching eye.

No mavrick or slick will be tallied
    In the great Book of Life in His home,
For he knows all the brands and the ear-marks
    That down through the ages have come.
But along with the strays and the sleepers
    The tailings must turn from the gate;
No road brand to gain them admission,
    But the awful sad cry "Too late!"

For the trail that leads down to perdition
    Is paved all the way with good deeds;
But in the great roundup of ages,
    Dear boys, this won't answer your needs.
But the way to green pastures, though narrow,
    Leads straight to the home in the sky;
And Jesus will give you the passports
    To the land of the sweet by-and-by.

No. 123
The Cowboy's Soliloquy

Biblical reminiscences stimulate the singer in this virile song which exposes realistic facets of the cowboy code—muscular involvement in a rugged out-of-doors setting, self-reliance, free enterprise, the competitive spirit—shall we call it pragmatic Christian materialism? Whatever the name, it is still very much with us. (Melody: Victor 21402, Carl T. Sprague. Text: *Kansas Cowboy,* Dodge City, April 25, 1885.)

THE COWBOY'S SOLILOQUY

All day o'er the prai-ries a-lone I ride,— Not e-ven a dog to run by my side; My— fire I kin-dle with chips gath-ered round,— And boil my cof-fee with-out be-ing ground. Bread lack-ing leav-en I bake in a pot, And sleep on the ground for want of a cot; I wash in a pud-dle and wipe on a sack And car-ry my ward-robe all on my back.

All day o'er the prairies alone I ride,
Not even a dog to run by my side;
My fire I kindle with chips gathered round,
And boil my coffee without being ground.
Bread lacking leaven I bake in a pot,
And sleep on the ground for want of a cot;
I wash in a puddle and wipe on a sack
And carry my wardrobe all on my back.

My ceiling the sky, my carpet the grass,
My music the lowing of herds as they pass;
My books are the brooks, my sermons the stones,
My parson's a wolf on a pulpit of bones.
But then if my cooking ain't very complete,
Hygenists can't blame me for living to eat.
And where is the man who sleeps more profound
Than the cowboy who stretches himself on the ground?

My books teach me constancy ever to prize,
My sermons that small things I should not despise,
And my parson remarks from his pulpit of bone
That "The Lord favors those who look out for their own."
Between love and me lies a gulf very wide,
And a luckier fellow may call her his bride;
But Cupid is always a friend to the bold,
And the best of his arrows are pointed with gold.

Friends gently hint I am going to grief,
But men must make money and women have beef,
Society bans me a savage and dodge,
And Masons would ball me out of their lodge.
If I'd hair on my chin I might pass for the goat
That bore all sin in ages remote;
But why this is thusly I don't understand,
For each of the patriarchs owned a big brand.

Abraham emigrated in search of a range
When water got scarce and he wanted a change;
Isaac had cattle in charge of Esau,
And Jacob "ran cows" for his father-in-law.
He started in business clear down at bedrock
And made quite a fortune by watering stock,
David went from night-herding and using a sling
To winning a battle and being a king.

And the shepherds when watching their flocks on the hill
Heard the message from heaven of "Peace and Good Will."

No. 124
The Glory Trail

The theme of "The Glory Trail" is the eternal triangle, not between a man and two women—but between man, humdrum existence, and a quest for the universal. Hooking your wagon to a star, or taking a bull by the horns, are but play compared to High Chin Bob's task when he threw his lasso on a mountain lion. The author is Charles Badger Clark (Melody: "Away High Up in the Mogliones," as sung by Rudolf Bretz, *A Treasury of Western Folklore,* ed. B. A. Botkin [New York: Crown Publishers, 1951], p. 765. Text: Charles Badger Clark, *Sun and Saddle Leather* [Boston: Richard G. Badger, 1920], pp. 70–73).

THE GLORY TRAIL

Way high up the Mo - gol - lons, A -mong the moun-tain tops, A

li - on cleaned a year-lin's bones And licked his thank -ful chops, When

on the pic - ture who should ride, A - trip -pin' down a slope, But

High - Chin Bob, with sin - ful pride And mav 'rick hun - gry rope. "Oh,

CHORUS

glo - ry be to me," says he, "And fame's un - fad - in flowers! All

med -dlin' hands are far a -way; I ride my good top - hawse to - day And I'm

top - rope of the Laz - y J! Hi, kit - ty cat, you're ours!"

'Way high up the Mogollons,
  Among the mountain tops,
A lion cleaned a yearlin's bones
  And licked his thankful chops,
When on the picture who should ride,
  A-trippin' down a slope,
But High-Chin Bob, with sinful pride
  And mav'rick hungry rope.

  "Oh, glory be to me," says he,
    "And fame's unfadin' flowers!
  All meddlin' hands are far away;
  I ride my good top-hawse today
  And I'm top-rope of the Lazy J—
    Hi! kitty cat, you're ours!"

That lion licked his paw so brown
  And dreamed soft dreams of veal—
And then the circlin' loop sung down
  And roped him 'round his meal.
He yowled quick fury to the world
  Till all the hills yelled back;
The top-hawse gave a snort and whirled
  And Bob caught up the slack.

  "Oh, glory be to me," laughs he.
    "We hit the glory trail.
  No human man as I have read
  Darst loop a ragin' lion's head,
  Nor ever hawse could drag one dead
    Until we told the tale."

'Way high up the Mogollons
  That top-hawse done his best,
Through whippin' brush and rattlin' stones,
  From canyon-floor to crest.
But ever when Bob turned and hoped
  A limp remains to find,
A red-eyed lion, belly roped
  But healthy, loped behind.

"Oh, glory be to me," grunts he.
  "This glory trail is rough,
Yet even till the Judgment Morn
I'll keep this dally 'round the horn,
For never any hero born
  Could stoop to holler: ' 'Nuff!' "

Three suns had rode their circle home
  Beyond the desert's rim,
And turned their star-herds loose to roam
  The ranges high and dim;
Yet up and down and 'round and 'cross
  Bob pounded, weak and wan,
For pride still glued him to his hawse
  And glory drove him on.

  "Oh, glory be to me," sighs he.
    "He kain't be drug to death,
  But now I know beyond a doubt
  Them heroes I have read about
  Was only fools that stuck it out
    To end of mortal breath."

'Way high up the Mogollons
  A prospect man did swear
That moon dreams melted down his bones
  And hoisted up his hair:
A ribby cow-hawse thundered by,
  A lion trailed along,
A rider, ga'nt but chin on high,
  Yelled out a crazy song.

  "Oh, glory be to me!" cries he,
    "And to my noble noose!
  Oh, stranger, tell my pards below
  I took a rampin' dream in tow,
  And if I never lay him low,
    I'll never turn him loose!"

No. 125
The Hell-Bound Train

The dance of death has been a motif in Christian art and literature since the early Middle Ages. It appears in stone over the portals of the Gothic cathedrals where one sees the Angel of the Balance weighing up the souls of the departed and directing them toward the lap of Jesus on the right, or toward the caldron of Hell on the left. Here we have it in the nightmare of a drunken cowboy. (Melody: FMC I 974, sung by Phyllis Stocks and Evelyn Ward. Text: JL 55.)

THE HELL-BOUND TRAIN

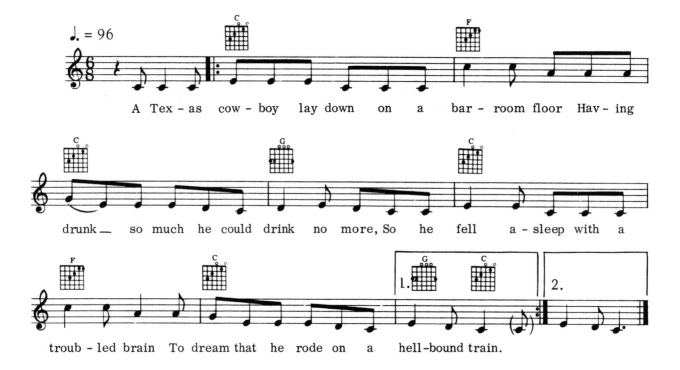

A Tex-as cow-boy lay down on a bar-room floor Hav-ing drunk— so much he could drink no more, So he fell a-sleep with a troub-led brain To dream that he rode on a hell-bound train.

A Texas cowboy lay down on a bar room floor
Having drunk so much he could drink no more,
So he fell asleep with a troubled brain
To dream that he rode on a hell-bound train.

The engine with murderous blood was damp,
And was brilliantly lit with a brimstone lamp.
An imp for fuel was shoveling bones
While the furnace rang with a thousand groans.

The boiler was filled with lager beer,
The devil himself was the engineer;
The passengers were a most motley crew,
Church members, atheist, gentile and Jew.

Rich men in broadcloth, beggers in rags,
Handsome young ladies and withered old hags;
Yellow and black men, red, brown, and white,
All chained together, oh God, what a sight!

While the train rushed on at an awful pace
The sulphurous fumes scorched their hands and face;
Whiter and whiter the country grew
As faster and faster the engine flew;

Louder and louder the thunder crashed,
And brighter and brighter the lightning flashed;
Hotter and hotter the air became
Till the clothes were burnt from each quivering frame.

And out of the distance there arose a yell,
"Ha ha!" said the Devil. "We're nearing hell."
Then, oh, how the passengers all shrieked with pain
And begged the devil to stop the train.

But he capered about and danced for glee,
And laughed and joked at their misery.
"My faithful friends, you have done the work,
And the devil never can a favor shirk.

"You've bullied the weak, you've robbed the poor,
The starving brother you've turned from the door;
You've laid up gold where the canker rusts
And have given free bent to your beastly lusts.

"You've justice scorned, and corruption sown,
And trampled the laws of nature down;
You have drunk, rioted, cheated, plundered, and lied,
And mocked at God in your hell-born pride.

"You have paid full fare so I'll carry you through,
For it's only right you should have your due;
Why, the laborer always expects his hire,
So I'll land you safe in the lake of fire;

"Where your flesh will waste in the flames that roar,
And my imps torment you forevermore."
Then the cowboy awoke with an anguished cry,
His clothes wet with sweat and his hair standing high.

Then he prayed as he never prayed till that hour
To be saved from his sin and the demon's power;
And his prayers and vows were not in vain,
For he never more rode the hell-bound train.

No. 126
The Cattleman's Prayer

The frontier represented not only challenge but insecurity. It is little wonder that first- and second-generation Westerners place a high value on material things, especially the cattle, unique source of income for many. Hence we can excuse the naïve self-interest expressed in this cattleman's prayer (one of many). (Melody: Victor 21402, Carl T. Sprague. Text: Clifford P. Westermeier, *Trailing the Cowboy* [Caldwell, Idaho: Caxton Printers, 1955], pp. 265–266, quoted from *Socorro* [New Mexico] *Bullion*, Nov. 21, 1885.)

THE CATTLEMAN'S PRAYER

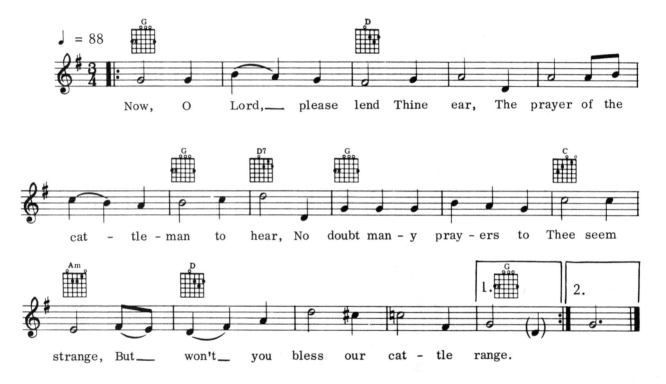

Now, O Lord,__ please lend Thine ear, The prayer of the
cat - tle - man to hear, No doubt man - y pray - ers to Thee seem
strange, But__ won't__ you bless our cat - tle range.

Now, O Lord, please lend Thine ear,
The prayer of the cattleman to hear;
No doubt many prayers to Thee seem strange,
But won't you bless our cattle range?

Bless the round-up, year by year,
And don't forget the growing steer;
Water the land with brooks and rills,
For my cattle that roam on a thousand hills.

Now, O Lord, won't you be good,
And give our stock plenty of food;
And to avert a winter's woe,
Give Italian skies and little snow.

Prairie fires won't you please stop?
Let thunder roll and water drop;
It frightens me to see the smoke—
Unless it's stopped I'll go dead broke.

As you, O Lord, my herds behold—
Which represents a sack of gold—
I think at least five cents per pound
Should be the price of beef the year around.

One thing more and then I'm through—
Instead of one calf, give my cows two,
I may pray different than other men,
Still I've had my say, and now, Amen!

No. 127
The Buffalo Range

"Buffalo Range" is most likely a creation of the 1930's. Yet by its candor, artistry, and faithfulness to the cowboy and western image it deserves a place in this repertoire. We especially like its gentle and subdued artistry in shaping the cowboy mood to the needs of camp and gospel singing. (Melody and text: Melotone M13082, Frank Luther Trio.)

THE BUFFALO RANGE

♩.= 80

Yip-pee - yay— get a-long lit-tle do-gie, get a-long, Yip-pee-yi,— you and I through the fold;— Oh, I would-n't ex-change the buf-fa-lo range For the world and all of its gold.— On a buf-fa-lo range I'll build me a home, And set-tle down, no more to roam;— And the moon o-ver-head will tuck me to bed, Lit-tle

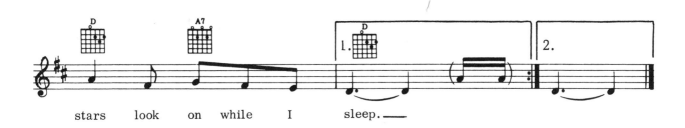

stars   look   on   while   I   sleep. ____

CHORUS:

> Yippee-yay, get along little dogie, get along,
> Yippee-yi, you and I through the fold;
> Oh, I wouldn't exchange the buffalo range
> For the world and all of its gold.

On a buffalo range I'll build me a home,
And settle down, no more to roam;
And the moon overhead will tuck me to bed,
Little stars look on while I sleep.

On the buffalo range the antelope play
And little birds sing all the day;
And at night mellow beams like a bundle of dreams
Send a picture of a beautiful land.

On the buffalo range I'll live and I'll die,
And thank the Great Boss in the sky
For the privilege dear we know down here
On the good old buffalo range.

No. 128
A Cowboy's Prayer

Charles Badger Clark's "A Cowboy's Prayer" is a fitting conclusion to this collection of songs because it evokes the code of the cowboy on its highest moral plane: the godliness of unkempt nature, the freedom of the wide open spaces, generosity for the faults of others and the expectancy of the same for oneself, perseverance in one's journey up the long dark trail. Vigny and Camus offer us the same stern ethic. We have found no music for it. (Charles Badger Clark, *Sun and Saddle Leather* [Boston: Richard G. Badger, 1920], pp. 35–37.)

A COWBOY'S PRAYER

Oh, Lord, I've never lived where churches grow.
   I love creation better as it stood
That day You finished it so long ago
   And looked upon Your work and called it good.
I know that others find You in the light
   That's sifted down through tinted window panes,
And yet I seem to feel You near tonight
   In this dim, quiet starlight on the plains.

I thank You, Lord, that I am placed so well,
   That You have made my freedom so complete;
That I'm no slave of whistle, clock or bell,
   Nor weak-eyed prisoner of wall and street.
Just let me live my life as I've begun
   And give me work that's open to the sky;
Make me a pardner of the wind and sun,
   And I won't ask a life that's soft or high.

Let me be easy on the man that's down;
   Let me be square and generous with all.
I'm careless sometimes, Lord, when I'm in town,
   But never let 'em say I'm mean or small!
Make me as big and open as the plains,
   As honest as the hawse between my knees,
Clean as the wind that blows behind the rains,
   Free as the hawk that circles down the breeze!

Forgive me, Lord, if sometimes I forget.
   You know about the reasons that are hid.
You understand the things that gall and fret;
   You know me better than my mother did.
Just keep an eye on all that's done and said
   And right me, sometimes, when I turn aside,
And guide me on the long, dim trail ahead
   That stretches upward toward the Great Divide.

Lexicon

(We refer frequently to *Adams* in this section of our study. Full bibliographical reference is: Ramon F. Adams, *Western Words: A Dictionary of the Range, Cow Camp and Trail* [Norman: University of Oklahoma Press, 1946].)

adiós. Spanish for goodbye.

adobe. In Spanish, *adobe*—dried brick. Clay, mixed with water and straw, is placed in molds about 18 × 10 × 6 inches, then removed to dry and bake in the sun. It was a common building material in the Hispanic Southwest. Adobe gives excellent insulation but requires protection from moisture which causes rapid erosion.

alkali. The Great Basin and other regions of the Southwest present innumerable instances of small basins that accumulate alkaline wastes due to the nature of soils and lack of drainage. These range all the way from dry basins crusted with whitish soil and supporting a limited vegetation to such phenomena as the Great Salt Lake itself. As an adjective, alkalied means: "acclimated to the country; a person or animal ill from drinking alkali water; one who is drunk." Also a colloquial name for whiskey.

americano, n., adj. American.

amigo. Spanish for friend.

amor. Spanish for love.

antelope. Also called "pronghorn" (*antilocapra americana*). Unique to North America, this svelte denizen of the sage is in no way related to species of African ruminants bearing the same name. Unlike the deer family, male and female both have horns. Their range once extended from the northern reaches of Arizona and New Mexico through the Rocky Mountain area and on up into the prairie provinces of Canada.

arroyo. Spanish for small stream. In the Southwest it means a precipitous gully or channel cut in soft earth by the waters from sudden violent storms.

barbed wire. *See* FENCES.

bedground, bedded, bedding (cattle). On the range or on trail drives the bedground was the place where cattle gathered and got off their feet to spend the night. On drives range cattle were skittish: getting them "bedded" took some riding, and guards rode circle on them all night long.

bedroll, *n.* Next to horse and saddle, the wandering cowboy's most treasured possession. It consisted of a tarpaulin about 7 × 8 feet containing quilts and most of his personal possessions. On roundup or trail drive it was carried in chuck or equipment wagon: when the cowboy was floating between jobs it was tied behind his saddle.

bellota. *See* BLACKJACK OAK.

bit, *n.* Metal bar that traverses a horse's mouth. There are many types, ranging from a straight metal bar to variously curbed or articulated types. Silver mountings and gaudy designs were, like boots, spurs, and sombrero, symbols of affluence or the quest for status.

blackjack oak. *Quercus Emoryi,* a scrub oak of the dry foothill areas of West Texas, Arizona, and New Mexico, sometimes known as *bellota.* It grows to fifteen feet in height with a trunk up to two and a half feet in diameter. Adams (p. 12) notes "blackjack steer" to designate a scrawny critter from the timber country.

bolero. Spanish dance done to castanets and lively music in three-quarter time.

Brahma (cattle). Species of East Indian cattle gray in color with legs and underside shading off to white. They are distinguished, especially the males, by a notable hump over the shoulders. Legend has it that Ringling Brothers' Circus imported and exhibited them, with little or no success, prior to 1900. These animals were later sold and ended their days among the cattle herds of the King Ranch, Texas. Because of their tolerance for heat, disease-resistant qualities, and their resistance to insects, they have been used to interbreed with the familiar strains of beef cattle imported from Europe. In rodeo shows they are used especially for the bull-riding contests.

brand, *n.* Mark burned into the hides of cattle or other animals to identify ownership. *v.* To put such a mark on an animal. To assure that brands for each owner were distinctive, registration thereof by a state official came into being, and brand books were, and still are, issued periodically. Brands were inflicted with a "branding iron," "running iron," or simply an "iron." Under open-range conditions irons were heated in a small fire. Critters were roped, thrown, and tied, then branded and released. "Reading" or "calling" brands was a necessity whenever cattle of different owners were to be separated. When cattle were sold, old brands were canceled (also with an iron), and the new brand burned on. The expert rustling of branded cattle necessitated careful modification of brands using appropriate irons. Often the brand also became the recognized name for the home ranch; the rancher might even be known by his brand in lieu of his family name, and hands long employed there likewise. In a figurative sense, to "start a brand" meant to get married and rear a family. In a transcendental sense, brands (of God or Satan) are worn by Christians in a state of grace or disgrace.

brogan shoe. Coarse shoe made of untanned leather.

bronc, bronk, bronco, broncho. *See* HORSE.

bronc(o) buster. Cowboy who specializes in riding, subduing, and breaking to the saddle previously ungentled horses. The job calls for nerve, physical dexterity, and acumen lest the horses he has trained persist in bad habits which make them unusable as cow ponies.

buck, *v.* The efforts of an ungentled horse or wild steer to unseat its rider. Prior to being "broken," almost any range horse will make a most vigorous struggle to "throw" its rider. Adams (p. 22) lists a half column of names to identify the pitches and other movements that characterize bucking, this terminology being developed as systematically and as comprehensively as is the lingo of boxing or wrestling. *n.* Webster defines the noun ("beans and the buck") "buck" as lye or soapsuds in which clothes are soaked in washing or bleaching. Here it seems to be a pejorative for the liquid in which the beans have been cooked.

buckaroo, *n.* Probably derived from Spanish *vaquero,* influenced by the verb *buck.* It is another name for the cowboy, but generally designates one who is a bit on the rough and cantankerous side. Note its use as an endearing epithet in the lullabies.

buffalo. Popular name for *Bison americanus.* Vast herds roamed the plains of the central and western United States into the 1880's. They were ruthlessly exploited for hides and for sport (so called). The hump was considered a delicacy. Their droppings, dried, made satisfactory fuel for campfires (buffalo chips).

buffalo gnat/black flies. *Simuliidae,* species of blood-sucking fly which can bedevil both man and beast. They are up to a quarter inch in length and hump-backed: hence their name.

buffalo-hide canoe. The hides of cattle or of buffalo were commonly known as bull hides. The bull-hide or buffalo-hide canoe was a circular boat with a frame of bent willow covered with buffalo hide. It was used extensively on the Missouri River by Mandan and Hidatsa Indians.—A. H. Woodward, Patagonia, Arizona.

bull, *n.* Bull Durham, or simply "bull," was a grated tobacco sold in small pocket-sized cotton bags along with a sheaf of cigarette papers, and from which any self-respecting cowboy "rolled his own." With practice it can be done with one hand while the pony jogs doggedly on.

bush up, *v.* At midday, especially in hot weather, critters (and the wiser humans) on the open range take to the shade of mesquite, chaparral, or other available foliage.

button-hole door. According to Bill Koch, Professor of English at Kansas State University in Manhattan, a button-hole door consisted simply of the cured pelt of a cow, bison, bear, or other large animal stretched across the opening and attached to pegs on one side so that it could be slipped off to give access to the dwelling.

buzzard. Otherwise called a turkey vulture. *Cathartes aura*, a large hawklike scavenger whose range extends from the plains to the Pacific, and from Canada south into Central and South America. Applied to men, it is an epithet of derision.

caballada. Spanish for a band of horses. *Syn. remuda.*

caballo. See HORSE.

casa. Spanish for house.

case-hardened. Said of iron having a thin hard surface.

catclaw. Species of *Acacia greggii*. Widely spread in the arid regions of the West and Southwest.

cavvy (cavyard, cavvy yard, covy-yard). From the Spanish *caballada. Syn. remuda.*

cayuse. A scrubby, undesirable horse said to be named from a Northwest Indian tribe that liked horses.

cellar. It was typical on the plains and in the inter-mountain area to build a one-room food storage facility about one rod behind the back door of the dwelling. It consisted of an excavation about five feet below the ground level, lined with sod or stone and covered over with timbers which were then covered with earth. The resulting room resisted frost in winter and was impervious to heat in the summer.

chaparral (chapparral). Term applied to *Atriplex, adanostroma arctostaphilos*, and other genera of thorny evergreen shrubs of the Southwest. Usually more than stirrup high, they form thickets and areas of cover ideal for the protection of range cattle despite the annoyance to punchers constrained to ride therein.

chaps, chappies (*chaparajos, chaparejos, chapareras*). Leather trousers or overalls. Worn over the ordinary trousers to protect the horseman's legs from injuries caused by brush fences, etc. *Syn.* leggings.

chaw. Not encountered elsewhere. Could it be an erroneous reading for "squaw"? A residue of "chawbacon," meaning a country bumpkin?

cholla (chola, choya). *Opuntia fulgida mammillata*. One of the small, treelike cacti of the arid regions of the Southwest. Being nearly spineless, it was found edible by cattle, sheep, and rodents. Curio shops sell lamps, flower holders, and other objects made from its dried shell. It grows to five feet in height.

chuck. Range name for food. The chuck wagon was a mobile kitchen for cowboys on trail or roundup. It had a chuck box extending across the rear and bolted to the wagon bed: its sturdy hinged door could be dropped down to form a table. A cowboy floating from ranch to ranch between jobs, especially when no work was available, was said to be "riding the chuck line."

chute. A narrow, fenced lane, usually connecting one corral with another; also a narrow passage designed for loading cattle into railroad cars, or passing them through into dipping vats. At a rodeo it terminates in a cage just big enough to permit the buckaroo to adjust his gear and mount. When he is ready the gate is sprung and the animal goes into action.

cinch. From the Spanish *cincha*—girth, cinch. Girth that passes around the horse's body to anchor the saddle. For heavy work there are generally two.

circle (herding). On roundup a crew of punchers fans out to gather all the cattle on a certain range. The circle riders are those who take the outer perimeter; a circle horse is one chosen with sufficient stamina ("bottom," in cowboy lingo) to endure the greater mileage.

claim. *See* GOVERNMENT CLAIM.

cocinero. Spanish for a male cook. At roundup or on trail herd, the role of the cook was extremely important. He didn't have to ride but he managed almost everything except the herd. He took charge of the teams and wagons hauling food, bedding, water, and supplies. He managed the *remuda*, assisted, of course, by the wrangler. Often the Anglo-American punchers reduced *cocinero* to the more manageable *coosie.*

Colt. In 1875 Colt produced a single-action 45-calibre pistol known as the Peacemaker. Three years later it appeared in a model accommodating the same 44-40 cartridge used in the Winchester rifle, thus permitting a westerner to carry a single type of cartridge for both rifle and pistol. This new weapon acquired further utility in the West because its sturdy frame recommended it for the gruesome sport of pistol-whipping, a practice by local marshals of clubbing tough hombres over the head, or by outlaws to intimidate their victims.—Summarized from Larry Koller, *The Fireside Book of Guns* (New York: Simon and Schuster, Inc., 1959), pp. 131–132.

corazón. Spanish for heart.

corn dodger. A hard-baked bread of cornmeal made in small pones.

corral. Enclosure designed to hold cattle, sheep, or horses in a restricted area, usually made of pole fences from five to eight feet high. The "home corral" is the final abode of the human spirit.

coulies (also coolies). From the French *couler*, to flow. *Syn.* arroyo. The term still persists on Rocky Mountain and northern cattle ranges in preference to the Mexican term.

cow. Term used to designate cattle generally, regardless of sex or age. *Syn.* critter.

cow horse. *See* HORSE.

cow pony. *See* HORSE.

cowboy. Used to identify the cowboy by almost everyone except the cowboys themselves who prefer puncher, cowpuncher, hand, cowhand, as general terms, and a list of other epithets so long that it takes Adams (p. 42) almost a full column to give the ones familiar to him. In Revolutionary days, and again in the early conflicts with Mexico, the term, as a proper name, was applied to certain mounted troops who marauded behind enemy lines. Now it comes near being universal, American movies having taken the cowboy's image and name to all parts of the world.

cowhand, cowman, cowpoke, cowpuncher. All these terms apply broadly to men who work cattle as their principal occupation. "Cowman" tends to be reserved for an owner or manager; the others for the brawn and muscle men. "Poke," "hand," and "puncher" often stand without prefix, but with the same meaning. (The work these men perform is known as "cowpunching" or "punching cows.")

coyote. From the Mexican *coyotl. Canis latrans* is of the same genus as the dog and the wolf. His range extended from the Mississippi to the Pacific Coast and from well down in Old Mexico to Arctic regions. He has survived well against the inroads of civilized man: specimens have recently been seen in Los Angeles. Gregarious animal that he is, nights on the prairie he did close harmony with sundry companions scattered far and wide.

crack-a-lou. Gambling game consisting in pitching coins to or toward the ceiling in a room so that they would fall as near as possible to a crack in the floor.

critter. Cattle. By extension, other domestic or wild animals, including women.

cross-herd, *v.* Our first and only encounter with this word. It could refer to the zigzagging movement of a puncher behind cattle moving slowly on a wide front so that there are no laggards and no critters spreading too far out on the wings.

curocos. Spanish. We have not encountered the term elsewhere in print; however, Mexican and New Mexican friends assure us it is the popular name for bugs that infect the peon's stores of dry beans or *frijoles.*

cut, *n., v.* At a roundup, the range cattle were assembled into smaller units for any number of purposes. It took an expert hand and a well-trained "cutting" horse to ride into the herd, locate, and isolate the animals desired. A "cut" was used to identify an animal or a herd separated from the main group for whatever purpose. The image, transferred to man, meant the selection of souls at the Final Judgment.

cutting horse. *See* HORSE.

dally, *dalebueltas.* In Mexican, *dale vueltas!* "give it some twists." Anglicized to "dally welters," then simply "dally." In roping cattle a full turn is taken around the horn of the saddle at the moment of making a catch. This is done in such a way that the rope can be released at once, or so that slack can be taken up. If the lasso is tied fast, saddle and rider may be torn from the horse. To "take your dally welters according to California law" meant to use a dally rather than to tie the lasso fast to the saddle horn, so that a "snake steer" could be released if rider and mount got into trouble.

deer. Two species are prevalent in the Rockies and the Southwest. The mule deer, *Odocoileus hemeonus,* is a large deer whose range is from parts of Old Mexico to the Arctic Circle. It prefers coniferous surroundings. Its popular name, "mule," is substantiated by its prominent ears. The white-tailed deer, *Odocoileus virginianus,* prefers hardwood or second-growth vegetation, and is somewhat smaller than the mule deer.

diamondback. *See* RATTLESNAKE.

Digby pine. This has not been encountered elsewhere. It may be an erroneous reading for "digger" pine, *Pinus sabiniana,* which grows among the dry, hot California foothills, especially in the Mother Lode country. Soft, crooked, and knotty, it produces a very inferior lumber.—Dr. Hector Lee, Professor of English, Sonoma State College, California.

dog, *v.* Rodeo sport in which a horseman rides alongside a critter, drops on its neck and throws the animal off its feet. Adams (p. 23) says a Negro puncher, Tom Pickett, was the first to practice the art, that it appeared first in rodeos as an exhibition only. Now it is a regular part of the rodeo repertoire.

dogies. Scrubby calves, orphan calves, unbranded calves, or calves generally. Derivation is uncertain: Spanish, *dogal, n.,* slip or hangman's knot, i.e., a calf fit to be killed? English, dough-gut, a lean potbellied calf carrying the scars of malnutrition?

dude. Applied by genuine range folk to the city-bred man out in the wide-open spaces merely for kicks.

dungre grass. Neither biologist colleagues nor Webster has been able to inform us about this plant. Is it derivative of *dungaree,* defined by Webster as "a coarse cotton cloth used for tents, sails, work clothing, etc."?

earmarks. Earmarks as well as brands are used to assert ownership: both were frequently inflicted upon the animal at the same time. At roundup the brand caller shouted the name of earmark and brand. Adams (p. 56) lists the names of more than thirty earmarks.

elk. *Cervus canadensis.* A magnificent denizen of the virgin lands from coast to coast and from southern Arizona, New Mexico, and Texas to sub-Arctic tundra. It frequents forest areas that are interspersed with open meadows. Its range has been greatly reduced by the civilizing activities of man. It is also known by the name *wapiti.*

fan, *v.* To slap a bucking horse on its sides while in the saddle. Adams (p. 57) says it served, as a pole does for a tightrope walker, to preserve one's balance.

faro. A gambling game with cards, in which the players bet on the cards to be turned up from the top of the dealer's pack. In one of our texts a "faro wheel" is mentioned. Perhaps the reference is to the use of a "faro box" which prevented delivery of more than one card at a time.

fences. Since fences permit the selective and specialized use of land, their importance cannot be overemphasized. In the West they ultimately changed the whole pattern of life. Barbed wire (twisted wire with short sharp spikes inserted) became common in the late '80's; earlier settlers had used mostly various types of pole fences, including the "Arkansas fence," made of poles stacked on diagonal planes.

flaps. There were *sombreros* made for use in cold seasons which had flaps that could be let down from the inner band to protect the ears.

forty-five. *See* Colt.

Four X. A popular brand of flour whose sacks were stamped conspicuously with four gaudy X's; reused for the making of children's clothes, the situation of the four X's sometimes produced ludicrous results.

frijoles. Spanish for dried beans.

Gentiles. In Mormon usage the term encompasses Christians except those born or baptized in the Mormon church.

government claim. A plot of farm or range land acquired under the Homestead Act of 1862. This Act offered any citizen who was the head of a family and over twenty-one years of age 160 acres of surveyed public land upon five years' continuous residence and payment of registration fees, or upon six months' residence and payment of $1.25 per acre.

grasshopper. General term applied to members of the *Acrididae* family, especially those whose wings are not highly developed and, hence, are primarily hoppers. They are to be distinguished from locusts who fly long distances in black droves. *Tetigoniidae* identifies grasshoppers popularly called "Mormon crickets." Many varieties of grasshoppers reach plague proportions and wreak a cruel destruction on all plant life, especially on farm crops.

graybacks. *Pediculus humanis corporis.* The common body louse, as popularly called in the mid-1850's and later.

grazin bit. Good general-purpose lightweight bit with a small curb in the mouthpiece.

Greaser. The "gringo's" (Anglo-American's) name for the common run of Mexicans.

greenhorn. *Syn.* tenderfoot.

grizzly bear. *Ursus horribilis,* a formidable denizen of the Northern Rockies whose range is now restricted to the most remote areas. His almost black fur is silvery and resplendent at the tips. He has a moderate hump over the shoulders, and a slightly swayed back. Specimens weigh up to a thousand pounds. Though basically vegetarian, this formidable and powerful animal is known for horrible deeds of carnage among wild and domestic beasts and, though rarely, among men.

grub. *Syn.* chuck.

grubstake. An advance made to a prospector in exchange for a share of his findings.

gulch. Deep, narrow ravine.

gut-line. *Syn. reata.*

hardtack. Cowboys on trail herd or riding range carried the same coarse, hard, unleavened bread which was the staple of soldiers at the frontier outposts.

haze, *v.* To drive cattle slowly, thus permitting them to graze.

heel fly. There are two species: (1) *Hypoderma bovus,* about thirteen millimeters in length and encountered in the northern parts of the United States, and (2) *Hypoderma lineatum,* the common heel fly widely distributed in the United States. Eggs are laid on the fetlock and belly of cattle, horses, and the larger ruminants; larvae, upon hatching, penetrate beneath the skin, travel through the muscles, and build their nests just beneath the skin.

hen-skin bedding. Bedcover stuffed with feathers.

hoecake. A thin bread made of cornmeal, water, and salt, originally baked on the blade of a hoe.

holdup man. *Syn.* outlaw. A man who detains and robs a person, train, stage, bank, etc.

hominy. Parched corn, hulled and coarsely broken; prepared for food by boiling in water.

horse. The horse has many names among Westerners. In this collection the following appear: bronc, broncho, *caballo,* cayuse, cow horse, cutting horse, hack, nag, Normans, outlaw, roping, steed, top horse.
   (1) bronc (bronk, bronco, broncho). From Spanish *bronco, adj.,* meaning rough, coarse, harsh. It is used to designate ungentled or semigentled horses, cow horses generally, but especially tough, lively, and cantankerous specimens whose behavior matches that of the wild breed of western men. *See* BRONC BUSTER.
   (2) *caballo.* Spanish for horse. Direct use of the Mexican term, or its anglicized counterpart *cayuse,* was usually pejorative and hence reserved for cantankerous or ugly but tough specimens.
   (3) cow horse, cow pony. A general term for the adaptable, sturdy, general service mount used by punchers in any and all jobs encountered.

(4) cutting horse. To see an expert rider work a well-trained cutting horse is equal to an evening at the classical ballet. The object is to separate one particular critter from the herd. Once the cutting horse has this animal identified he will parry its every lunge and end up with the critter backed into a corral corner exhausted, confused, and alone.
(5) hack. Probably derived from "hackney," meaning to the cowboy a beaten-down carriage horse.
(6) nag. Nondescript, common, inferior, ugly, or broken-down horse.
(7) Norman. A stock breed of dray horses, not suitable for the speed and quick reactions required of a cow horse.
(8) outlaw. Wild, mean, untamed or untamable horse—just the kind to foist upon an unsuspecting tenderfoot.
(9) roping horse. Roping and cutting place more demands upon the horse than any other range skill: speed, sudden and violent maneuver, a calm temperament under maximum pressure. The roping horse requires the further skill of keeping a taut rope in the second following a catch so that the puncher can dismount and throw and tie the critter. The well-trained roping horse will face the caught animal and keep backing off just enough to avoid the hazards of a slack rope.
(10) steed. Pre-cowboy name for a sturdy and trustworthy mount: the term survives in cowboy and western verses, especially those written by cowboys who had a mite of book learning.
(11) top horse. On trail or roundup each puncher kept a string of from three to six animals and changed as often each day as the work at hand permitted. The one he liked best, and hence harbored for the real delicate jobs, was of course the top horse in his string.

hot roll. *See* BEDROLL.

iron (branding). *See* BRAND.

jackrabbit. Two species are commonly known as jackrabbits: (1) the black-tailed variety, *Lepus californicus,* a desert dweller (Utah to California) whose color does not change with the seasons; and

(2) the white-tailed *Lepus townsendi,* whose habitat is foothill and mountainous areas from Utah eastward to the Great Plains. It is grayish-brown in the warm seasons but wholly white in the wintertime.

johnnycake. Variety of corn bread baked on a griddle. As the song is frequently interpreted it becomes quite clear that johnnycake is also a special dish stirred up by young men a-courting.

keno. Game of chance played with numbered balls and cards. Westerners used it to mean that the outcome of almost anything is very acceptable. It is still used, often shortened to "Keen!"

kerchief (also bandanna). Essential item in the cowboy's costume. It was worn knotted around the neck where it could be brought up over the nose as a dust shield, or, in the case of mounted bandits, to conceal their identity. It was typically blue or red in color, with white polka dots.

lariat. From the Spanish *la reata,* a rope used to tie pack animals in single file. Later extended to mean any rope used in working cattle.

larrup. To thrash or beat up. "I'll larrup the daylights out of you!" Webster says it has East Anglican origins, though we think that, in the American West, it may have been revitalized by association with lariat.

lasso. Portuguese *laço,* noose. *n.* A long rope, usually made of hide, with a running eyelet or *honda* at one end for making a loop. Also used as a verb. *Syn.* rope.

loco, n. Spanish—mad, crazy. Species of *astragalus* producing a drug which affects animals, especially horses. Several species are spread widely in the mountain West. The effect is cumulative. Used also as an adjective.

longhorn. A name given early cattle of Texas, because of the enormous spread of their horns; also the name for native men of Texas, the home of the longhorn cattle. The saga of the longhorn is interesting, and for a valuable and the only complete study of this historic bovine, we recommend *The Longhorns,* by an able recorder of the West, J. Frank Dobie (Boston: Little, Brown, 1941). (Adams, p. 93.)

lucerne. *Syn.* alfalfa. *Medicago sativa,* clover-like deep-rooted plant of the pea family imported to the West from Europe and now serving as one of the most important forage and cover crops.

madre. Spanish for mother.

maguey. Rope made from the fibers of various species of the century plant (especially *Agave americana*); used now only by trick ropers.

maverick. An unbranded calf of uncertain ownership. As a verb it is the act of placing one's own brand on such an animal. Adams (p. 97) derives it from the name of Samuel E. Maverick who sold a range herd to a neighbor. Since many of the Maverick cattle were unbranded the purchaser of the Maverick brand claimed and branded every animal he encountered, including some that did not belong to Maverick: hence, to "maverick" came to mean to steal and brand unbranded cattle.

mesquite. In Spanish, *mezquite.* A spiney shrub of the pea family growing in the Southwest and Mexico.

milling. The movement of cattle in a compact circle. This formation is forced upon a herd to stop a stampede. As the cattle mill in a circle, they wind themselves up into a narrowing mass which becomes tighter and tighter until finally it is so tight they can no longer move. When the same action takes place with horses, it is spoken of as "rounding up," the term "milling" being reserved strictly for cattle. The milling of cattle on the bedground where they should be off their feet was a symptom of restlessness foreboding a stampede.

monte. A gambling game of Spanish origin, played with a special deck of forty cards, in which the players bet against a banker on the color of cards to be turned up from the deck. It is a nickname often carried by a Westerner.

mountain lion. Although there are several species of large cats in cowboy country, the largest and most publicized is *Felis concolor* whose range, now restricted to very remote areas, once extended from Canada to Florida and Old Mexico, even on into Central and South America. Large specimens run up to eight feet in length and weigh up to two hundred pounds. They are of tawny color with tinges of gray shading off at the flanks to an off-white. The long tail ends in a small black tuft. The popular nomenclature is ambivalent and there are regional peculiarities: cougar, puma, panther, painter, or simply lion may serve for this and other members of the Western or Mexican cat family.

nag. *See* HORSE.

neck-up. This word, in range lingo, has a very different meaning from that which is used in metropolitan circles. On the range, an unruly cow or one with roving disposition will often be *necked* or tied to a more tractable animal. This practice was especially resorted to in the days of the longhorn. After the two animals had worn themselves out trying to go in different directions at the same time, the wilder one was enough subdued to move along in company of its fellows. A good neck animal is valued highly by its owner. (Adams, p. 103.) In the particular case cited in this book the unruly critter was necked-up to a scrub oak.

needle gun. A long-disused western slang term for any of the breechloading Springfield military rifles of the models of 1865 through 1884, so called from their long slim firing pin. Not to be confused with the Prussian "needle gun" of 1848, which was probably entirely unknown in the American West.— H. J. Swinney, Blue Mountain Lake, New York.

nester. A squatter who settles on state or government land. This term is applied with contempt by the cattlemen of the Southwest to the early homesteaders who began tilling the soil in the range country. Viewed from some ridge, the early nester's home, as he cleared his little patch of brush and stacked it in a circular form to protect his first feed patch from range cattle, looked like a gigantic bird's nest. The cowboy, ever quick to catch re-

semblances, mentioned it to the next man he met, and the name spread and stuck to every man that settled on the plains to till the soil. (Adams, p. 104.)

niggerhead rum. Not encountered elsewhere. The term "nigger" as a noun epithet and meaning dark in color, potent, unpalatable, etc., is common. *Niggerhead* also designated a black rounded boulder. Here we venture that the drinking of the niggerhead rum alluded to "sorting out the men from the boys."

night herd. On a cattle drive it was necessary to ride circle around the bedded cattle all night long lest they stampede or scatter. Guards spelled each other at two-hour intervals. The night horse was chosen for his keen sight, sure-footedness, and unfaltering sense of direction and calm under adverse circumstances. Riding night herd gave a puncher time to speculate about the nature of the cosmos and his personal involvement therein. Night-herd songs capture these transcendental experiences in rhythms gauged, like lullabies, to calm the restless cows.

Norman. *See* HORSE.

ocotillo. Fouquireria splendens: also called slimwood or coachwhip. A beautiful desert cactus whose whiplike stems flare out from its central base like a vase.

outfit. All the hands engaged in a given cattle operation, as a roundup, a trail drive, etc.: the supplies, wagons, gear, equipment, and mounts of such a group; a ranch together with its herds, buildings, and equipment; wearing apparel.

outlaw. *See* HORSE. The term is extended to vicious, untamable cows.

owl. Of the many *Bubo* in the West it is probably the species *virginianus,* or great horned owl, which interested Western pioneers the most. He ranges throughout most of North America, has a wingspan up to two feet, and gets his name from his conspicuous ear tufts. There is also a smaller burrowing owl, *Speotyto cunicularia,* which cohabits with the prairie dogs. It has a wingspread of about nine inches.

panther (painter). *See* MOUNTAIN LION.

picket. In the military encampments of the Western frontier, pickets, i.e., guards, were placed at strategic points along the perimeter of the installation. Gangs of bank robbers used a similar device to spot officers of the law and to distract them from the center of operations.

piñon. One of three open-branched evergreens of the mountain West: *Pinus edulis,* from which pine nuts are harvested; *Pinus monophilla;* and *Pinus cembroides.* The latter is encountered especially in Mexico.

prairie dog (gopher). Several burrowing rodents of the genus *Cynomys* that are confined to areas of moderate rain. They breed in colonies, building mounds that cover a hole that is dangerous to running cattle and to cow ponies, for if the hoof should penetrate down into the burrow a fall and almost inevitable injury are in store for both mount and rider.

prickly pear. General term applied to cacti of the genus *Opuntia,* characterized by flattened stems; widespread from Montana south.

prove up on (a claim). *See* GOVERNMENT CLAIM.

Pullman coach. George M. Pullman (1831–1897) built the first railroad sleeping car and, in 1867, organized the Pullman Palace Car Company.

punch, *v.* To "punch" cows is a general term covering all of a "puncher's" direct work with cattle— driving, roping, branding, cutting, earmarking, etc. By extension and a bit derisively, "punching dough" covered the camp cook's work with food.

punchboard (puncheon) floor. When metal was scarce, hardwood pegs about one-quarter inch in diameter were used to join flooring and to hold it in place. Flooring is still sold which, though se-

cured by nails, has pegs inserted to preserve the antique punchboard design.

puncher/cow puncher. Usual name for a man who worked with cattle; probably derived from the necessity of prodding cattle that lie down in a railroad car: they must be kept on their feet to avoid being trampled by the other cattle. Appears also as a verb, "to punch cows."

quirt. In Spanish, *cuerda*—cord; becomes Mexican *cuarta,* meaning whip. It consists of a wooden or leaded stock braided over with rawhide tapered into three or four loose rawhide thongs. The stock may serve as a blackjack or to pacify horses that tend to rear. A loop in the butt of the stock serves to anchor it on the rider's wrist or the saddle.

rag. Ann Charters places the origins of ragtime in banjo improvisations or "licks" and the possibilities for syncopation inherent in the piano and as developed among "flesh-pot" artists of New Orleans and St. Louis. "Old Black Joe: Paraphrase de Concert" by Charles Gimble, Jr., is identified as the first instance of printed ragtime (1877). A quarter century after its appearance on the "Tenderloin Circuit" (brothels of the cities mentioned above), it gained respectability when Ben Harney took the trick of piano syncopation, admittedly learned from Kentucky Negroes, to New York (1896). *The Ragtime Song Book* (New York: Oak Publications, 1965), pp. 8–34.

railroad speculators. From 1850 to 1871 the federal government made substantial grants of land— more than one hundred thirty million acres, in fact —as a stimulus to the construction of railroads. Typically the grants consisted of alternate sections, six miles in depth, on either side of a railroad right of way. Entrepreneurs, either in the employ of the railroads or under other auspices, conducted land sales operations throughout the eastern seaboard states and in Europe, inciting thousands to come and take up lands. *Dictionary of American History,* 2nd ed. (J. T. Adams and R. V. Coleman, eds. New York: Charles Scribner's Sons, 1942), Vol. III, p. 237.

ranch. From the Spanish *rancho.* A farm, especially

one devoted to the breeding and raising of live-stock. Note also: rancher, ranchman, ranch hand, etc. The "home ranch in the skies" appears as an image of life after death.

range. Unfenced country where cattle graze. In U.S. public surveying, a row of townships lying between two consecutive meridian lines, which are six miles apart, and numbered in order east and west from the principal meridian of each survey, the townships in the range being numbered north and south from the base line, which runs east and west; as "township No. 6 N., *range* 7 W., from the fifth principal meridian." It is in this latter sense that the word is used in the famous "Home on the Range" song. The term is extended to mean death (i.e., to change ranges), or the hereafter.

ranger. One of a body of mounted troops for patrolling a region. *See* Texas Rangers.

rattlesnake, rattler. Several species of poisonous reptiles of the *Crotalidae* family are widely distributed in the United States. Most typical in cowboy country was *Crotalus viridis,* or the prairie rattler, of which there are several subspecies. They grow to three feet in length; their range extends from Alberta into Old Mexico, and from the western plains states to the Pacific Coast. The diamond-back, *Crotalus astrox,* has a more southern range (from Arkansas south and west to Old Mexico). It is much larger, up to eight feet in length, and more deadly: the name derives from a distinctive patterning along its back.

rawhide. Many frontier crafts depended upon use of the tanned hides of cattle; ropes, chaps, saddles, horse gear, chair seats, clothing, and other items too numerous to mention were contrived by the use of rawhide.

reata. Spanish. Rope to tie pack animals in single file; rope of braided leather or rawhide. *Syn.* gut line, lariat. At a branding on the open range, after a critter was roped by the horns, the *reata* man threw a loop on the hind feet: the animal was then stretched out between the two horsemen and thrown for branding.

red pepper. Any one of several plants of the *Capsicum* or nightshade family, especially *Capsicum annum* which produces a fruit or berry widely used as food seasoning in the Southwest and Mexico.

remuda. From the Spanish *remudar,* to exchange. The herd of extra saddle horses not under saddle, used by the cowhands on roundup or trail drive. *Syn. caballada, remontha, remonta,* cavvy, cavyard, or simply the hosses or string (of horses).

rimming, *v.* To ride circle on a herd so that their grazing area is restricted within desired limits.

rimrock, *n.* The vertical escarpments of southwestern plateaus, buttes, or mesas are known as the rimrocks; seen from the valley floors they rise like the architectural remains of a cosmic temple.

ringy. Angry or riled.

rodeo. From Spanish *rodear,* to surround. In actual ranching operations it was a synonym for "round-up," the driving of cattle together for whatever purpose; more recently it is applied to the conventionalized and highly developed "western show" where cowboys compete in riding, roping, and dogging.

roll, *n.* Cowhands on trail herd were typically paid in cash. The greenbacks were rolled up and carried in the hip pocket. The demonstrative way in which the puncher drew out his roll and peeled off his cash was no doubt a temptation for cardsharps and prostitutes in the trail head towns.

rope, *n.* The cowhand's rope was the very sustenance of life itself, weapon and slave. With it he captured animals, both domestic and wild; he dragged firewood to camp, staked his horses; dueled; tied his packs. As a verb it meant to do almost anything you can do with a rope, especially to rope cattle. *Syn.* lasso. In a square dance it meant to join hands for a new figure.

roundhouse. A building circular or semicircular, with a turntable in the center, used for storing, repairing, and switching locomotives.

roundup. Probably derived by translation from the Spanish *rodeo,* action of surrounding. This represented the cattlemen's annual harvest: used transcendentally as a symbol of death.

rustle. To herd the *remuda;* to steal cattle; by extension, to choose partners at a dance. *Rustler,* one who steals cattle; is extended to mean "sinner."

sabe, savy, *v.* In Spanish, *sabe,* know. In cowboy lingo it survives as a verb and also as a noun meaning to know, skill, know-how.

sage hen. *Centrocirius urophasianus.* A large game bird whose range is tied to the sagebrush on which it feeds. It is noted for the use it makes of traditional breeding grounds where elaborate ritualistic mating dances are enacted. Also applied to the women at a cowboy square dance.

sagebrush. *Artemisia tridentata.* Typical vegetation of the arid and semiarid West. It adapts to many climatic conditions and serves as food for the larger mammals, especially sheep.

sand burrs. A spreading grass (up to four feet in diameter), *Cenchrus pauciflorus,* which produces a hard pea-sized burr which can be irritating and downright dangerous when, as a practical joke, it is placed under the saddle blanket of an already cantankerous horse!

sassafras. Any of a number of related trees of the laurel (*Laurus*) family whose dried roots were used in medicine and for flavoring.

seago. From *la soga.* A rope. Applied more particularly to a loosely twisted hemp rope which is used for lassoing purposes.

seagull. Two species are involved: (1) the black-headed variety, *Larus pipixcan,* or Franklin's gull, an inland dweller who loves to feed on freshly turned soil: he is about the size of a crow; (2) *Larus californicus,* or California gull, all white in color and as big as a raven. He ranges from Utah westward and is sacred in Utah where, as the well-known legend goes, he saved the first settlers from famine by consuming hosts of "Mormon" crickets that threatened to destroy their precious crops.

setfasts. Saddle sores.

seven-up. A card game played widely in the West since the days of the trappers, then commonly known as "all fours." *See* J. R. Bartlett, *Dictionary of Americanisms* (Boston, 1860).

Sharps rifle. Any of the single-shot breechloading rifles on the system invented by Christian Sharps, popular in percussion form in the 1850's and 1860's, and modified into cartridge rifles in the late 1860's. The most-used powerful western rifle, particularly by buffalo hunters, until the advent of repeaters and the end of the hide trade put the Sharps company out of business in 1881.—H. J. Swinney, Blue Mountain Lake, New York.

six-gun, six-shooter. Colloquial name for pistols or revolvers that could be fired six times before reloading. "Six-gun law" reigned in the absence of genuine law and is probably the touchstone to the popularity of the "Western" in all the popular arts.

sleeper. A calf earmarked by a cattle thief who intends to come back and steal it later. (Adams, p. 146.)

slick, *n., adj.* Name for an unbranded animal; also a man who has smooth but dishonest ways, especially an outsider.

slicker, *n.* A smooth and heartless deceiver of innocent girls. Also, a raincoat resembling an oilskin, used by cowboys; it was carried tied to the cantle drop of the saddle, ready to be worn when needed.

snapping out broncs. Breaking wild horses.

soap root. Yucca, a member of the lily family found widely in the Southwestern portions of the United States. It grows to about four feet in height, producing swordlike leaves and a single cluster of white blossoms. Early settlers used its roots in the making of soap.

sod shanty. In the very first years of settlement upon the frontier the simplest kinds of shelters were built for human occupancy. Among these, especially where timber was scarce, was the sod shanty, which consisted of an excavation into the side of a hill, shored up on the sides and front by stones or sod. A few timbers were placed across and brush and earth piled thereon to form a roof.

sodbuster. Name applied to Westerners who established farms and grew crops, as opposed to the cattlemen or sheepmen. Songs about homesteading and farm life are frequently known as sodbuster songs.

sombrero. The Spanish *sombra* (shade) gave rise to *sombrero,* a hat, especially one that casts plenty of shade. Such hats became a "tag" of the cowboy's gear. Though movie and TV specimens exaggerate both crown and brim, a cowhand found a good hat extremely useful—as a barrier to sun and rain, as protection against twigs and leaves, even as a temporary basin for water.

sourdough biscuits (bread). On roundup or trail drive the cook kept a sourdough keg ever fermenting. It contained a batter of flour, water, and salt, kept in a state of constant readiness by exposure to the sun during the day and by wrapping in blankets at night. Whenever the cook withdrew dough for baking, he added sufficient flour and water to replace it.

Spanish dagger. Several species of yucca are popularly identified as "Spanish dagger." They flourish in arid regions of the Southwest. They produce a spray of narrow pointed leaves capped with a sharp spine and a blossom that cattle find edible; grow up to five feet in height.

spike. Freight wagons were designed most typically to be drawn by one or more teams of horses. If for any reason the teamster wanted to add an extra animal, he improvised a way of hooking it to his load. This process was known as "putting the animal out on spike."

spurs. Metal instruments worn on cowboys' boots to assist in controlling the mount. They became an essential piece of cowboy equipment seldom removed from his boots. They may have been more useful as a status symbol than for riding. One of the simplest and most commonly used was the "OK" spur. Their silvery shine, ornate designs, and especially the jingle of the rowels as a cowboy walked gave his gait some real "pazazz" and caused the hearts of impressionable maidens to go flip-flop.

stake. Money or other goods risked at cards, or in gambling: by extension, capital accumulated through earnings, loans, theft, etc., the wise use of which gave a frontiersman hope for the passage from "hired hand" to owner-manager. *See also* "grubstake."

stampede. From the Spanish *estampida,* the running of cattle. Cattle raised on the open ranges were wild animals. Any sudden noise or other unusual occurrence might send them in a mad run dangerous alike to man and beast. Many western songs and stories tell of the drama, excitement, and tragedy of cattle or buffalo stampedes. The meaning of the term is extended to include the rush of men to mining strikes.

States: term used by Westerners for the eastern and relatively highly developed areas of the United States, as opposed to the territories or primitive regions of the West.

steed. *See* HORSE.

steer. "Cow" was used to designate cattle of either sex; the term "steer" is reserved for the castrated males.

Stetson. Name given by Westerners to the big hat that is an earmark of the cattle country, whether made by Stetson or not. Adams (pp. 155–156) gives two full columns to its composition, ornamentation, tilt, practical uses, and symbolic meanings.

stranger. Beyond its usual meaning, the term was also applied to a cow or horse on a range where it didn't belong. *Syn.* stray.

stray. Used to designate cattle grazing on a range where they don't belong. Ethics called for their being headed back toward their own grazing area. If, however, a range crew just happened to be fresh out of meat, and if a stray just happened to be handy, its life was not nearly as secure as was that of a cow bearing the home brand. By extension, used to designate humans who have deviated from "the strait and narrow way."

strike, *n.* Mining term used to designate the discovery of a rich new source of ore.

stud, *n.* Variety of poker in which each player is dealt five cards, the first face down and the others face up, the betting proceeding after each round of open cards is dealt.

suggan. Blanket for bedding, a heavy comforter often made from patches of pants, coats, or overcoats. A suggan usually weighs about four pounds, as the cowboy says, "a pound for each corner." Also called *soogans* or *soogins,* camp quilts, boys' room quilts.

sull, *v.* Cowmen use this verb in speaking of a cow which, in a state of shock or exhaustion, goes down on its front knees and refuses to move.

sunfishing, *v.* A bucking term used in describing the movements of a horse when he twists his body into a crescent, alternately to the right and to the left; or, in other words, when he seems to try to touch the ground with first one shoulder and then the other, letting the sunlight hit his belly. (Adams, p. 159.)

tadpole pie. Bill Koch, Professor of English at Kansas State University in Manhattan, thinks that "tadpole pie" is a pejorative for frog legs: for the early plainsmen they were considered not a delicacy but rather were resorted to out of necessity when more palatable foods were scarce.

tail down. The throwing of an animal by the tail in lieu of a rope. Any animal can, when traveling rapidly, be sent heels over head by seizing its tail and giving it a pull to one side. This method was resorted to frequently with the wild longhorns, and a thorough tailing usually knocked the breath from

them and so dazed them that they would behave for the rest of the day. The act requires both a quick and swift horse and a daring rider. J. Frank Dobie, *Vaquero of the Brush Country.* (Dallas: Southwest Press, 1929), p. 15.

tally. At spring roundup one hand kept a ledger or tally book in which he recorded the number of animals branded—the only device whereby an owner could know the size of his increase. The term is used transcendentally to designate God's record of souls saved by His divine grace.

tapaderas. Spanish. Hispanic-American horsemen attached leather guards known as *tapaderas* in front of the stirrups to prevent the feet from penetrating too far. They also protected the feet against brush and prevented the dreaded tragedy of being dragged to death when, on being thrown, one's foot slipped all the way through the stirrup. Anglo-Americans shortened the term to "taps."

tarantula. Applied to several species of large spiders of the southwestern United States. Their superficial resemblance to a European spider of the same name caused our Anglo- and Hispanic-American forebears to carry over the name. Their bite is mildly toxic. Genus *Eurypelma.*

tarpaulin or **tarp.** Canvas in which a puncher rolled bedding and the few personal effects which he carried, tied behind his saddle whenever away from the home ranch. It also served as a waterproof cover on his bed.

tenderfoot. *Syn.* greenhorn, greener, dude. According to Adams (p. 164) the term was first applied to cattle imported to the Southwest, later, to men new in the region.

tequila. Spanish. Alcoholic beverage distilled from the juice of the century plant.

Texas Rangers. By 1826 Texas colonists had from twenty to thirty "rangers" in service against Indians. By 1840 an organized corps had come into being: it achieved fame in the war with Mexico. By 1870 it had reached its zenith, imposing order on the Rio

Grande in operations against Indians, horse thieves, outlaws, and disorders of the Reconstruction years. They carried six-shooters and saddle guns but were otherwise un-uniformed. They did not drill, their guns were never notched, there was no saluting of officers. J. Frank Dobie, *Dictionary of American History,* 2nd ed. (Vol. V, pp. 256–257.)

tlaco. Spanish. Coin, one-eighth of a Spanish *real;* obsolete.

tommy gun. A Thompson submachine gun; loosely, any submachine gun.

top hand (man, rider, roper, cutter, screw, shot, etc.). The best, the man who excels in and is, hence, in charge of a particular punching activity.

tortilla. "A large, round, thin unleavened cake prepared from a paste made of corn, baked on a heated iron plate or stone slab; used in lieu of bread in Mexico."—Webster.

tough. We have not encountered elsewhere "tough" used as a noun and referring to food: here it may simply mean pork (cooked and served with boiled beans) without the prior removal of gristle or skin.

trading post. From the founding of Jamestown (1607) furs were exchanged for guns, ammunition, hatchets, knives, blankets, etc. In 1796 the U.S. government established trading posts, and frontier military outposts became centers of trade between the Indians and the Anglo-American colonists. After the Louisiana Purchase (1804) they were established over a wide expanse of the area west of the Mississippi. They persist today on the Indian reservations, where the Indians procure a wide variety of manufactures, and where tourists buy the products of Indian craftsmanship.—*Dictionary of American History,* 2nd ed. (Vol. V, p. 302).

trail (trail drive, trail herd). Perhaps the most dramatic of all cowboy activities. Drives over great distances began in the 1830's and continued into the 1880's. Driven hard during the first day or so in order to get them off the home range, the cattle were subsequently trailed easily along so that they could graze and put on fat en route. The work of trail driving was highly organized, with riders cooperating as skillfully as the members of a professional athletic team. The cattle being driven were known as the trail herd.

tree. The frame of wood or pressed rawhide over which the saddle is constructed. Saddles are commonly named from the shape of the tree on which they are built.

tumbleweed. *Amaranthus graecizans* or *Salsola kali tenuifolia* (Russian thistle). Annual weeds that break off at the root at the end of the growing season and which, because of spheroid shape, blow across the country, scattering their seeds and piling up on every fence line. They came into the West from Eurasia, have been eaten as greens, and their seeds even ground for flour. Some reach a diameter of six feet.

"Turn out there!" One of the camp cook's duties, on trail drive or roundup, was to get the hands up, fed, and mounted. Each had his favorite "gettin' up holler" or "chuck call," some of which look all right in print.

twisted hay. What little wood that was produced in the plains from Canada to Oklahoma in pioneer days was all too precious to be burned. The long grasses of the marshlands were twisted into knots by a small hand-operated machine designed specifically for this task. Moreover, there were specially designed stoves called "hay-burners," still to be seen in museums of the region. Bill Koch, Professor of English at Kansas State University in Manhattan, says that his father's family, living in Brown County, North Dakota (territory), were still using hay-burning stoves in the early '80's.

vaquero. Spanish for cowboy. The term gives rise in cowboy lingo to buckaroo, admitting contamination from the verb buck. (Recall that an initial *v* in Spanish is pronounced like a *b.*) In all probability it served to fix the term cowboy, which is a faithful translation of *vaca* (cow), and *ero,* a suffix meaning a person who deals with something.

waddie. Name for an ordinary cowboy, usually one who floated from ranch to ranch, being engaged for seasonal work only. Adams (p. 173) thinks it may be derived from wad, i.e., something you use temporarily to stop a leak until you can do the job up good and proper.

wagon boss. Man in charge of a roundup or trail drive; undisputed leader of an operating outfit. The movies have glorified particularly the wagon bosses who piloted groups of pioneers in the wagon trains that moved West to stay.

waterfall. Chignon or roll of hair worn low on the neck, popular in the 1860's. Also a hat of the same period, usually one with a long, drooping feather in back. It may also designate a figure in a square dance.

Winchester. An early model repeating rifle named for its maker and still a favorite with Westerners.

wire grass. *Junicus balticus,* a worthless blue-green grass that produces coarse stalks up to eighteen inches high, appearing typically in wet meadows.

wolf. *Canis lupus* once ranged widely in North America, though he is now restricted to the most remote areas. He is about the size of an Alaskan husky dog, weighing up to one hundred twenty pounds. Pioneers were fearful of wolves, especially because they roved in packs and preyed alike upon domestic or wild animals, even the most hardy ones. Two other species, *Canis occidentales,* the timber wolf, and *Canis ladrans,* the prairie wolf or coyote, were probably not always differentiated by the folk who used the term "wolf" for largest specimens and "coyote" for the smaller ones.

wrangler, wrangle. From the Mexican *caverango*— hostler. The man on roundup or trail drive who took care of the *remuda,* typically the least experienced hand in the outfit. It is extended to mean the performance of the duties of camp cook, and to the restless milling of cattle.

yip. Cry or shout used by punchers to get the cattle to move in a desired direction; prettied-up and stereotyped, yips serve well in the refrains of western songs and verse.

zapatero. Spanish for shoemaker.

Index of Titles and First Lines

[First lines are set in italics; titles are set in roman type]

General Index

Indexing of geographical and personal names presents real difficulties since the songs do not particularize which "Red River," which "Lincoln" (city), or which "Sheriff Brady" is involved. We have still thought it useful to enter them in the index: in the context of a given song researchers may find them useful.